CW00420511

RAF
BOMBER
STORIES

RAF
BOMBER
STORIES

Dramatic first-hand accounts of British and
Commonwealth airmen in World War 2

Martin W. Bowman

Patrick Stephens Limited

© Martin W. Bowman 1998

All rights reserved. No part of this publication may be reproduced or stored in a retrieval system or transmitted, in any form or by any means, electronic, mechanical, photocopying, recording or otherwise, without prior permission in writing from Patrick Stephens Limited.

First published in February 1998

British Library Cataloguing in Publication Data
A catalogue record for this book is
available from the British Library

ISBN 1 85260 567 7

Library of Congress catalog card no. 97-76834

Patrick Stephens Limited is an imprint of Haynes Publishing,
Sparkford, Nr Yeovil, Somerset, BA22 7JJ.

Tel: 01963 440635 Fax: 01963 440001
Int. tel: +44 1963 440635 Fax: +44 1963 440001

E-mail: sales@haynes-manuals.co.uk
Web site: http://www.haynes.com

Haynes North America, Inc.
861 Lawrence Drive, Newbury Park,
California 91320 USA

Designed & typeset by G&M, Raunds, Northamptonshire
Printed and bound in France by Imprimerie Pollina s.a., Luçon, France - n°73819

Contents

Acknowledgements

I AM MOST GRATEFUL to the following people, all of whom graciously contributed either stories or photos, and sometimes both, for this book:

Steve Adams; Mike Bailey; Carl Bartram; Dr Theo Boiten; Len Bradfield RAF Retd; Mrs Susannah Burr; Nigel Buswell; Noel Chaffey; C. H. 'Chick' Chandler RAF Retd; Oliver Clutton-Brock, Editor, RAF Bomber Command Association; the late Basil Craske RAF; Tom Cushing; Edward A. Davidson DFM RAF Retd; Squadron Leader Bob Davies AFC RAF Retd; Dr Colin Dring; Howard 'Tommy' Farmiloe RAF Retd; Captain E. D. Fieldson DFC; Bill Garrioch RAF Ret; Peter Gibby RAF Retd; Alan Hague, Curator, Norfolk & Suffolk Aviation Museum; Wing Commander Brian R. W. 'Darkie' Hallows OBE DFC; Roland A. Hammersley DFM RAF Retd, who kindly allowed me to quote from his book *Into Battle with 57 Squadron*; the late A. J. S. Harrison RAAF Retd; Bill Hough RAF Retd; Mike Lewis; Geoff Liles; Wing Commander Gerry F. McMahon DFM RAF Retd; Larry Melling RCAF Retd; Jack Parker RAF Retd; Squadron Leader Charles Patterson DSO DFC; Dr Keith Percival-Barker RAF Retd; Bill Reid VC; Albert E. Robinson; Squadron Leader Malcolm Scott DFC RAF Retd; Steve Snelling, *Eastern Daily Press*; George Turner DFC* RAF Retd; Ken Westrope RAF Retd; Tom Wingham DFC RAF Retd; Ray 'Bob' White RAF Retd; Jenkin Williams MBA RAF Retd, 2nd TAF Medium Bombers Association; Mrs Phyllis Wood; the late J. Ralph Wood DFC CD RCAF.

Introduction

OF ALL THE STARK, cold, statistics that emanate from WW2, there is one set of figures which even today, outweighs all others when one talks about RAF Bomber Command. No matter what historians and commentators have to say about the ethics and the prosecution of the day and night bombing offensive, the inescapable fact is that no less than 55,500 aircrew in Bomber Command were killed in action or flying accidents, or died on the ground or while prisoners of war.

Approximately 125,000 aircrew served in the front-line, OTU and OCUs of the Command and nearly 60 per cent of them became casualties. In addition, almost 9,900 more were shot down and made PoWs to spend one, two or more years in squalid, desolate oflags and stalags in Axis held territory. Over 8,000 more were wounded aboard aircraft on operational sorties. Bomber Command flew almost 390,000 sorties, the greatest percentage of them by Avro Lancasters, Handley Page Halifaxes and Wellingtons. Theirs of course were the highest casualties.

To try to encapsulate every dramatic episode of RAF Bomber Command's long and distinguished history in one volume is therefore impossible, but the unique selection that follows is wide-ranging and significantly, each experience is related by British and Commonwealth airmen themselves. Their endearing bravery and fortitude, and sometimes their despondency and cynicism, shows through in these stirring, daring, often irreverent, humorous, and sometimes sardonic, but memorable stories. All reflect the ethos, camaraderie, fear and bravery of the largely ordinary men, most of whom were plucked from 'civvy street' and thrust into a frightening, bitter conflict which was made even more dangerous by the lethal advance of technology. Death would normally come from an anonymous assassin, either in the black of night, or from behind a cloud or out of the sun, or simply from the Flak gunner on the ground. And, if all this was not enough, the often unmerciful weather was no respector of mortality.

There was no escaping the all-embracing shock wave that rippled through the bomber squadrons after a heavy mauling over enemy territory. Nothing could be more poignant than the vacuous places at tables in the depleted mess halls, the empty locker of the departed, or the dog pining by the barracks for its missing master. Each man had to deal with tragedy in his own inimitable way. Some hid their feelings better than others only for the pain to resurface months or even years later. Some who had survived the physical pressures and who completed their tours then succumbed to the mental torture that had eaten away at their psyche during the incessant and interminable onslaught day after day, night after night. There was little respite. The valorous men of Bomber Command were, in turn, the Light Brigade, the stop gap, the riposte, the avengers, the undefeated. Always, they were expendable.

Martin W. Bowman, Norwich. 1997

1: The Grey Monk
Albert E. Robinson, Observer, 115 Squadron

BOMBING BY NIGHT presented a formidable barrier to the young crews of the Wellington bomber during the crisis years of 1940–41. So much so that if groping blindly through the curtain of darkness that had descended over Europe was to be overcome, it became crystal clear that in the initial stages an awful lot was going to depend on the crews themselves. Trial and error mostly could only result, and it did, a situation that brought about a high casualty rate for the pioneer crews. Unfortunately, it was with little result for so great an effort, a pot-pourri of calculated risk, personal skills, and circumstances that favoured the more successful crews. The 'X' factor, a quality difficult to define, but one that enabled them to take advantage of more than a full share of luck, lifted them high above average.

Whatever the mixture, a fierce determination to succeed in spite of the numerous setbacks was a common denominator, and it united the crews almost without exception. With such resolution, the crews attempted to face up to their task. It was not made any easier by briefing officers who spoke at length about the necessity for precision bombing. It would not be too critical to suggest that some of these briefings were out of touch with reality. Truthful crews considered it a reasonable effort if the city itself was found, let alone a specific aiming point.

There were many reasons for this, but the principal culprit was night navigation. This was based almost entirely on the age-old theory of dead reckoning. There was no problem if all the links in the chain were known, but if not, it could turn out to be a hit-or-miss affair, especially with little or no radio assistance to help

An RAF crew boarding their Wellington bomber.

with the calculations. The basic requirement for success was to establish the wind speed and direction, but in order to assess these it was necessary at various times during the flight to define the position of the aircraft in relation to the ground – obtain a 'fix', as it was known to the navigator. Under variable conditions this was not always possible. The flight could be blown well off course, sometimes miles away if there were adverse winds, and with it went little chance of finding out the true position of the aircraft. This in turn usually added up to wasted effort, with bombs being brought back or jettisoned in the sea.

Inexperienced crews could end up on the slopes of a mountain or in the grey wastes of the sea. The North Sea in particular was a big enemy to Bomber Command, a heaving predator, menacing in its vastness to any crippled bomber struggling to maintain height over its darkened wilderness. The enemy coast to the hoped-for landfall in England offered little hope if a crippled bomber had to force-land, and most certainly so if contact had been lost with any listening post as a result of a damaged radio.

A bomber aircraft then was a lonely and desolate figure, struggling against the odds and with the chilling thought that no matter how expertly the aircraft was set down on the sea – turbulent or calm – the bomber would sink within minutes. There was the rubber dinghy, of course. It could be paddled, but when exhaustion came and effort faded it would just drift along with the wind and tide, aimlessly and without hope, to a tortured end, unless providence took a hand. God knows how long this would take. Perhaps better not to have taken the dinghy at all.

That's how it went. Such possibilities could only be accepted by crews with a philosophical shrug of the shoulders. It came with a host of other things, but even so most crews were optimistic and they set their sights on completing the mandatory, magical number of 30 operations before being taken off for a rest at some training squadron. In comparison to the numbers involved, very few managed to achieve this; the average could have been as low as five missions before the Grim Reaper called the tune.

Given the conditions, the chances of survival on any one operation, whether it was

'The enemy coast to the hoped-for landfall in England offered little hope if a crippled bomber had to force-land, and most certainly so if contact had been lost with any listening post as a result of a damaged radio.' (Bart M. Rynhout)

the first or 30th, were not good. The betting odds would be rated low by any discerning bookmaker. All aircrew were volunteers to a man, but in saying this, they needed to be. Each raid was equivalent to 'going over the top' in the 1914–18 war. However, if one were to put the clock back to the briefing room in 1940–41 and peer through the haze of cigarette smoke that hung in swirling clouds, no one would have guessed it. It was more like a gathering at any sports club. We were boisterous, outgoing and extrovert, but underneath this cloak there was a quiet confidence and rugged determination. Such an outlook was essential. The effort needed to penetrate Germany, certainly with the out-dated aircraft at the crews' disposal in the years 1940–41, required a deep-seated motivation and a special quality.

We were lucky to have the Wellington. It was probably the best of the bunch when compared to the other bombers. A good old warhorse, it was as loyal and forgiving as the crews were to the bomber, but the fact remains that it was outdated, unable to reach much height over the target, poorly armed, had no internal heat, and when carrying a full bomb load of 4,000lb had a speed of less than half that of an enemy fighter. Freezing temperatures often coated surfaces with ice and frost, froze controls and radio sets and brought instant ice-burn should metal surfaces be touched without a glove. Engines were often suspect (they invariably coughed and spluttered) and the dials on the instrument panel were constantly watched with anxious eyes, hoping that the readings would not give reasons for concern.

Should one engine fail, as they often did, it was a heart-stopping moment with the certain knowledge that the Wellington would not be able to maintain height over a sustainable period. Its flying range would then be determined by irreversible factors such as the state of the aircraft, height at the time, angle and speed of descent, and the skill of the pilot to nurse the aircraft along. They were always apprehensive lest the extra workload would cause the remaining engine to overheat – not the least of the problems was the possibility that it too could fail.

If all this sounds gloomy, then add for good measure the fact that from take-off to return the Wellington would be flying in isolation. In many respects the raid would be one of individual effort and self-planning by the crews. Often the route to the target would be varied by crew preference. They normally took into account the known Flak areas, but defences could alter their tactics or geographical position, so even the most carefully thought-out plans could go astray and bring the sting of the serpent at an unexpected moment. Strict radio silence did not help, but this was essential because of the enemy's rapidly increasing radar detection. To break this silence was to invite trouble, the equivalent to sending a telegram to the Luftwaffe notifying them of intent!

But all these shortcomings were shrugged off with an unflagging optimism. Metaphorically speaking we were all in the same boat, and in any case anything bad happened to the other fellow – or at least so said the mind's defence mechanism. The more missions that were flown, the easier it became to believe this. It could also induce a state of mind dubbed by the crews as 'Flak happy'. This could loosely be interpreted as over-confidence, a mistake for which many usually paid dearly, joining the list of doomed aircraft. These unfortunate souls just took off and literally vanished, never to be seen again – just like a conjuror's rabbit. The toll under this category became harder to stomach as the casualty list mounted.

Replacement crews to fill the gaps, proud of their newly won wings, keen and enthusiastic, came to the squadron like an endless belt at some factory complex. The crewroom became a platform on which the passengers were ever-changing. There was barely time to get to know their names. Sadly, within a month, the fresh young faces who had been so eager to prove their worth would move along up the belt, often within days as crews were called upon to fly operations that were near impossible. Some were lucky, some not, but in all cases there was the same unpredictability as a name drawn at random from a hat. Not all were fresh faces either. The Grim Reaper was not choosy and some were veterans of many operations. They *always* came back, and their demise sent an ice-cold shock through every level in the squadron. The sorrow of their passing gave everyone food for thought.

With Bomber Command heavily committed, in principle any retrograde step was out of the question, and Command was compelled to allow for these losses when planning. It was not a very happy thought for the squadron commanders to lose so many of their valuable, well-trained crews, but it is not possible to make an omelette without breaking eggs, a fait accompli that just about fitted in with a Wellington bomber squadron. Even so, Command intensified its efforts. There would be no respite, no let-up, and the battle, if Britain was to keep intact its position as the sole bastion in the struggle against a Nazi Germany, must continue to be fought.

Orders filtered down from high command to the squadrons, and in smoke-filled rooms the crews were briefed in detail. If it was a tough target, an unrestrained groan would echo through the briefing room. On the other hand, an easier one would produce a mild cheer, and if the squadron commander even as much as hinted that there was the smallest chance of cancellation, this was met by much stamping of feet and an enthusiastic round of applause. The CO would listen and a faint smile would cross his face. He had heard it all before. He had flown many operations and he understood the crews' outlook. To him this show of humour, usually expressed in an offbeat way best described perhaps as black humour, was quite normal. Whatever it was, it covered up quite a lot. This was just as well, since in the few hours following the briefing the adjutant would be reaching for his telegram pad to write out the condolences to loved ones waiting at home. The sight of the telegram boy always caused a chilling premonition and a clutch at the heart.

There was much to do before an op. There were maps and charts to prepare, target approach to consider, known fighter bases to ring round in red ink and a whole host of other things to do. It was a busy period, but preparation was vital. Much had to be examined in microscopic detail and the better the grasp of this, the more likely the success of the operation and, in all probability, the chances of survival too. Even so, with all the work and concentration required, somehow it always seemed to be completed with a good hour to spare before take-off time.

That hour always took its toll. Irrespective of experience or how many operations had been completed, that hour became the waiting time. It passed with a dreadful slowness. A jumbled-up mass of crews muffled in their flying leathers watched the clock tick over and urged it on, for it gave them time to consider the possibilities that lay ahead and above all offered so much time to think. They were a cheerful, resourceful, happy-go-lucky bunch, mostly in their teens, and in almost hourly touch with death, but on the surface at least, they had an apparent fatalistic acceptance of this role. The mess had an atmosphere of its own. People talked in hushed whispers or on a higher note than usual, and there was an edgy tension. Some wrote letters to a loved one, others thumbed through magazines in a restless way. Some were fidgety, some composed, while others just sat, deep in their own thoughts. Yet, once in the air, with the onset of danger, such thoughts would evaporate completely. The operation would be all that mattered and it called for an authoritative grasp of the nettle. The game would be on.

For the crews that came back, life on the squadron was almost a world on its own, and not only in the world of bombing either. The close-knit relationships were evident in their off-duty times too, and these were celebrated, perhaps not too wisely, at the Red Lion, an old-worldly hotel with a thatched roof and a wealth of oak beams already blackened by the smoke of ages. A much favoured meeting place for the crews, it saw many boisterous, heavy nights with endless frothy pints of beer and a piano banging out bawdy songs with an emphasis that threatened to lift the timbered ceiling that almost brushed our heads. Even when the casualty lists were running at a high level, these carefree times carried on as usual and the frothy pints continued to be hoisted high and drunk with perhaps even more appreciative relish.

Callous? Uncaring? Not so. That way some sort of sanity was preserved. Each one had to take his chance. Who would be next? So, live for today, enjoy it while possible. Most crews did just that. Even so, very few left the hotel without a backward glance at its panelled walls and glittering brasses, always with the thought that it could quite likely be for the last time.

That this comradeship, both on the scene of battle and during these relaxed off-duty periods, bore relationship to the atmosphere in which school games were played was no accident. In fact, this attitude was actively encouraged by many squadron commanders and, in a sense, was a convenient hat and coat hook fixed in some mythical pavilion on which to hang the trauma, a contrivance that also acted on carefully defined lines to help mould the team spirit with which these games were played. To cast this mould was easy. Most of the crews were barely out of school anyway. It was only the setting that was different.

It was apparent right from the very moment on an operational day when the crews strolled over to the mess for breakfast. An early morning mist might be floating over the base in grey wispy patches, a hazy cloak settled over the runways. It became a familiar sight to the crews, and almost a permanent feature of the flat, moisture-filled greenness of the open farmland that surrounded the base and stretched for miles.

At dispersal points the Wellingtons, stark and austere in their camouflage paint, stood waiting – a colossus in their own right with their six Browning machine-guns jutting from their turrets and ominous in their setting. A petrol bowser stood alongside some of the aircraft. Soon it would pump the high-octane fuel into the tanks and a tousled-haired mechanic would peer from the cockpit waiting for the signal. There was always a scene of great activity as the ground staff fussed around, each to their own job, and a lot would depend in their attention to detail.

A Wellington bomber at its dispersal. (via Dr Colin Dring)

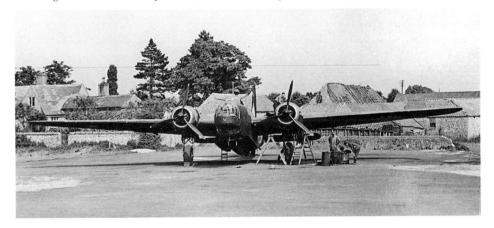

A bomb train for a Wellington of 149 Squadron at Mons Wood, Mildenhall, in 1941. (via Dr Colin Dring)

The aircrew by now had dispersed, each caught up with the technicalities of their own job. They would not meet again until briefing. As for the navigator, he had a recently introduced system of astro-navigation to study. In reality it was a basic affair, consisting of a sextant, a rather splendid watch for time-keeping, and a hooded projector set over the navigator's table. There was illuminated astronomical data on the chart, on which the sextant readings were plotted. It was a brave effort by the boffins to help offset the weakness in night navigation, but under operational conditions it had its limitations. One of the drawbacks was that it was necessary to fly a straight and level course at a constant speed for a protracted period – a gift-wrapped present for German radar. The bumpy, wallowing Wellington could not, by any stretch of the imagination, be described as the ideal platform from which to take hand-held sextant readings. Also there was the question of the stars' visibility themselves, for they were often blotted out by heavy cloud. On the nights when the Plough in Ursa Major could be seen, this was not only useful in the construction of a mental star map, but it was easy to pick out Polaris, the Pole Star. Poised several light years above the North Pole to an accuracy of one degree, it had guided travellers throughout the ages. Now, with its ancient origins and religious beliefs, it was to come ironically to the aid of bomber crews.

However, crews at that time gave little significance to such significant or philosophical meanderings. Operations were not the Holy Grail, just a job, which in the interests of their nation they had been called upon to do, and that was their sole object, nothing else. Any personal feelings could not be allowed to swerve or distract. With this in mind and the completion of briefing, it was time to go.

At dispersal points, in the already darkened sky, the crews at their stations, the pilot made ready to start the two Pegasus radial engines. Starter buttons were pressed and there was a cough and a roar as they fired. A column of grey smoke with a sheet of flame shot out from the exhaust. The crews settled down in their positions. Engines were throttled back to tick-over position and, with the pilot's thumb-up signal to the waiting ground staff, the chocks were hauled away from the wheels. Throttles were pushed forward and the engines answered with a roar. Guided by twinkling lights, the Wellingtons, gorged with the bomb loads tucked in their bellies, trundled slowly to take-off position. It was all systems go.

The training manual made it look so simple. Throttles were manipulated to gain full power. The aircraft responded with gathering speed and if all else was carried out correctly, the Wellington took off. But, sitting at the end of the runway, waiting for the green flashing light that was cleared for take-off, it did not seem so simple. In fact, there was a sense of disbelief that nagged at the stomach that the lumbering, heavy Wellington, laden to the maximum with bombs and petrol, would ever leave the ground at all. But it did – well, usually – but if there was ice or frozen snow on the grass airstrip and this affected lift, or there was a significant splutter from either of the engines at the critical point of lift-off, then either of these could threaten disaster. The normal load of 650 gallons of petrol for an average run, plus the 4,000lb bomb load usually carried, could make quite a hole in the ground. Tense moments these, broken only by a sense of relief when the bomber left the ground and began to make its circuit of the airfield ready to set course for far-off Germany.

The Wellington gained height slowly, very slowly. High above on a clear night a myriad of stars pin-pricked the sky with their brilliance. The black nose of the Wellington tilted towards them and the defiant roar of the two engines filled the air with vibrating noise. A lot would depend on those engines. They would have to blast effortlessly away for a good many hours, and more than one aircrew said a silent prayer as they listened to the roar. But there were many other items to consider, and the list was compounded with problems that seemed endless.

Weather could be problematical. Accurate forecasts, with the scant information available to the meteorology officers, were rare. It was more successful to wet a finger, hold it up, and hope. Since all operations were dictated by requirements of war, often this meant flying in appalling conditions. High gusty winds, fog with thick cloud up to high levels, and particularly ice, were common enemies. Ice could layer itself over the wings, and create drag to the point of stalling as the Wellington lurched and sagged in a series of sickening movements. Adverse conditions could make themselves known in the space of a short time, sometimes before leaving the English coast. Then it became a lonely trek flying through the murk until the Dutch coast was reached.

A Handley Page Hampden of 144 Squadron, pictured at Hemswell in 1939. At the outbreak of war Hampdens equipped No 5 Group Bomber Command and were used on daylight operations until heavy losses caused the aircraft to be used solely at night. Along with the Whitley and Wellington, Hampdens carried the night offensive to Germany until 14/15 September 1942, when the Hampden operated with Bomber Command for the last time. (Jock Galloway via Theo Boiten)

A Bf 110 night fighter of II./NJG2 with Lichtenstein radar aerials at Leeuwarden airfield, Holland, in 1942. This aircraft was flown by Oblt Sigmund, who at this time had seven victories against RAF bombers. (Collection Schmitt, via Rob de Visser/Theo Boiten)

Flak, either from the coastal guns or the numerous flak ships anchored off the Frisian Islands, would come up. An umbrella barrage and dotted tracer like a giant firework display were joined by the probing searchlights spreading their light like some huge, luminous spider's web trying to lure the victim into its mesh. Ahead, blips bobbing and dancing on electronic screens indicated our position to the controller. Then the night fighter bases were alerted. We hoped, with some measure of callousness, that the blips would be caused by another aircraft. Since it was an invisible thread that connected the Wellington to the night fighter, the gunners in our aircraft did not know until the actual moment of interception, so we, the crew, sat, tensed, waiting for the sight of the Messerschmitt night fighter. From now on the Wellington was in grave danger.

This was never more true than on a moonlit, cloudless night. The art of crossing the Dutch coast was by concealment in the clouds. But this too had its drawbacks since it was necessary for navigational purposes to 'fix' the exact crossing point, and naturally this meant emerging from the cloud cover. This we hoped would be over the Frisian Islands or, to be more specific, the island of Schiermonnikoog. Mere hiccups on the chart maybe, but an area with which we had become familiar, especially Schiermonnikoog. If we were correct when we broke cloud cover, it boiled down to a quick movement, 'fix' the position as soon as possible, then head back to the concealment of the cloud with full boost and airspeed.

It sounds reasonably simple, but even so it may have been just the moment for which the night fighter crew was waiting. Individual aircraft flying in isolation – and that's how it was for us in 1940–41 – were comparatively easy meat. German radar used the time that this early warning afforded to put the night fighter in a position to suit themselves, usually from astern and below, and always it seemed when the Wellington broke cloud for the 'fix'. The Me 110 night fighters were only too pleased to take advantage of this and were quick to exploit these favourable circumstances.

Then the bomber would break into a stomach-heaving routine of carefully rehearsèd evasion – not so much to shoot down the fighter, but purely as an evasive tactic. A fighter claimed may be exciting news in the mess, but the successful completion of the operation took precedence. Anything else was a bonus.

Of course, this assumes that the fighter had been spotted before the attack. If not, the first indication would come with a staccato crackle as the red tracer streaked across, and the cannon fire of the Messerschmitt was vicious, both in range and effectiveness, far more than the .303 machine-gun fire of the Wellington. An unexpected attack usually spelled disaster, but it must be said that given an early sight of the enemy fighter, he did not have it all his own way. The Wellington, with alert gunners, could give a reasonable account of itself, and facing aggressive, accurate fire the enemy fighter would often break away and seek easier meat. Even so, it was an apprehensive moment for the crews, and as the gun turrets rotated in the sky, searching with an intensity for the fighter, it was essentially a moment of quick reaction. An off-guard, dreamy relaxation or a split-second delay would quickly decide the issue.

Even with this risk of interception it was of paramount importance to get a 'fix' as the Dutch coast was crossed. This enabled the ground speed and track over the territory to be calculated and made it easier to pick out the landmarks as we flew over Holland. It was a strange, eerie feeling as we did so. To us, Holland was a territory of friendly people and there was a sense of outrage that it was occupied by the Nazis. We liked to think that when the Dutch people heard the drone of our Wellingtons they recognised it as a gesture of hope. This was confirmed on numerous occasions when flashing lights from down below spelled out a welcome in no uncertain terms. Such a sight made our flight more personal and acted as a strong fillip to morale.

Naturally the German defences did not see it that way, and the inevitable flak came up. If this flak was widespread and heavy, it sometimes made diversion necessary, and this, in many instances, could take the Wellington far away from the calculated track. This caused a period of frustration, since it was not always easy in the darkness to refix the aircraft's position. At such moments of indecisiveness the poor navigation facilities came into question. As one crew member put it succinctly, as we strode out to our Wellington for take-off: 'Here we go again with a map, pencil and rubber. Oh well, the target is only 600 miles away and as for the return, well, just forget it.'

It was not quite like that of course, but in the early days of the bombing campaign it just *seemed* like that. Certainly the loss of compass course and a confused meander over hostile territory provoked high irritation when the search turned out to be fruitless. But it was not all failure. Success came along too, and then the flush of achievement took on a positive and welcome role. It made all the effort and sacrifice worthwhile.

At such times, Essen, Cologne and Bremen were not cities, they were targets – seething holocausts with a glowing spread of a spitting shambles down below. Skies were made colourful by different shades of flak – greens and red predominated – and they were filled with a blinding light that dazzled and compelled the pilot to bank steeply as the searchlights wavered and probed in their systematic search for the raider. Often a whole series of searchlights positioned in a wide circle would take their cue from a master searchlight set in the centre of this circle. This vertical shaft in the sky stood quite still, until the operators felt that they had accurately calculated the height and speed of a particular aircraft. Then it would switch from the vertical with the swiftness of a striking snake in its attempt to centre its beam on the unfortunate aircraft. If this happened, then the other searchlights would simultaneously and instantly converge at an apex above the Wellington and in effect form a giant cone with the bomber trapped in a flood of light. Slowly they would bring the nose of the cone down forcing the bomber lower and lower and then, at a given signal, massed guns would fire up the cone with a fierce intensity that lit up the sky with its menace. When coned it was an almost impossible situation for any aircraft and the only escape lay in violent evasion, sometimes to the point where it put the aircraft's structure at risk, threatened catastrophe and gave the unfortunate souls nightmares. Most such endeavours were fruitless. Like a flickering moth trapped by light, the bomber was rendered impotent as it was pounded by the guns.

Often other crews over the target saw a blinding flash in the sky as a coned aircraft was blown into fragmentary pieces by a direct hit. It was not a very pleasant sight, or indeed one to inspire confidence, but whatever the feeling it could not be allowed to distract. It made sense to take all necessary precautions of course, but the task to seek out the aiming point was mandatory and still an issue to be solved – not easy for the bomb-aimer as he strained his eyes through the perspex panel let in the floor near the front gun turret and looked down at the blazing inferno. Often blinded by the glare of searchlights and the target obscured by smoke, it was difficult for him to pick out detail. The panoramic display by the entire pyrotechnics in full view was not the most reassuring sight. It needed strong nerves and a calm disposition, since at that moment, having established the aiming point, the bomb-aimer was virtually in charge of the aircraft. He guided the pilot by calling out steering instructions over the intercom. It was a big responsibility, and it decided the success or failure of the operation.

All bomb-aimers hoped to get it right with the first run over the target. Any repeat performance that he deemed necessary did not go down well with the crew, and it was an unhappy voice that came over the intercom when the bomb-aimer decided to abort the run-up for some particular reason and requested the pilot to go around again. To use a bomb sight effectively meant that a straight and level course had to be flown through the thick spread of flak, not a happy thought, especially since this usually meant fleeing through the centre of its seething core. It was an effort that stretched nerves to the full. It brought on a pulsating trepidation and caused butterflies in the stomach. The stark reality was that the outcome would only rate as high as the chance spin at a roulette table, with always the disquiet that out of the hundreds of shells layered in the sky, just one hit in the right place would be enough. So, given all this, it was a welcome moment when the bomb aimer, satisfied with his sighting, pressed the bomb release button and yelled over the intercom 'Bombs gone!'.

This was the signal to get the hell out of it, and the Wellington was dived, twisted and turned in its dash to break clear of the flak-infested area. Full boost, full airspeed, full everything was applied and the bomber shuddered and creaked under the strain. It was an apprehensive feeling for the crews, since the next few moments would be decisive and all eyes looked for some sort of opening in the fierce barrage set up by the guns. Anywhere would do. Direction was unimportant. Just an opening that could offer some sort of chance. The decision was made – the crew held their breath – and the bomber hurtled through the chosen path. The flak – vivid orange splotches and fragments of hot metal – burst around, rattling the fabric of the bomber. Then, as the Wellington screamed away, there was a numbed realisation that the sky had cleared as if by magic. The iron curtain had been breached. With composure gained, and clear of the danger zone, there was a compelling fascination to bank the Wellington steeply and take a look at the holocaust as it receded. It was an awesome sight, truly a Dantean inferno, as the illuminated tracer streaked up forming an illusion of the wires of a giant birdcage covering the area. Set in its midst was the dull red glow of the stricken city.

For the crews it was not the moment for reflection. The raid must be viewed in context and judged as a success.

Now all efforts had to be centred on the struggle to get home. This was tempered by the thought that the long trip to base would be a virtual repeat of the perils that had loomed getting to the target. It was always a sobering thought, but not one without some advantage, with the comforting knowledge that radio locations in England would be listening out for any message, however faint, to give what help they could. This would include a QDM, a radio bearing for the aircraft to home base, a navigator's dream, but with one vital snag – the aircraft had to be within a short range of the English coast before the beam became effective. For the Wellington crew flying in the remote depths of Germany it had to remain a wistful dream for the time being. Even so, the feeling as the course was set for base was simplicity itself: 'We'd made it coming in and we'd make it going back.'

Even the Wellington seemed to enter into the spirit of things. Shorn of its burden of bombs, all 4,000lb of them, it became buoyant again, easier to handle, much faster and able to reach greater heights. These factors gave the crew a feeling of superiority as the light flak was unable to reach us. The heavy stuff was still there of course, but with some knowledge of their position and the evasive courses we flew, it was possible to avoid the brunt of their fire.

The Wellington droned on, each minute bringing it nearer to home. Crew morale grew higher with every mile. Then at length the Dutch coast came up and so did the flak and searchlights. It was the usual reception, but down below there was the familiar sight of the Frisian Islands, and from now on, if the night fighters left us alone, it was a straight run over the North Sea – a happy thought if all went well. There was the added

A Whitley bomber coming into land. At the outbreak of war Whitleys equipped six squadrons in No 4 Group Bomber Command, and flew night raids throughout 1940–41 until being retired from first line service in the spring of 1942. (Flight)

reassurance that the radio people would be listening, ready to give the all-important heading that would bring us over the red flashing light – with its coded letter of the day, and its proximity to base. That is if all did go well, but it would be unwise to rely on this. Often, with success within grasp, the roulette wheel could throw up the wrong numbers. If it did, the perils were by no means over. A pea-soup fog or densely packed mist – common enemies to the returning bomber – could shroud the home airfield, close down the base and make diversion necessary, sometimes quite a distance away. Often other areas had conditions almost as bad, so a weary aircrew, after many hours in the air, had an unwelcome trek as the aircraft flew on its long tiresome path through the murky halflight of a breaking dawn. It was a journey with petrol gauges mostly running at danger level, which in the long run usually meant little alternative but to put down wherever possible. This was a risky business, especially on an airstrip ill-equipped to receive a heavy bomber.

Even when the home base was fully operational, the dangers had not yet passed. An enemy aircraft, usually a Ju 88, could be prowling around the base ready to pick off the unwary – and their proficiency at this was never to be doubted. Sometimes, to achieve an easier kill, it was not unknown for the more audacious German pilots to enter the circuit, navigation lights full on, hoping that their bluff would work as they intermingled with the bombers circling the airfield. If this ploy did succeed, they would then wait until a bomber prepared to land, and attack. This was when the Wellington was at its most vulnerable, with braking flaps down, landing speed adjusted and all attention being paid to touchdown. It was a hapless situation for the bomber, which had no chance at all of surviving this attack; a sad ending on the very last lap of a gruelling operation. Such a disaster was a stark reminder that with the hazards of operational flying nothing was finally settled until the Wellington was safely down, had taxied to dispersal and the exhausted crew had clambered out.

Emotions ran high at this point. At de-briefing most crews were over-stimulated, excited and shaken up, but at least the kitchen staff on the squadron were down to earth and many bomber crews will recall the tempting smell of the bacon and egg breakfast served in the mess on return. With the crews reasonably calm now, it was a pleasant, relaxing moment. Not only did the food titillate the palate, but it was also an opportunity to reflect on the reprieve – temporary or not – swim with the sweetness of life, and with the not unwelcome thought that the crew would be stood down for a possible two days. Not a lot in terms of time, but enough to prepare mentally for the next operation, and psychologically this was important if the composure to face the future was to be achieved.

Traumatic days, grave days, and the responsibility that had been thrust upon Bomber Command in the years 1940–41 had become not so much a battle but a crusade to hold the fort until the nation gathered strength. This carried with it a vital significance, not only to Britain but to the whole of Europe, perhaps even to the whole world.

As for myself, an Me 110, operating from the German base at Leeuwarden, made a copybook attack from astern and below on our Wellington at 1930 hours on the night of 31 October 1941. We never saw him until it was too late. We were never in with the chance of a shot. He just loomed out of the murk with a startling suddenness and opened up with a prolonged and devastating burst of cannon fire. It was all over in a matter of seconds. No time to consider. One minute we were happily on course and the next we were plunging down and about to crash, ironically, on Schiermonnikoog itself. Fate decreed that I should survive this, plus some enlightening, even if somewhat dreary years in German prison camps before liberation by Russian troops in May 1945.

Now, some 50 years on, there are some who hold the view that Hitler's war must be put aside and forgotten. I do not concur. But even if there were any substance in this belief, and as I write this with the memories crowding in, the very people who say this should also tell me how.

2: The last flight of *'H for Harry'*
Bill Garrioch

BY THE END OF 1940, the Battle of Britain was over, as was the threat of invasion, due to a large extent to the constant bombing of the Channel ports by Bomber Command. The RAF was building up its strength to go on the offensive.

In February 1941 I was a Sergeant Pilot in 15 Squadron, B Flight, stationed at RAF Wyton, near Huntingdon, operating Wellington 1C bombers of No 3 Group. Monday 10 February opened as any other day except that we expected to be on 'ops' that night, and our names on the battle order posted in the mess confirmed this. Speculation as to the target ranged from Bordeaux to Berlin, and finally settled on Hanover. We were a happy crew and worked hard to become as efficient as possible, being very much aware that good teamwork could enhance our chances of survival in an emergency. We never really believed that 'it could happen to us', and therefore tried to prepare ourselves to cope with the possibility of being 'shot up' or 'down'.

Our Navigator, Sergeant Bob Beioley, and WOP/AG Sergeant G. 'Taffy' Rearden had completed 12 operations with me in Blenheims prior to converting to the 'Wimpy', while second pilot Sergeant Bill Jordan was on his second trip with me for familiarisation. WOP/AG Sergeant George Hedge RNZAF and Sergeant J. Hall, rear gunner, a Scotsman with many trips in Coastal Command to his credit, made up the rest of my crew. This was our 16th raid.

Prior to air test in the morning, Taffy Rearden expressed the wish to be front gunner that night as a change from being cooped up inside the cabin. I agreed, as George Hedge was also a fully qualified WOP/AG. I was allocated T2702 *H-Harry* (Flight Lieutenant Morris's aircraft), as my *D-Dog* was being repaired after I had accidentally hit my wing-tip on the control caravan during a previous

A Wellington crew board their aircraft at a desolate and snow-covered airfield for another night raid over Germany. It was on a night like this, on 10/11 February 1941, that Sergeant Pilot Bill Garrioch and his crew in 15 Squadron, B Flight, took off from RAF Wyton, near Huntingdon, in Wellington IC T2702 H-Harry for Hanover on their 16th operation of the war.

take-off! As was the custom, a late morning air test at Alconbury, our operating satellite, was followed by lunch and briefing.

The briefing officer announced the target, the route in and out, and the bomb load, 4,000lb made up of seven 500lb bombs and the balance in incendiaries. The Met Office forecast clear skies, strong westerly winds, a full moon and very cold. The CO, Group Captain Forster, said that this was to be the biggest show of the war to date, wished us all the usual good luck, and told us to beware of moving stars (night fighters)! This great man, a First World War pilot, still wore a steel brace on his back caused by spinal injuries received in a crash. Even so, he flew with us occasionally, and when we went missing, thinking we might be down in the North Sea, he led a 6-hour search looking for us.

Take-off was timed for 1730 hours and the flight duration expected to be about 7 hours. Then followed the usual pre-flight planning between pilot, navigator and crews. We then went to the mess for our tea of bacon and eggs, back to our quarters to change into warmer clothing, and of course to empty our pockets. The ritual of this act always gave me a momentary feeling of apprehension until I put some small change back into my pocket in case we had to land away from base on return. The funny thing is, I had only half a crown in small change, which I put into my pocket, that being the only article carried on my person.

We then boarded the Bedford crew bus for the 6-mile journey to Alconbury, our satellite airfield. Generally during these bus journeys there was the usual chatter, pocket chess, or cards, but I remember vividly that on this occasion everyone seemed quiet and preoccupied with their thoughts, so much so that Bob remarked on it. Soon we arrived at our dispersal. I signed the Form 700, and as I climbed the ladder into the aircraft I remember Chiefy Wright saying to me, 'If you break this one, don't bring it back!' I laughed and said that I would be a good boy and nurse his precious Wimpy. I glanced at my watch and at the other aircraft around the dispersal area.

Time to start up. Fuel on, first port, and the starboard engines coughed, burst into life, and warmed up at 1,000rpm. Soon we ran each engine up to take-off rpm (2,650), tested the magnetos, oil pressure and temperature, and cylinder head temperature, and checked and set the gyro, cooling gills, flaps, etc. All the crew reported ready. The time was now 1725 hours. I gave the signal and with a final wave to our much-appreciated ground crew, we moved out towards our take-off position near the end of the runway. We were No 2 to go.

At precisely 1730 hours No 1 started his take-off run, and as he reached the end of the runway I lined up and got my green light from the caravan. Brakes off, I opened the throttle slowly to maximum power as we started rolling. As we gathered speed the noise was deafening and seemed to reach a crescendo that vibrated throughout the loaded aircraft. I kept the nose down until the last bit of the all-too-short runway loomed up, then, pulling up, she lifted clear, a light kiss on the concrete, and off. Wheels up and nose kept down to increase flying speed. I throttled back to climbing rpm to reach operating height, and the engine noise now changed to a welcome hum. All was well.

Bob gave me the course, which I confirmed from my knee-pad. As the snow-covered countryside receded far below in the darkness, Bill Jordan flew the aircraft and the gunners entered their turrets while I visited each member of the crew to ensure that all was in order. Soon we reached the coast at Orfordness and levelled off at 11,000 feet. The navigator and wireless operator were at their stations, and the lighting was very subdued, creating an eerie yet efficient atmosphere tinged with the smell of dope and fuel, amid the roar of the smooth-sounding Pegasus engines. When we were over the sea Taffy and Jock test-fired their guns. From now on we were on the alert for night fighters.

It was cold and clear. The patches of white cumulus would make us an easily identified target seen from above. I took over before we reached the Dutch coast, which we crossed at 1850 hours – another 213 miles and 65 minutes to the target. We had a very strong tail wind and ground speed was nearly 200mph. Bob got a pin-point. We were almost dead on track – a slight course alteration and all was well. We were lucky so far.

It was unbelievably quiet. We flew towards the target and still there was no flak. We were very much alert, but it was the easiest run-in so far, and the ground was easily identifiable. Only 5 minutes to the target. Then we saw it. Bob was a good navigator – we were almost spot on. On the eastern horizon the rising moon assisted target identification. With bomb doors opened and bombs fused, Bob went down to the bomb sights. He saw the target nestled in the crook of the 'Y'-section of a big road junction. We had a following wind, so I throttled back a little and kept the aircraft steady. Right a little . . . I did not see any activity at all, not even a little flak.

The first Wimpy's bombs burst, then suddenly there was a series of flashes close to Gilmore's aircraft. Bob called, 'Left . . . left . . . left . . . a bit more . . . steady now . . . steady.' Flak now curled lazily up towards us, then there was heavy ack-ack to our left. It was accurate for height, but was not near us. Must be the other aircraft in trouble.

Bob called 'Bombs gone!' and I immediately turned steeply to port. Jock in the rear turret watched our bombs burst. There were only six flashes. Where was the seventh? Gilmore's aircraft started a fire and our incendiaries were well alight. Ack-ack was almost non-existent with us, but as we flew away we saw other aircraft getting a hot reception and the sky was full of flak. All this time the fires seemed to grow in intensity – Hanover was visible 40 miles away. The moon was up and it was like daylight. We watched for enemy fighters but all was quiet and we could not even see other aircraft.

Against a strong head wind our ground speed was now only 85 knots; it was going to be a long haul home. Large white cumulus clouds were building up below. As we crossed the eastern coast of the Zuider Zee at Kampen, Jock suddenly called out 'Fighter below and behind!'. I put the engines to cruising revs, and steep turned to starboard to face him. As I turned I saw an Me 110, which was turning to meet me. I turned violently to port to avoid him. Jock gave him a long burst, but he still attacked, hitting the aircraft in the fuselage and port engine. I put the flaps down and soon the shooting stopped. He had overshot.

I heard the cannon fire hit the aircraft somewhere behind me. Jock said that he had been hit. Could we get him out of the turret? The port engine was on fire. I turned off the fuel and full throttle. Bob called, 'Are we on fire?' It seems strange to relate, but I vividly remember that with my mind concentrating only on the job in hand, avoiding the fighter attack, Bob's sudden announcement on the intercom must have paralysed my senses if only for a fleeting instant, because as I was looking through the cockpit window, superimposed in space, just outside the windscreen, was a very clear picture of my grandfather and a great uncle looking directly at me. It was so clear that I even recognised my uncle's old tweed jacket! Then it was gone and I was back to reality. It frightened me because these two much-loved relatives had been dead for about seven years. Much later George told me that cannon shells came through the fuselage and exploded in his radio equipment. How he and Bob were not hit I'll never know. I was saved by the armour plate behind my head. At that moment I knew we had to survive, and I seemed to find added strength and courage to risk anything that would bring us out of this alive.

I looked back and the fuselage was full of smoke. I could not see anyone. Perhaps a flare was burning. Taffy moaned faintly, saying 'Get me out', and I saw the fighter turn to port over our port wing-tip. Bill Jordan went forward to open the escape hatch and to get Taffy out of the turret. I told the crew to prepare to bale out, and raised the flaps.

We were diving now. The fighter came in again and once more I put the flaps down and the aircraft yawed violently to port while I throttled back and side-slipped to almost stalling speed. Cannon and machine-gun tracer went just over the top of the cockpit, but miraculously we were not hit. This time, as the fighter went over the top of us, I raised the flaps and control was easier. I think only the starboard flap worked, but I am not sure.

I told Taffy to shoot the fighter down, position 10 o'clock. He did not answer. Bill Jordan tried desperately to operate the turret door release and get him out. George Hedge was standing beside me ready to help when Bill opened the floor escape hatch. Bob and Jock were still back in the smoke-filled fuselage. Were they alive? I did not know. I decided that unless we baled out or landed quickly we would all die.

We were blazing very badly now. I signalled to George not to jump as I had not given the order, and I dived for the ground in the hope that a crash landing might save some of us. The aircraft persisted in turning to port. We were diving very steeply and fast, over 300 knots. Through the cockpit window I saw the port engine, and that the inner wing was now on fire – off all fuel and full throttle starboard engine. We did not see the fighter again after the second attack.

The frozen expanse of the Zuider Zee was hurtling towards us. I tried to level off but the elevators were sluggish, and we hit the ice slightly nose down and skidded for what seemed to be miles. Then, suddenly, she broke through the ice and the nose filled up with water and ice through the open escape hatch. Then the aircraft stopped.

It was very hot, but we did not explode as I imagined in my initial fright at the sound of Bob's cry of 'Fire!' I opened the cockpit escape hatch and lifted myself out on to the cockpit roof. George followed, together with Bob and Jock, who was wounded and burnt. Bill appeared and assisted Bob with Jock. I jumped down on to the ice, which was melting, and with George's help took Jock from Bob and Bill.

Wellington IC T2888 LN-R of 99 Squadron pictured at Newmarket Heath. This aircraft was one of 22 bombers that crashed in heavy fog, R-Robert crashing at Stags Halt, Wisbech, on the night of 11/12 February 1941, the night following that during which Bill Garrioch's Wellington went missing. (RAF Museum)

I looked at the front turret. It appeared to be undamaged but was tilted slightly forward. Taffy was inside. He did not move, although George said he appeared to move his arm. We tried in desperation to smash the perspex cover with our bare fists, but to no avail. The turret was sinking and the ice we were standing on was already below water to our knees. Taffy, sadly, was gone.

The heat rapidly melted the ice and the ammunition in the rear of the plane was exploding. We moved away quickly and, fearing an explosion, dragged Jock with us. Some of us fell through where the ice looked black. We dragged each other out with difficulty. We were 100 yards away now, and still there was no explosion. It was impossible to carry Jock and still remain upright on this slippery ice. He was badly injured: his foot looked to be almost severed, and he had bullet holes in his burned clothing. His face was red and his hair was burned because he removed his helmet. Someone produced a penknife and we cut off my parachute harness and improvised a tourniquet for Jock's leg behind his knee as he was bleeding badly. We strapped his good leg to the wounded one and the four of us proceeded to drag him on his back using another parachute harness as a trace. I wrapped my angora wool scarf, which was a bit scorched, around his head to keep him warm. He was very weak but conscious. We told him to cheer up, as we would try to get help.

Glancing at my watch I saw that it was 2320 hours. We must have crashed at about 2230. We could not see any land except for a small white light that flashed intermittently on the horizon to the east. We heard a series of explosions from our aircraft, which finally sank from sight. We were alone in what appeared to be a sea of ice with no land visible. I estimated that we must be approximately 15km west of Kampen, so we decided to walk towards the distant light. I now realised what the Arctic wastes must be like. I felt very sad at leaving Taffy. Was he fatally wounded in the air, or killed in the crash? I would never know. A strange twist of fate had killed Taffy and saved George.

Some time later a heavily laden He 111 circled us as he flew towards England. We also heard some of our aircraft flying home and wished them better luck than us. If only one could have landed and picked us up – wishful thinking! Without any doubt we were saved by the ice. Hitting dry land or water at that speed would almost certainly have killed us all. Five out of six survived and only one wounded. It seemed like a miracle!

The wind was very strong and cold and the icy spindrift swirled across the surface of the ice making it difficult to see, at times reducing visibility to almost nil. Three of us pulled Jock along while the fourth walked ahead to test the strength of the ice. At intervals I opened the tourniquet on Jock's leg to let it bleed freely for a minute, but eventually I had to stop, as we were afraid he might die. It was now daylight, almost 8am, and the wind was still very strong, but thankfully at our backs, which made things a little easier. All at once we noticed that seagulls were flying down to collect bits of flesh that had fallen off Jock's foot. I could see that it was turning a strange colour and thought that it must be gangrenous. He moaned a lot and said he wanted to sleep and that we should leave him and try to get help. At that time we were resting for 5 minutes in every hour, sitting in a circle to shelter him from the biting wind. I do not remember feeling very cold, even though we were all wet from the waist down. I think it was the fear of Jock dying and of us all falling through the ice if it melted that kept us going.

Eventually we reached a channel of very thin ice where an icebreaker had gone through the day before. We rested again while George searched for a way across. Luckily he did find an ice floe big enough to cross to continue our journey. We could now see a slight rise on the horizon, and the flashing light had gone out, so we aimed for that point. We could not see any sign of life in the distance and we almost prayed aloud that we would be seen and rescued before Jock died from exposure.

During the forenoon Bill saw some people running along the shore. We had been seen! We kept on walking, dragging Jock, who was now almost delirious and probably suffering from frostbite. When we were close to the shore Bob and I decided to walk or swim ashore and give ourselves up to get help. Bob showed great courage here as I learned later that he was a non-swimmer and neither of us knew the depth of the water. We checked our pockets to ensure that we had nothing on us that would identify us with 15 Squadron or Cambridgeshire.

As we approached the shore the ice gave way and we sank up to our waists. Two German soldiers shouted at us and as we raised our arms they waded into the water and helped us out. We could not, because of our language difficulties, communicate with them, but we did manage to convey to them that one of our crew was wounded. Several other soldiers now appeared on the scene and with a small boat broke a channel through the ice and brought Jock, Bill and George ashore. We were taken into the Flak unit and given schnapps, and Jock, who was by now in a very low state, as much as he could drink. He still managed to request a visit to the toilet and we carried him and tended to his needs. One German who spoke a little English tried to make him say what aircraft he was in, but we would not let him talk.

About 2 hours later an ambulance arrived and we were loaded aboard and driven very fast around the perimeter of the Zuider Zee to the Queen Wilhelmina Hospital in Amsterdam. The journey was hair-raising! It was a small converted van that had two stretchers on either side with a gap of about 18 inches between them, with the result that the lower occupant could only lie on his back and not turn over. The driver was travelling at 100kph whenever possible because of Jock's condition (for which we later thanked him), so it was of necessity a very rough ride!

It was now getting dark. We were treated and allowed to wait while Jock was operated on, which they did immediately. His leg was amputated just below the knee. The doctor said that he would be fine. We were all sincerely grateful for this. In his delirium, Jock said that he thought he had hit the fighter. Two Luftwaffe pilots who later came to visit a comrade said that the encounter had been on the previous night. This was also confirmed by a Dutch nurse. However, I do not know if it was as a result of action on our part, because I saw the fighter break away to port very close, and his rear gunner did not shoot at us.

After Jock's operation the four of us were taken in a van under guard to the city gaol and locked up in one cell. A German orderly brought us each a packet of raw herring, one slice of bread and a mug of ersatz coffee. The cell was very warm. I took off most of my clothes and sat nearly naked on the two planks that served as a bed. I looked at my watch – it was still going, although it was wet, and the time was 8pm, 26½ hours after taking off from Alconbury. In those few hours we had lost our freedom and were reduced to prisoners with nothing but the wet clothes we stood up in. I wondered what my parents would do when they received the 'Missing' telegram. I was to have met my father and a fellow pilot at Holyhead for three days leave in Ireland after the raid.

While I was gathering my thoughts I heard banging on the wall of the cell and I had a shouted, guarded conversation with Pilot Officer Green, a Canadian who was shot down the same night in a Hampden. The guard in the corridor soon told us to keep quiet. At about 10pm I heard the welcome drone of Wimpies flying overhead. Suddenly, without warning, a light flak gun opened up outside my cell and started shooting at the bombers. Later I must have fallen asleep from exhaustion because I woke to find a guard opening the cell door and offering me a mug of mint tea, which tasted horrible and I did not drink it.

At about 7.30am we were taken out of the cells and P/O Green, his two surviving crew, Don Bristow and Bert Fisher, and the four of us were put into a small truck and driven at speed through Amsterdam over cobbled streets full of people going to work. Through the slits in the canvas awning we could see that our driver had knocked down two cyclists without stopping – our first taste of the Nazi boot in Holland! Soon we stopped at the station, where we were escorted under heavy guard through the travellers on to the platform. The guards pushed people out of the way with their rifle butts. I thought of escaping and hung back hoping to get lost in the crowd, but the guards were too experienced and the officer behind me pulled out a small revolver and pointed me very much in the direction he wanted me to go! Nothing was said but I kept on walking. Bill Jordan looked at me. I think that he had the same idea!

The crowds parted and made way for us, while some gave us slaps on the back and wished us good luck. A carriage was reserved for us and we were told to sit down. A lot of people on the platform crowded around and gave us the 'thumbs up' sign. A platform vendor tried to give is some chocolate from her trolley, but the guard hit her and knocked the trolley over, spilling the contents on to the ground, which caused an angry scene. I think the guards acted through fear of the people and their understandable aggressive attitude towards them.

As the train moved out we stood and waved, which brought an immediate reaction from one of our four guards, the officer having now left us and having put an NCO in charge. He told us in English 'For you the war is over', and that we would have a pleasant journey if we behaved, because he said escape was impossible, and in any case if we tried we would be shot. We felt that at least this guard meant it! The ration for the journey consisted of two slices of Dutch meatloaf and a tin of pork fat between two persons. Soon after leaving the station I saw two big hoardings indicating the docks departure area for Dublin and Glasgow – so near and yet so far, especially as we were heading south-east and into captivity.

In 1969 Bob Beioley sent me a copy of *Shell Aviation* magazine and suggested that I read the article on the 'Harvest of Iselmeer'. As a result I wrote to Colonel De Jong of the Royal Netherlands Air Force, giving him all the details that I could remember of the crash. By an amazing coincidence my letter arrived the same morning that a Dutch farmer, Mr Aalbrink, uncovered a Wellington wreck in the mud about 17km west of Kempen. It consisted of approximately 1,000 kilograms of geodetic scrap, one Bristol Pegasus 18 engine, some live and unexploded 1936, 1937 and 1940 .303 ammunition, and, sadly, the remains of Taffy Rearden, our front gunner. The assembly jig number T2702 was found stamped on a serial number-plate affixed to a piece of geodetic framework. Colonel de Jong obtained the night fighter combat report, which stated that the fighter was a Bf 110 flown from Middenmeer north of Schiphol by Hauptmann Walter Ehle of II./NJG1 at 2335 hours. Ammunition expended by him in the attack was 560 rounds of 7mm mg and 100 rounds of 20mm cannon.

Taffy's remains were buried at the military cemetery at Jonkersbosch. In 1970 my wife and I visited Holland as guests of the RNEAF. Together with my cousin, who lived in Amsterdam, we spent a day with Colonel de Jong and Gerry Zwannenberg, the Chief Salvage Investigator. No praise could be high enough for these two men and their team, who have worked ceaselessly for many years to uncover and establish the identity of hundreds of crashed aircraft that have lain hidden in the mud of the Iselmeer. We met the farmer, Mr Aalbrink, who presented me with the steering wheel of T2702, and we visited the actual spot where the aircraft sank.

Next day we visited Jonkersbosch to pay our last respects to Taffy. It was a sobering thought when standing amid seemingly endless rows of white headstones to realise how much the free world owes to such people as Taffy, and how easily we could have been lying beside him. Later, while speaking to George Hedge, whose front turret position Taffy occupied on that last raid, he confided to me that he started to pray and say aloud the Lord's Prayer as we dived for the ground, and then watched the propeller blades bend like paper on hitting the ice. I think his prayers were heard, as my hands were guided that night.

3: Whitley wanderings
Basil Craske

THE WHOLE ATMOSPHERE of an operational squadron as opposed to a training unit was very apparent as soon as we arrived at Leeming, Yorkshire, in January 1941.

It is rather difficult to describe but it was quite obvious that 10 Squadron was there to do a job and everything seemed geared to that end. A serious approach certainly, but not without its humorous interludes. The Squadron motto was and is *Rem Acu Tangere* ('Straight as an arrow to the target'), and I recall some artistic wag amending the plunging arrow to become two fingers raised amongst the flames, with the caption *Ram Acu Rectum* – all beautifully drawn in coloured chalks on the blackboard in the crewroom. There were periods of boredom when waiting for the next assignment, but the time of inactivity did not last for long.

Quite apart from operational flights there were many test flights for the aircraft, experimental navigation exercises and even a crash course in astro-navigation and the use of a sextant, which was invaluable, bearing in mind that from take-off until landing no radio communication was allowed except in emergency. Consequently, all navigation was by dead reckoning, directional loop aerial and the stars, none of which were very accurate more often that not. Navigation in 1941 was very basic. At

Sergeant Basil Craske, Whitley pilot, No 10 Squadron, 1941. (Basil Craske)

briefing there was a large wall map with a red tape extending from Leeming to the target. Aircraft were expected to leave the country more or less at the approved coastal feature, but getting there and back was very much in the hands of the pilot and navigator.

An example of suspect navigation could be seen on the very large map of Europe and the British Isles in the crewroom, which had a suitable pin and flag indicating the targets bombed by *Shiny Ten*. In the very middle of England at Bassingbourn there was a pin where some crew had unloaded their bombs upon an inviting but dimly lit runway! There were many others on the other side of the water, one of which showed a successful raid on Turin in Italy.

Our first operation was to bomb the docks at Rotterdam. The captain of the aircraft was a Flight Lieutenant, and I was second pilot. This Flight Lieutenant was an RAF 'Regular' whose basic raison d'être was as an armament officer. I am sure that he was a better armament officer than a pilot. All his night landings were straight down from 15 feet – 'Hang on, chaps, we've arrived'.

The normal bombing run was carried out on a straight and level basis with the bomb-aimer, the second pilot in a Whitley, directing the pilot 'left' or 'right' as the case may be. The height was constant and this figure was set into the bombsight together with other factors such as speed, type of bombs and order of release. There was another method of dropping bombs, which was the glide approach; this would only be considered by an armament officer.

The relative merits of one system over the other are that a straight and level run at a constant height and speed and direction gives the ack-ack gunners a significant time in which to plot the position of the aircraft, and the flak becomes increasingly accurate. With the glide approach method the theory is that the throttled-back engines allow the aircraft to silently glide down towards the target, the glide factor having been set on the bombsight, and hopefully the enemy on the ground will not notice your presence. All very well in theory, but if the glide approach is commenced too far from the target, the aircraft arrives over the target at a dangerously low height.

It was a beautifully clear night with something approaching a full moon and the target docks were plainly visible. I lined them up at the top of the graticule – the fine optical lines of the bombsight – and waited for the target to centre, when I could press the tit to operate 'Mickey Mouse' (the bomb release mechanism). We glided lower and lower and the flak became thicker and thicker. It is OK if you can see the bursts, OK if you can hear the explosions, but when the cockpit fills with cordite fumes it is time for some concern! The impatience of our pilot was becoming increasingly obvious, but in the end I did manage to make a good drop, although we did get a bit plastered in the process.

The bombsight is situated in the 'greenhouse' at the nose of the aircraft and is surrounded by perspex. I was naturally in rather a hurry to return to the body of the cabin, but having forgotten that I had plugged my oxygen tube into the bomb-aimer's position, my hasty retreat was rather like an internal bungy jump. However, all's well that ends well, and we managed to find our way back to Leeming for our 15-foot drop, having learned quite a lot from our baptism of fire.

Our next target was the Kiel Canal itself, and the same crew duly took off on another moonlit night. On the face of it, operations to Kiel, Hamburg, Bremen and Emden were not so hazardous or taxing as those to inland targets, as the majority of the flight was across open sea, leaving Yorkshire by Flamborough Head and flying due east. Apart from the flak ships off the islands of Texel, Terschelling and Borkum, if you got too close to the coast, and the very strong defences of Heligoland, there was not much

Armstrong Whitworth Whitley I K7188 of No 10 Squadron, one of 34 Mark Is built for the RAF. These aircraft were powered by two 920hp Armstrong Siddeley Tiger IX engines. (BAe)

to worry about until it was time to approach the target. To get to north German targets we would leave the coast at Flamborough Head and there take a drift sight to check and adjust if necessary for a change in predicted wind direction. The lighthouse at Terschelling was usually operative and on a good night taking a bearing from it could confirm your position. Otherwise, it was astro-navigation all the way, always assuming that the stars could be seen.

On this occasion the sea crossing went without incident, and from a considerable distance the renowned defences of Kiel and the Canal could be seen blasting away. The closer we got to the heart of the matter the more agitated became a certain ex-armament officer. I had the night's target in my bombsight, but I regret to say that I did not have the opportunity of declaring 'Bombs gone!' – they were jettisoned early and short of the target from within the cockpit.

There were some rude words expressed by the rest of the crew and at de-briefing. As diplomatically as possible without 'dropping him in it', we made our feelings apparent. It was not long afterwards that the Flight Lieutenant departed 10 Squadron, presumably back to his 'arms'. An unfortunate episode, but these things did happen, as we found out.

Our next captain was Pilot Officer Willi Freund, a Czech by nationality. I cannot recall the target attacked, and presumably all went according to plan. I do remember his 'Zees ees Rarbit Zee for Zebra calling Bandlor'. That was the last trip I made as a second pilot/bomb-aimer, and thereafter I had my own crew and aircraft. I was still only 20 years of age.

Hamburg was a well-defended city, but I remember one very clear night when we had made a particularly good bombing run and had seen our bombs burst on target producing the usual rectangular box pattern of explosions. Many other aircraft were hitting the target and so impressive was the sight that I circled Hamburg to enjoy the view! It was not often that I hung around waiting to be shot at.

I recall on one occasion with a full moon, not a cloud in the sky and at about 12,000 feet, I spotted a Ju 88 heading towards us and from abeam, but at about 2,000 feet below. I hastily changed places with the second pilot, who was 'driving' at the time, but I am pleased to report that the Jerry obviously had elsewhere to go. We did have regular practice in evasive action in conjunction with Spitfires from Catterick, which amounted to the rear gunner telling the pilot when to pull up the nose and do a semi-stall turn, hopefully to get the fighter to overshoot – quite effective, although the 'arse-end Charlie' usually ended up being sick.

On the way home on these runs it could be a pleasant experience, if the cloud top was around 8–10,000 feet, to engage 'George' (the automatic pilot) and spend time taking sextant shots of Polaris, which gave a pattern of latitude progress and was a good check for me on the navigator's prowess. 'George' was not very efficient and gently undulated the aircraft in and out of the cloud top – a very pleasant memory. There was always the constant monitoring ear for any imperfection in the drone of the Merlin Vs, but I never did have the least spot of bother from a purely mechanical aspect.

Targets to the south involved the warships *Scharnhorst* and *Gneisenau*, which were very much part of Bomber Command's itinerary in 1941. I came into the picture while they were at Brest, and I recall two trips there, mainly because the German defences produced the best fireworks display in Europe. In order to protect the warships, which were extremely well camouflaged, the Jerries used to 'hosepipe' the tracer flak in order to maintain a curtain of fire over the whole target area. All very lovely to look at, but invariably all aircraft suffered some damage. The bombing run at Brest was always exciting, to say the least. Despite, or perhaps because of, our efforts to cripple these ships, the *Scharnhorst* slipped out of Brest in July 1941 and re-positioned herself at La Pallice, near La Rochelle and a long way south from Brest. Nevertheless, it was decreed that we should let her know that we were still after her.

The distance to be covered necessitated the fitting of auxiliary fuel tanks to the inside of the fuselage, so moving from one part of the aircraft to another required a crawl on your belly for part of the distance. The unusual weight distribution did not do a lot for the trim of the aircraft and, coupled with the extra fuel plus the bomb load, the take-off was a bit dicey, but with brakes on at the extreme end of the runway, with full boost and almost full throttle, I could get the tail off the ground almost before we started to run. As the other end of the runway approached a little bouncing technique got us safely airborne and on our way.

The route was compiled specifically for this raid, and took us down the eastern side of England to leave these shores eventually at Southampton, where the defensive balloons were grounded. Across the Channel to the French mainland, we had to go straight for La Pallice as opposed to an over-sea route because of the distance, but our bombing run was, I recall, to be from the seaward side of where the *Scharnhorst* was known to be 'parked'. Apart from the odd spot of flak, the journey there was not too difficult and, having arrived, the target area (but not the ship) could easily be pin-pointed from the pattern of the shoreline, which is unique with its promontory at this point. Flak over the target was fairly intense, but nowhere near as severe as at Brest.

And so to the return trip – again back across France and in at Southampton with balloons still on the ground. The next point of reference was the Abingdon beacon, and from there up the country to Leeming and home. Unfortunately, after leaving the Abingdon beacon the cloud cover was 10/10ths up to about 3,000 feet, but flying on a dead-reckoning course we stooged on . . . Dawn was just breaking as I made a reasonable landing and taxied behind the vehicle sent to lead to me to dispersal, where an airman with the usual two torches saw me safely parked and shut down. A ground crew appeared and secured the aircraft, and as we emerged the question had to be asked: 'Where are we?' The answer was 'Squires Gate', which meant that we had been flying around Blackpool Tower in the dark. In the mess they were amazed that we had been airborne for more than 10 hours, as the Beaufighters they were flying had a maximum duration of just 1¼ hours. A good breakfast and a few hours shut-eye saw us off again and back home to Leeming. A subsequent check of the aircraft suggested that the compasses were not producing the correct readings. Perhaps they were being kind.

The Channel ports (theirs, not ours) were fairly frequent destinations at this time, and usually a nice easy operation to complete. On one occasion the target area was found without difficulty, even to the extent of seeing rows of invasion barges awaiting our attention. I was flying *Q-Queenie* (my regular partner and the nicest and fastest aircraft of the squadron; being the oldest, she was not encumbered by the bulbous addition of an astrodome). The bombs were dropped to good effect, and my intention was a heading back home to our ritualistic eggs and bacon breakfast in double quick time.

It was a pleasant night and *Queenie* enjoyed the straightforward flight home above the clouds. Bandlor (Leeming) responded to our call dead on ETA. I was given a QBB (cloud base) of 400 feet and, in accordance with usual practice, I confirmed that I would descend towards Linton and hedge-hop home. The Leeming to Linton track avoided the Yorkshire Moors to the east and the Pennines to the west. Down and down we went and at 400 feet we had not broken cloud – nearer to 200 feet, visibility was just about passable by wartime standards, remembering that it was all happening just after dawn. The River Swale or the main railway line could usually guide us near enough to base to see the runway, but that night the visibility was such that I found no landmarks.

In no time at all the cloud base came down and the ground went up, leaving me to take some quick evasive action to avoid an oak tree. I didn't quite succeed, and the underside of the port wing scraped across the upper branches. A loud exclamation from my wireless operator came through the intercom and, in wireless operator's expressive language, apart from wanting to know what the hell was going on, he informed me that he had lost his trailing aerial, around somebody's chimney he thought. He did add that he had forgotten to reel it in!

I considered that enough was enough and quickly climbed into the clouds; while gaining height I instructed my Canadian second pilot to call up base, telling them what the true cloud base was and requesting a QFX (diversion airstrip). Unfortunately my second dickie had left the TR9 on transmit, and when he eventually did get through to Leeming their immediate response was, 'Would you please moderate your language as there are WAAFs listening out at Dishforth?' At least they knew what I thought of their 400 feet cloud base!

Eventually we got our QFX to Silloth on the Solway Firth. Being the first aircraft to return, I had the same problems with the ground crew at the beacon and did a lob down ahead of every other aircraft on duty that night; there was a full house at Silloth that morning. The underside of *Queenie*'s port wing, which was canvas-covered, was in shreds, so we had a pleasant day or two at Maryport while they patched it up before returning to base. Another narrow squeak.

On another occasion we were bound for St Nazaire with the intention of demolishing the U-boat pens, which were well concealed and embedded in massive concrete structures. The weather was far from ideal with bags of cumulus cloud producing thundery conditions, particularly over France. In such conditions it was common for the propellers to look like giant Catherine wheels, with the blade-tips having a visible electrical charge producing this effect. This in itself caused no problem, but having emerged from one cloud bank and entered another almost immediately there was a terrific sudden and violent noise with an accompanying flash sufficient to temporarily blind me. I think we must have gone from a positive cloud to a negative cloud, or vice versa, and we were the spark between. In any event, we were at about 12,000 feet, and both engines decided that they had had enough and cut out. The Sperry panel (ASI, altimeter, artificial horizon, etc) also decided to go on strike, and the radios had blown, not to mention the compasses, which had been demagnetised. My first instinct was to maintain a 'flying attitude' and accordingly, once I had some sort of vision back, I put the nose down and hoped for the best.

The propellers were still rotating even without power from the engines, and apart from varying the throttle settings and altering the propeller pitch, there was little I could do. Much to my relief, at about 8,000 feet the Merlins began to show some signs of life and eventually resumed reasonable health. It was later explained to me that in all probability the electrical charge had caused the magnetos to fail, but the continued turn of the engines by the free-spinning propellers had had the effect of making them workable again.

So there we were over France, virtually without instruments, but with a glimpse of Polaris we could deduce that England was 'over there'. Fortunately the night was clear and over the Channel the bomb load was jettisoned manually. Having crossed the coast it was possible to establish our position by means of the flashing beacons and reference to the rice-paper 'flimsy', and I virtually beacon-hopped all the way back to Leeming. Without a functional TR9 we could not announce our arrival, and not having gone the whole distance we were not expected. However, the usual three 'glim' lamps indicated the runway and without instruments on a pretty dark night I made a good landing and taxied round to my dispersal point to wake up the ground crew! I actually got a pat on the back from the CO for this exploit!

The last area of operations relates to Germany itself, and the targets were many and varied. The nature of the operations was more hazardous for two basic reasons: the defences were more efficient and concentrated, being in defence of the 'Fatherland' itself, and the time spent over enemy territory was much longer.

One of the most significant features of the defence system was a mighty bank of searchlights some 20 miles or so across, stretching from about Emden in the north to almost the French/German border in the south. Not only were these searchlights used in collaboration with flak batteries, but night fighters also prowled in abundance waiting for an intruder to be 'coned'. It must be remembered that in 1941 with a full bomb load it took a long time to struggle up to 12,000 feet, which was about the Whitley's ceiling, and at that height the indicated airspeed was in the region of 120mph, so the searchlight barrier was something to be taken seriously. At 12,000 feet a single searchlight could not pick out an aircraft, but a concentration of light working in a cone shape certainly lit up the cockpit. By extraordinary manoeuvres and a bit of good fortune the 'cone' could usually be lost, but the safest method was to hang around outside the searchlight band until two aircraft were separately 'coned', then, nose down, nip smartly between them and through the danger area while the Jerries were otherwise engaged.

As well as the searchlight problem there were many and changing areas of concentrated flak batteries, which necessitated taking avoiding action at all times when over enemy territory. If a constant course, speed and height were maintained for only a short period of time these factors could be plotted, and even without the help of computers a shell could arrive in the same piece of airspace as occupied by the aircraft. Thus the continuous procedure was 2 degrees left, 2 degrees right, 50 feet up, 25 feet down, adjust your speed and hope you've kept close to the average course required for navigation purposes. Believe me, when you've been doing this for 2 or 3 hours non-stop, you end up with a sticky shirt.

I can recall targeting Frankfurt on one night, which meant 5 hours over enemy territory with 5 hours' evasive action. This was not a particularly memorable operation, but reasonably successful and home to bacon and eggs for breakfast and head down until lunchtime. The rub was that there was an early afternoon briefing to do exactly the same thing again that night. I was not very enthusiastic, but having revisited Frankfurt and returned safely, my memory of these two raids on consecutive nights is the shattering physical experience.

Towards the end of 1940, for the defence of Germany the Nachtjagd had been formed as an elite night fighter force within the Luftwaffe. Prior to that time there were very few night fighters, most being Me 109s, and they did not have any effective ground co-ordinated control. As time progressed Me 110s and the new Ju 88 fighters came into prominence. The greater development, however, related to the German radar and its ability to pin-point an intruder and guide a night fighter to it, and this facility was used to great effect along the Kammhuber searchlight barrier now stretching from Schleswig-Holstein in the north to Liege in Belgium in the south. Against such odds it will be appreciated that the chance of finishing a tour of 30 operations was somewhat remote. In the early part of June 1941 I had ten days leave, and upon my return to Leeming there were very few faces that were familiar. There was less than a handful of pilots who had any length of operational experience. My beloved *Q-Queenie* had failed to return, and with her my navigator Bill Rice, with whom I was very friendly and with whom I had completed a fair number of trips. He was an excellent navigator (he had his 2nd Mate's ticket in the Merchant Navy before the war) and a number of his 'logs' of trips we had completed together had been used as training examples at 4 Group HQ.

Certainly in my time all targets in Germany were of military importance or were industrial centres, and of course the Ruhr was high on the list of target priorities and a constant source of attention by Bomber Command. Cologne, Düsseldorf, Essen and Dortmund were visited frequently, with peripheral targets such as Hamm marshalling yards and Mannheim included for good measure.

For much of the early part of August 1941 I was not called upon to take part in every operation flown by the squadron, and bearing in mind the imminent conversion to the Halifax as the squadron aircraft, my egocentric thoughts produced the idea that as one of the few remaining pilots with operational experience I was being saved for this event. I had taken part in 25 raids and had more than 250 hours of operational flying under my belt; a complete tour consisted of 30 trips.

A relatively easy trip to Cologne came my way on 16/17 August. My crew consisted of Sergeant Harold P. Calvert, navigator, Sergeant King, WOP-AG, and Sergeant Bruce Robertson, rear gunner. We took off in Rabbit *G-George* at 2203 hours, having been fully briefed in the afternoon. The meteorological part of the briefing promised us cloud cover from the Dutch coast to the target. Accordingly, as was the practice I sat down with Calvert to plot our route and discuss possible problems. In view of the promised cloud cover we agreed upon a track directly to the target, as opposed to going in by the back door.

It was a relatively calm night as I remember it, and after a bit of a stooge across the North Sea we obtained a good fix and some flak around the Hook of Holland. It was fairly obvious by this time that the promised cloud cover was a figment of the Met man's imagination, as it was as clear as a bell. But our die was cast, our course plotted, so we continued as planned. The searchlights were obviously working overtime, and it was not going to be easy to sneak through by playing the waiting game. However, this was our best bet and, sure enough, the dancing beams of light merged into strong cones both to port and starboard, balancing an aircraft, in full glare, on the tip of the cone like a jet of water holding a ping-pong ball target on a fairground rifle range. Our chance had arrived, and with all the power that *G-George* could muster, I went for the gap. Alas, not much progress had been made through the searchlight belt when the cockpit was filled with dazzling light. Normally, with a few hectic manoeuvres there was a fair chance of losing the lights, but on this occasion the centre light had a bluish colour and had fastened on to *G-George*, and no amount of twisting and turning could shift it and its accompanying beams. It was obviously a DHF development that was new to me. Being so occupied with trying to get out of the illumination, it was something of a surprise to hear and to see cannon tracer shells flying around the aircraft and in particular flashing up through the unoccupied front gun turret.

I had no doubt in my mind what to do next. I put the nose straight down and kept it that way. I can well remember the ASI registering 320mph. In the meantime Robbie in the rear turret was more than a little disturbed and was yelling all sorts of things into the intercom. He thought we had all 'had it' and certainly I was not able at that time to put his mind at rest. We had been at our usual 12,000 feet, and at about 7,000 feet I tried to get back on an even keel, which was easier said than done. At that speed the port wing had dropped and the only way in which I could get sufficient purchase on the 'stick', which in fact was a large wheel, was to put my feet against the dashboard and heave like blazes with the wheel turned as far to the right as I could get it. With some relief I got *George* out of the dive and regained straight and level flight once again. I took stock of our situation, having firstly calmed Robbie with the news that I was still alive and flying. The engines were sounding good, and while we were somewhat battered, there seemed no reason not to go to the target.

However, before I had managed to check all aspects and make a final decision, a further attack from the starboard saw cannon shells whistling through the starboard engine, through the cockpit and within inches of my feet and out the other side. The starboard engine caught fire, and although I managed to extinguish it from within, the port engine sounded a bit sick, to say the least. Thus I was left flying on less than one engine, and in such circumstances it is necessary to trim the aircraft as far as possible. This was achieved by adjusting the rudder tabs by means of a wheel at the side of the pilot's seat. However, when I endeavoured to do this all I found was a coil of wire that, having been shot through in the fuselage, had sprung to the other end of its tension – next to me.

It was amazing to me that the pilot of the night fighter did not finish us off, but presumably he lost us in the darkness. I have often wondered whether the original attacker had followed us down and then made another pass, or whether by chance another night fighter had picked us up. It was obvious from the damage reported by the crew that the first attack had been from below and mercifully the rear turret was missed, but gaping holes had been blasted in the underside of the fuselage even to the extent of losing the Elsan (I wonder who was the lucky recipient beneath). Having observed the cannon shells coming up through the front turret, I am led to the conclusion that the bombs, being positioned beneath the cockpit, had acted as armour plating and had saved the three of us in the cabin – a sobering thought.

Having survived, if that is what you can call it, and being unable to maintain height, the next problem was where to go. It would be impossible to back-track through the searchlight belt with any hope of success, so I had little option but to head in a northerly direction with a view to reaching Holland and possibly a friendly face or two. As we were gradually losing height, even with full boost applied to the damaged and only engine, the crew were busy jettisoning everything moveable they could lay their hands on. The bombs were the first to go, followed by hatch covers, bombsight, ammunition and indeed anything that was detachable. I was flying marginally above stalling speed and the ASI hovered around the 60mph mark. It was something of a difficult juggling act to feel the balance of the aircraft and keep it flying, with one leg stretched to the limit to counteract with rudder the one-engine factor.

I decided that both King and Robertson should depart as soon as possible as they would stand a better chance of evading capture if they descended silently from above and away from a crashed aircraft. King went out of the front hatch without any problem. The rear hatch was in fact on top of the Whitley's square fuselage and Bruce Robertson later told me that, having clipped his parachute on to his harness, he emerged from the hatch on to the fuselage, stood up and had to literally run off the rear and over his turret – there was insufficient strength in the slipstream to whisk him away as we were flying at such a slow speed.

Cal and myself stooged on hoping to reach a friendly reception. After Cal had rescued my 'chute from beside the open hatch, he went back to writing his log. We were getting lower and lower and eventually I persuaded him that it was more important to get his backside through the hole in the floor than to complete his log! He too disappeared, leaving me to find my own way out. By this time I had clipped my parachute on to my harness and had engaged 'George' for good measure. It was then my intention to make a quick dash for it, which entailed getting out of my seat, descending a few stairs to the well, turning round and facing backwards with legs through the hole. However, I encountered a hiccup in the first part of the intended procedure. When I left and moved towards the open hatch, I found that my intercom cable, which was still plugged in, had somehow got around my 'chute, which meant that I had to retrace my steps to disentangle the cord. By this time I could see that the aircraft was dropping a wing quite severely and I had to disengage 'George', straighten things up, then make a sharp exit. I can clearly remember falling away from the aircraft and being on my back, seeing it fly over my head and quickly going to ground.

You will have gathered that my parachute opened and for a few moments I experienced complete peace. The contrast from total mayhem to almost complete silence – from non-stop action to passivity – is an experience that I am sure could never happen again. But as I have implied, this heavenly suspension lasted but a very short while, as in no time at all tree-tops were whistling past my feet. It had been less than 1,000 feet above ground when I had left G-George to go it alone. We had never had any instruction about parachute jumping. I found the best solution naturally; let the breeze take you and make sure you land facing backwards – no problem at all! G-George did not have such a soft landing and was well ablaze some 200 yards away. I must admit that when I landed my heart rate was off the clock, but I did have time for a quiet 'thank you'.

My immediate problem was the disposal of my 'chute and harness and the two £1 notes I had with me, which I should not have carried. I had gathered my equipment together and had buried the cash when I heard the clanking of chains. My first thought was that I had landed in some sort of concentration camp, but the inmates turned out to be tethered cattle, presumably belonging to the farmer who emerged from his house to investigate the burning aircraft. He was followed in line astern by wife and two children. (Fifty-three years later I visited the farm and met the children, Derk-Jan and Johann-Willem Hesselink.) As I was in direct line between the house and his intended investigation he quickly spotted me and turned tail back to the safety of the homestead. Still in line astern the children were calling 'Papa, Papa', which sounded to me reasonably civilised, and having been seen in any event, I joined the line and called 'Papa', hoping that this might be the Dutch for 'How's your father?' I never found out as the door was slammed and bolted.

Simultaneously around the corner of the farmhouse came a German policeman with gun at the ready, who made it clear that I was his prisoner. I did not like to gamble that he could not properly fire his revolver and push his moped at the same time. I did, however, win one small argument with him when he endeavoured to make me pick up my 'chute and harness and carry it. This I refused to do. After all, I was aircrew! And he had to do it himself, draping the lot over his saddle and carrier. On this basis we proceeded through the village. It was surprising to me how many people were out and about at that time of the night. I did ascertain that the name of the village was Oeding, situated exactly on the border of Germany and Holland. For all the good it did me, I did take consolation in the fact that I had almost achieved my last target on this August night, that of reaching Holland.

I was eventually delivered to the German Army. Guards came and went during the next day but it was very much later that the Luftwaffe appeared in a large Mercedes and spirited me off to Munster, the Luftwaffe HQ. I was accompanied by Sgt Calvert, who had been picked up not far away. As the cell door slammed I was told, 'For you zee war if oofer'. But for me the war was just beginning – what followed was three years and ten months of captivity.

Later, after a mass escape from Stalag IIIE Kirchhain, during which Cal and I both got away, Cal and another escaper were apprehended by a member of the Polizei. He shot Cal when he attempted to replace his footwear. Apparently he could not cope with the two of them. Cal was somewhat older than the rest of us, and was 34 when he died.

4: Lucky 13
J. Ralph Wood DFC CD

MY WAR BEGAN in Woodstock, New Brunswick, while visiting the home and parents of my girlfriend, Phyllis Carter. This was the long weekend of Labor Day, September 1939, and I had rented a friend's car for the trip from Moncton to Woodstock and back. That Sunday I either volunteered or was talked into attending morning church services. I say my war began in Woodstock because as we left the church the newsboys were selling *St John Telegraph* newspapers on the street, and on a Sunday at that. Although by now this was not entirely unexpected, it still came as a bit of a shock. We were at war, and according to a certain quotation, 'War is Hell'.

Someone also once said 'Everyone has fears, but he who faces fears with dignity, has courage as well'. This looked a good long-range objective; I knew that I had fear of being labelled 'coward' or 'yellow' if I didn't volunteer my services to my country. I knew also that I had a fear of losing my life if I did volunteer. There was no contest. All that remained was to choose the service I would join. The Navy? No way! I'd probably be seasick before we left the harbour, let alone battling those 30-foot waves at sea. Also, it was a long way to swim to dry land. The Army? Well, according to stories of the First World War, which was the only reference we had to go by, this meant mud, trenches, lice, bayonets, etc. This was definitely not my cup of tea. Air Force? This was more appealing as it presented a picture of your home base in a civilised part of the country accompanied by real beds with sheets, fairly good food, local pubs with their accompanying social life, and with periodic leaves to the larger centres and cities. The hour of decision was at hand, but it didn't take me an hour to

Flight Sergeant Ralph Wood, RCAF Observer, sketched in the NCO's Club in Edinburgh by a European escapee. (Ralph Wood)

decide on the Royal Canadian Air Force. Being a fatalist, I was pretty sure my number would come up, and in the air it would be swift and definite.

(By early 1941, J. Ralph Wood had completed Air Observer School at Edmonton and Bombing and Gunnery School at Mossbank, Saskatchewan, and was a fully fledged air observer.)

Our proud moment came on a wings parade, when Wing Commander A. J. Ashton, CO, pinned on that one wing with the circle. With this insignia and my sergeant's hooks, I felt I was now an air observer. A 'one-winged wonder' – or, as we affectionately called ourselves, a 'flying asshole'. Sure, we were occasionally asked when we would finish our training and get the other half of our wings. There was an amazing amount of ignorance at this time about the air observer. As one English newspaper wrote, in part:

'The air observer is the boss once the plane leaves the ground. It is he who gives the pilot the course – It is he who checks the course, height and air speed – It is he who drops the bombs. It's not the pilot who does all these things – it's the boy with the wing on his tunic lying full-length on his stomach in the nose of the machine, sweating in the last seconds before zero hour. From the time of leaving their base until the return there is not a single moment when the observer can relax. He's busy all the time and he loves it. Even those trainees who have their hearts set on being pilots and who – through some minor defect – have been transferred to be trained as observers soon cease to have any regrets. He's the most important member of the crew. He's director general in the air – so – don't ask him when he will get the other half of his wings. Just shake his hand and say, "Thank you!"'

With that morale-boosting article under my belt, my air observer wing on my chest, and sergeant stripes on my sleeves, I headed for No 1 ANS (Advanced Navigation School) at Rivers, Manitoba. The next six weeks were spent trying to navigate by the stars. Using the sextant in sub-zero weather was anything but pleasant. I've never been so cold in all my life. Sure, says the Westerner, but it's a dry cold. Wet or dry, it damn near froze my ears and fingers off. It's a good thing we had those funny-looking round hats with the drop-down ear-tabs. They were comfortable, even though they looked like and were often called 'piss pots'.

(In April Ralph Wood bid farewell to Canada, next stop England. He embarked on the MV *Georgic*, a merchant vessel that was later sunk in the Mediterranean, then salvaged. Several aircraft appeared overhead to escort them up the Firth of Clyde to Gourock, Scotland. A long, sitting-up train trip to their receiving depot at Uxbridge was the next ordeal.)

It was here that we were introduced to English food, English pubs and English girls – in that order. The pubs were happy new experiences for Canadians used to the dingy taverns of home where one was made to feel uncomfortable, if not immoral. They were the Englishman's gracious way of living. The food was plain, palatable and rationed. The girls were friendly and good company. One thing I liked very much about English girls was that they seemed to use English so correctly and so naturally. It was a pleasure to listen to them. It almost didn't matter too much about the words; the sound of them was what counted.

From Uxbridge we were dispersed to the various RAF OTUs (Operational Training Units). Mine happened to be No 10 OTU at Abingdon, Berkshire. This station also contained a Group Headquarters, with lots and lots of senior officers to avoid.

At this stage of the war there were only two heavy bombers available, the Wellington, or 'Wimpy', and the Armstrong Whitworth Whitley. The Whitley – a rather unloved bomber but a much larger aircraft than the Anson – was often referred to as the 'Flying Coffin'. It had a crew of five and here, during May and June 1941, we trained day and night doing cross-country runs as well as bombing and gunnery exercises. A special event took place while we were here: King George, Queen Elizabeth, Princess Elizabeth and Princess Margaret visited our training unit and had high tea in the officer's mess.

Our off-duty hours were spent pub crawling in Abingdon and visiting nearby Oxford for a little sightseeing and dancing. Walking home from the Red Lion pub in Abingdon one night we witnessed a Whitley that was doing circuits and bumps (landings and take-offs) crash into the Commanding Officer's house. The pilots were natives of India and would never see their homeland again. What a mess! House, plane and crew a total loss.

Another nervous situation sometimes presented itself while one was landing, taking off or circling the airfield at night. The German intruders found this to be a desirable set-up for an easy killing.

No 10 OTU personnel were mostly RAF types interspersed with a handful of Canadians and the odd Australian and New Zealander. As soon as it was felt that we knew our way around the aircraft and could get to our target and, hopefully, back, we were posted to the various bomber squadrons located all over the country.

We were now moving up into the big leagues. No 102 Squadron, RAF station Topcliffe, Yorkshire, was to be my new home for a while, and I was now to operate and complete my first tour in RAF 4 Group, Bomber Command. At this time we were all on loan to the RAF, as the RCAF Bomber Command had not yet been established. Later, when it became active as No 6 Group, some of the Canadians transferred to the Canadian squadrons. Myself and several others preferred to stay with the RAF. We got along fine with the Limeys and, besides, we thought that where we were on loan, we might get away with a little more murder and less discipline.

I'll never forget my introduction to this first operational squadron. Arriving around midday, the officer commanding informed me that I would be on tonight's raid. Who me? Why, I hadn't even unpacked my kit bag. The flight's chief navigator suggested that he go in my place and I would watch him go through his routine preparing for the flight. I watched him prepare his flight plan, get the meteorology report, go to the intelligence office for his secret coded information – on rice-paper so that you could eat it if necessary – and other pertinent things to do before going off into that treacherous-looking sky. The navigator and crew never returned. This was a hell of an introduction, especially when stories were circulating about washing out the remains of a tail gunner with a hose, there was so little left of him.

I was on the next night, 25/26 July. The target was Hanover.

(Twenty-five Whitleys and 30 Hampdens were despatched, while 43 Wellingtons bombed Hamburg.)

Thirteen months after joining the RCAF I found myself in the briefing room nervously preparing my charts for the raid. I was trying to appear calm and nonchalant, this being my first op and not wanting to appear to be too much of a greenhorn. After the briefing, the navigators gathered around the huge plotting table on the operations room and worked out our DR (dead reckoning) courses to get us to the target and, far more important, home again. Our dead reckoning was based on the predicted winds as supplied by the met section, the airspeed, the groundspeed and the drift, as well as other information so important in our navigation. Many corrections and adjustments were made during our trip from new information obtained in flight. Our only navigational aids in these early days were from 'fixes' obtained from our wireless operator and good only up to a limited number of miles from the English coast. As a matter of fact, I soon learned to jokingly call my navigation 'guestimation'!

So here we were, a crew of five – two pilots, a navigator/bomb-aimer (observer), a wireless operator and a tail gunner. I never used a bomb-aimer during my tours – they appeared later on in the war, and there weren't always enough to go around. I felt that if I could get us to the target I should have the pleasure of bombing same.

My navigator's table was behind the pilot's seat in the cockpit. As we neared the target I unplugged my oxygen lead and my intercom and, dragging my parachute with me, made my way to the bombsight in the nose of our 'flying coffin'. It was a long

Sergeant Ralph Wood RCAF flew 13 night operations on Whitleys like these, as an Observer in No 102 Squadron, No 4 Group Bomber Command, from Topcliffe, Yorkshire, starting with a trip to Hanover on 25/26 July 1941 and ending with a raid on the same city on the night of 30 November 1941. (Ralph Wood)

Handley Page Hampdens in flight. When Ralph Wood flew his first op, on the night of 25/26 July 1941, 25 Whitleys and 30 Hampdens were despatched to Hanover, while 43 Wellingtons bombed Hamburg.

crawl in the darkness, and without oxygen the going was tough. Reaching the bombsight and front gunner compartment, I searched frantically for the oxygen connection to restore my strength. With the aid of a flashlight, partly covered so as not to attract any wandering fighters, I found my connection and began to breathe more easily. I was now lining up the target with the bombsight as I directed the pilot on our bombing run: 'Left . . . left . . . steady . . . right . . . steady . . . left . . . left . . . steady . . . Bombs gone!'.

Our Whitley leapt about 200 feet with the release of tons of high explosives. Now we flew straight and level for 30 seconds, the longest 30 seconds anyone will ever know, so that we could get the required photo of the drop for the intelligence officer back at base. Picture taken – now let's get the hell out of here.

Still in a cold sweat with the flak bursting around us and the searchlights trying in vain to catch us, I crawled back to my plotting table. The pilot was still taking evasive action as I gave him the course for home. Those black blobs of smoke surrounding the aircraft were flak, and when you could smell the cordite it meant that they were bursting too damn close.

Arriving back at our base without incident gave me a great feeling of relief and satisfaction (the Hanover force lost four Whitleys and one Hampden). It was hard to believe that I'd been over Germany, but harder to believe that I was back in England. Next came our de-briefing by the intelligence officers, accompanied by a cup of coffee laced with overproof rum. I was tired but happy after our 7$\frac{1}{2}$-hour trip. I guess I had that blissful No-1-op-behind-me look written all over my face. I kept thinking 'I've made it' – that first op I'd been dreaming about and working toward for 13 months.

As I settled into squadron life at Topcliffe I found that the best way to keep your sanity was to separate your pleasures from your work. I didn't want to become one of those casualties found walking around the airfield talking to himself. There was the odd one who cracked up mentally, and you really couldn't blame him.

Our commanding officer was a queer one. We called him 'Curly', but not to his face. He was RAF permanent force and had been stationed in India too long. We thought he'd gotten too much sun out there. He was baldish and had a remarkably long, red handlebar moustache, in which he took great pride. I noticed during my stay there that any time he put himself down to fly, the operation would be a comparatively easy one. How unlike Pilot Officer Cheshire, who was later to become Group Captain Cheshire, winning the DFC and other decorations. He was described as a madman who always picked the dangerous targets like Berlin for himself. Some say this was partly because his brother was shot down over Berlin.

My second op was Frankfurt, on 6/7 August 1941 – 7 hours of misery accompanied by engine failure. We were very glad to arrive back safely at base.

(Thirty-four Whitleys and 19 Wellingtons set out to bomb the railway yards, and two other raids were made, by Wellingtons on Mannheim, and by Hampdens on Karlsruhe. Two Whitleys and two Wellingtons failed to return from the Frankfurt operation.)

Hanover was my third op, on 14/15 August, and it proved as exciting as the first two. While over Europe we would drop thousands of propaganda leaflets down the flare 'chute. We also dropped flares from this 'chute as we approached the target area to enable us to pin-point the target itself. Before taking off we usually had a nervous pee beside the aircraft. This was much easier than trying to manipulate in the air. On our homeward journey we would get into our thermos of coffee and sandwiches of spam. Of course, our real treat was the ritual flying breakfast of bacon and eggs back at the base and our discussions of the attack with the other crews on the raid. Bacon and eggs were otherwise as scarce as hen's teeth. But after every mission there were empty tables – chairs, dishes and silverware aligned – for the men who weren't coming back.

(Nine aircraft – four Whitleys and five Wellingtons – failed to return from the 152 aircraft despatched on this operation. Of 314 sorties flown that night, 14 aircraft were lost.)

For relaxation we would frequent the pubs in the village of Topcliffe, Thirsk, Ripon and Harrogate. Weldon MacMurray, a schoolfriend of mine from Moncton, was stationed at RAF Dishforth. This was about 2 miles from Topcliffe, as the crow flies. We'd get together once in a while and exchange news from home. The nearest meeting place was the Black Swan pub, or, as we called it, the 'Mucky Duck', in the village of Topcliffe. On one such meeting he informed me that Johnny Humprey had bought it,

Ralph Wood flew his second op in a Whitley to Frankfurt on 6/7 August 1941, when 34 Whitleys and 19 Wellingtons set out to bomb the railway yards; two Whitleys and two Wellingtons failed to return. This Wellington II, W5461 R-Robert of 104 Squadron, failed to return from a raid on Berlin on 12/13 August. (via Mike Bailey)

and another time that Graham Roger's number had come up. This was followed by news that Brian Filliter was missing in action. One day at lunchtime I had answered the phone in the sergeant's mess and it was Weldon inquiring about me. He'd heard that I'd bought it the previous night. A few weeks later, friends of Weldon phoned me from Dishforth to say that he had failed to return from a trip. I found out later that he was a prisoner of war. Boy! Was I getting demoralised! Would I be next?

Frankfurt on 29/30 August represented about 9 hours flying time. I was getting to have a healthy respect for those searchlights. When they had you coned they would shoot tons of crap up those beams at you. After a bit they'd quit, leaving us to the fighters for target practice. The Whitley was a tough old bastard in spite of its ugly appearance. The damn thing always flew with its nose down, slowly at that, but it could take a hell of a beating, nonetheless.

(Altogether some 143 Hampdens, Whitleys, Halifaxes and Manchesters were despatched, on what was the first 100-plus raid on this city. Three bombers failed to return.)

Our target on the night of 31 August/1 September was Essen (with 71 Whitleys and Wellingtons being despatched to the city's Krupps Works, while 103 bombers attacked Cologne). This was a comparatively short trip over enemy territory, but still consumed 6 hours and provided us with plenty of activity. (Only one Whitley of the 43 despatched failed to return.) Our tail gunner decided to put his steel helmet, used for air raids, to some practical use. He'd take it on ops with him, and when things got hot over the target area he'd sit on his steel helmet. He said no way was he going to get flak up his ass!

Op No 6 to Frankfurt on 2/3 September presented us with an engine failure and we were unable to complete the operation (126 aircraft were despatched, including 44 Whitleys). If you carried the attack far enough you were given credit for an op, and an op behind you was one closer to a tour, no matter how you looked at it.

A rubber factory just north of Essen (Hüls) on 6/7 September was next on our list. This raid saw us with a rear-gun turret malfunction and an early and uneventful return to base. (Bombing results were described as 'good'. Five Whitleys and two Wellingtons from the 41 Whitleys, 27 Wellingtons and 18 Hampdens despatched failed to return.) One of my compatriots from Moncton, a navigator, missed Great Britain altogether when returning from a raid. He landed in Southern Ireland, which was neutral, and remained there in internment for the rest of the war, enjoying good food and drink while his pay and promotion continued. I still haven't decided whether he was a stupid navigator or a smart operator.

Op No 8 on 7/8 September was Berlin. Berlin in a Whitley? I don't believe it! (31 Whitleys were among the 197 twin-engined and four-motor bombers despatched.) Well, 10 hours later, as we were being de-briefed at interrogation, I felt quite elated. We had actually bombed the capital of Germany. But the trip hadn't been that pleasant. (Fifteen aircraft were lost, two of them Whitleys). I thought about that goddam 'Butcher Harris' – 'Butcher' was the deserved nickname of the RAF Chief of Bomber Command. He didn't give a damn how many men he lost as long as he was pounding the shit out of the Germans. He was just as willing to sacrifice Englishmen as Canadians.

I became involved in a heated discussion with my flight commander one night while partaking of some cheer at a favourite watering hole in Harrogate. I was complaining about not flying enough, and he came back with some derogatory remarks on my navigational ability. I told him that if that wasn't a yellow streak down his back, he'd put me down to fly with him. Sure enough, the next morning saw me listed as his navigator for that night. A little under the weather that morning, during our air test in the afternoon I made sure to take a few good whiffs of oxygen to clear the head. This was a tried and proven method of aiding your recovery.

Stettin, situated north-east of Berlin, was the target for our ninth op on 29/30 September (when 139 aircraft, 56 of them Whitleys, were despatched). It turned out to be the best trip I'd made to date. We threw out our flares, which lit up the target directly beneath us. We made two separate bombing runs, dropping one stick of bombs on each run. We never reached our base that night as were running short of fuel. (Five aircraft crashed in England and eight bombers, including four Whitleys, failed to return.) My flight commander was particularly pleased with this 11-hour trip, and my navigational abilities were never questioned again.

My tenth op was to Nuremberg on 12/13 October, but we ended up dropping our load on Frankfurt as the alternate target. (152 bombers were despatched and the majority fell outside the city, some 10 miles south of Nuremberg and as far as 95 miles west!). This turned out to be a $9^1/2$-hour trip. Our exactors, whatever they might be, were u/s (unserviceable), and we had to land at Pocklington, returning to base later that day. (Eight aircraft failed to return and five bombers crashed in England.) At this stage of the game we didn't fly as a set crew; the members were interchangeable for various reasons. For my part, I always made a quick appraisal of the pilot I was to fly with. How much confidence could I place in him? For that matter, how much would he have in me? We all had to depend on each and every crew member. We were a team – each relying on the other to do his job to the best of his ability. On this, and the following two ops, we had another Sergeant Wood as crew member, a Scotsman. During my stay overseas my nickname was usually 'Timber', or 'Chips', or just plain 'Woodie'.

Duisburg, on 16/17 October, was one of the easier trips in that 6 hours saw the operation completed and to our satisfaction (87 aircraft were despatched and only one was lost.) Making a good landfall on the English coast on our homeward journey always boosted the navigator's morale; by a good landfall I mean approaching the coast and hitting it just about where you were supposed to, right on track. I recall my pilot asking occasionally 'Where are we?' I'd shove a map or chart in front of him pointing wildly to the spot over the North Sea or Germany, depending on the occasion. This having satisfied him, I would return to my plotting table to work out our actual position undisturbed.

Operation number 12 was to Wilhelmshaven, on 20/21 October (when Bomber Command attacked four cities, three of them in Germany), and again we were forced to bomb the alternate target, Emden. This was an 8-hour trip, but we managed to return to our home base (nine aircraft failed to do so from the night's operations). The meteorology reports were very important to the success of our operations. The met section was at times about as accurate as it is today, leaving a lot to be desired. We called the meteorology information 'met gen', which usually turned out to be either 'pukka gen', meaning 'good information', or 'duff gen', meaning 'bad information'.

There was a story going around about a Whitley crew becoming lost and running out of fuel. The pilot set the automatic pilot and told his crew to bail out. This they did, with the exception of the tail gunner, whose intercom had become disconnected and he failed to hear the order. A short time later the aircraft made a remarkably good landing on a sloping hill in Scotland. The tail gunner, upon vacating his turret, commented loudly on the pilot's smooth landing. You could almost see him passing out when he discovered that he was the only occupant of the aircraft.

Hanover (181 aircraft started out for Hamburg) on the night of 30 November/1 December was my 13th op and destined to be my last in a Whitley. Number 13 – lucky

Halifax I L9530 MP-L of 76 Squadron. Ralph Wood flew 14 ops in Halifaxes in this Squadron between 8/9 May and 4/5 September 1942 from Middleton St George, Co Durham. (IWM)

or unlucky? (Thirteen aircraft failed to return.) I guess one had to call it lucky as we had a malfunction with our rear turret and we were forced to return to base.

The next five months were occupied converting to the Halifax bomber. This was done at Dalton, a satellite station near Topcliffe. This conversion course and some temporary duty at Lossiemouth in northern Scotland gave us a nice change of pace, including a rest from those bombing raids over Germany.

(Ralph Wood's 14th op was on 8/9 May 1942, to Warnemunde. He had been transferred to No 76 Squadron and operated from Middleton St George, Co Durham.)

Warnemunde was my first op in a 'Hallybag', with Pilot Officer McIntosh as my pilot. Our Handley Page bomber was a beautiful four-engined bird with three gun turrets, front, mid-upper and rear. She carried a 5½-ton bomb load, cruised at 300mph

A Halifax crew. (via Ralph Wood)

Last-minute check. (via Ralph Wood)

and had a 3,000-mile range. She had a crew of seven, or six in our case as I still acted as bomb-aimer, navigator and front gunner; the others were the pilot, a wireless operator, a flight engineer, a mid-upper gunner and a tail gunner. The dinky little navigator's compartment was below and in front of the pilot's cockpit. You went down a few steps and entered a small section with a navigator's metal table down one side, ahead and below the pilot's feet. A curtain in the nose end hid the even smaller compartment where I would huddle with my Mark 14 bombsight and other instruments

A little soccer before take-off. (via Ralph Wood)

P/O Ralph Wood took part in the first three 1,000 bomber raids, the first (his 17th op) to Cologne on 30/31 May 1942. The second, to Bremen, was flown on 25/26 June, and this time the Admiralty was ordered by Churchill to loan 102 Hudsons and Wellingtons of Coastal Command to swell the numbers to 960 aircraft. (Col Bill Cameron)

when we got reasonably close to the target. The gun I was supposed to operate when called upon was a Vickers gas-operated .303 machine-gun mounted on a swivel, which stuck out through the perspex nose, high above the bombsight. I recalled the short introduction lecture on the VGO: the RAF sergeant told us that the gun was famous for jamming.

There were many occasions when a navigator had to remove his gloves to work at his charts, and at altitude it was *cold*. Of course, a 'Hallybag' was always a deep-freeze

Short Stirling MG-L of No 7 Squadron. Eighty-eight Stirlings of 3 Group took part in the 1,000 bomber raid on Cologne on 30/31 May 1942, and 69 Stirlings took part in the similar raid on Bremen of 25/26 June 1942.

proposition, even at the best of times. There were supposed to be pipes giving off heat throughout the aircraft, but this was a laugh. I found my hands and feet were always cold by the time an op was over. You simply had to learn to live with it.

It was around this period that I was listed to fly with a Canadian pilot by the name of Flight Sergeant Bellows. We were all at least flight sergeants by now! Well, due to a rash on the inside of my thigh, the medical officer took me off the flying list that night. He figured that wearing a parachute harness would only irritate the rash, making it worse. So it was an application of medication instead. Flight Sergeant Bellows and crew, which included my replacement, bought it over the city of York, when their aircraft exploded on the way to Germany. Someone must have been looking after me that night, or I would have crapped out as well.

(Ralph Wood survived a terrible crash on a training exercise on 28 June 1942, which wrote off the Halifax in which he was flying, killing his pilot and injuring the flight engineer and wireless operator, while the tail gunner was found in the next field with 'a broken neck, a broken leg, a broken arm and a great many bruises'. In all, Ralph completed two tours (77 ops) by November 1944, 50 of them on Mosquitoes with 692 Squadron. It was certainly 'lucky 13' on Whitleys, but he says 'My lucky number was 77'.)

5: 'Darkie, Darkie'
Flying Officer Brian 'Darkie' Hallows DFC

NORFOLKMAN Brian Roger Wakefield Hallows was 11 years at Gresham's School, Holt, where his father was proprietor of the old market town's Steam Laundry. 'Darkie' later passed through Sandhurst and took a commission in the King's Liverpool Regiment, which he later relinquished to take up flying. In June 1938 he joined the RAFVR when he felt that a war was inevitable, so it was no surprise when all Reservists were called to report to their units around the end of August 1939. Then followed a wait until October, when he begun a 'Wings' course at No 9 FTS, Hullavington. They were an unruly lot, and finally the station commander got them all together and said that he was going to award them their wings, and commission all Sergeant Pilots to acting Pilot Officers. He added that they were not fit to be senior NCO pilots – how right he was!

Then it was off to Central Flying School, to become an RAF flying instructor, which had been Hallows's profession prior to August 1939. At CFS he won a trophy for 'Best all-round Cadet', and a reputation for the use of R/T language 'which caused some watch tower WAAFs to giggle, some to blush'*. Thence he went back to Hullavington as a Qualified Flying Instructor until July 1941. He had seen a rather odd notice in June 1941, asking for experienced twin-engined pilots to join Bomber Command, to fly Manchester bombers. Little did any of them know what a killer the Manchester was. Anyway, it was off to Finningley, with not a Manchester to be seen – they were all grounded with engine trouble. Eventually, in September 1941, Hallows got to 97 Squadron at Coningsby, where he actually flew a Manchester. On the squadron he was known as 'Darkie', not for his jet black hair and full moustache, but for an episode

* *The Augsburg Raid* by Jack Currie DFC (Goodall Publications, 1987)

Lancasters of Nos 44 and 97 Squadrons bombing Augsburg in one of the most daring low-level operations of the war, on Friday 17 April 1942. 'Darkie' Hallows in 97 Squadron flew 'B-Baker' R5537. (C. Stothard)

when he got lost and invoked the R/T get-you-home service of those early days: 'Darkie, Darkie'. Receiving no response, he had tried again, but still no reply. Once more he had transmitted to the void: 'Darkie, Darkie . . . where are you, you little black bastard?'*

'Darkie' had completed four operational trips by the end of January 1942 (Emden and Brest in daylight, Brest by night, and Hamburg). Throughout his first tour he kept a candid, unofficial diary in which he recorded in plain language his part in the bomber offensive. His experiences were typical of countless other pilots. His first diary entry read:

'Flight No I Target:- EMDEN. Railway yard or Town. Date. 15.11.41. A/C L7474 "Z" Crew No 5. Take off 1830 hours. Forty minutes late due to aircraft being unserviceable. Met forecast said no cloud at all. Climbed to 5,000 feet, met cloud, climbed to 10,000 feet, again in cloud up to 12,000 feet. Continued at 12,000 to DR (Dead Reckoning) position off BORKUM, thence to EMDEN. Cloud 8–10 tenths and observation was difficult. Spent 15 minutes in target area, but could not see anything. Flak all round us all time. Fire was seen through cloud, which we bombed, causing more fires. Heavy ice encountered in cloud. Landed Coltishall. Load 5 x 1,000lb. Time 6-30 hrs. Total times 6-30 hrs. No of Trips:- 1.'

Altogether, 49 aircraft were despatched to Emden and four Wellingtons failed to return. A similar operation, to Kiel, produced almost exactly the same results.

'Flight No II Target: "*Scharnhorst* and *Gneisenau* at BREST." Date. 18:12.41.

Avro Manchester B Mk 1A L7515 of 207 Squadron from Waddington, in November 1941.

Daylight formation Sortie. Remarks. A/C L.7525 "D". Crew No 5. Take off 0930 hrs. (Altogether, 47 aircraft – 18 Halifaxes, 18 Stirlings and 11 Manchesters – were despatched.) After much preparation in formation flying we were told we were to attack Brest to keep "Salmon and Gluckstein" (nicknames for the *Scharnhorst* and *Gneisenau*) penned in. The weather was good and eleven aircraft took off (nine in three flights in Vic and two reserves). There was some cloud about 5,000 feet with large holes so navigation was easy. I was on the right of second Vic. Fighter umbrella was provided. All went well up to the target area when very intense Flak was encountered. We were hit three times, self and navigator being hit on head by flying perspex, etc, but no damage. We bombed in formation at 15,000 feet and dived away to

On 18 December 1941 'Darkie' Hallows flew his second op when 47 aircraft – 18 Halifaxes, 18 Stirlings (photographed here) and 11 Manchesters were despatched in daylight to Brest to attack the Scharnhorst *and* Gneisenau. *Four Stirlings, one Halifax and the one Manchester were lost.* (via Mike Bailey)

right. Leading aircraft of No 1 section had starboard elevator shot off and rear gunner killed. On the way back tight formation was kept, but one aircraft (Pilot Officer Stokes, No 3 in third Vic) straggled and was shot down by a ME 109. Two seen to bale out seven miles approx N of French coast. On landing the leading aircraft (Wing Commander Baloden) crashed and killed all occupants. LOAD. 1 x 4,000 (HE bomb). 2 x 500. Time 6.10 (Total time 12.40).

Six aircraft – four Stirlings, one Halifax and the one Manchester – were lost.

'Flight No III, Target: "Scharnhorst and Gneisenau at Brest." Date. 9.1.42. Night Sortie. Remarks. A/C L.7475. "B" Crew No 5. (82 aircraft were despatched). Take off originally 0320 hours. 10.1.42. but it was put forward to 0004 hours because of weather. We had previously been briefed twice for this trip but each time it was cancelled. At take-off it was dark and no horizon. Cloud 1,500 feet. We kept to 1,000–1,500 feet to Upper Heyford when cloud thinned and up through it to 7,000 feet. Pinpoint Start Point and on to Brest. Cloud 1–3 tenths Channel but 10/10 target. Twenty minutes spent over target. "Nickels" (propaganda leaflets) dropped but as target could not be identified we brought bombs back. Flak heavy but inaccurate. 3 searchlights. (N.B. If trip had been original time we should probably have seen the target). Load. 1 x 4,000. 4 x 500 S.A.P. Time:- 6.00 HRS. Total Time:-18.40 HRS. No of Trips 3.'

'Flight No IV. Target: Hamburg Town. Fire-raising. Date. 15.1.42. Night Sortie. We took off at 1700 hours in daylight and set course for Denmark, arriving there at 1915. From there to Hamburg. Over the target we saw little until another aircraft dropped a load of incendiaries. In the subsequent glare we saw the river and docks and the Binnen Alsten (inner harbour) clearly. We then ran in easterly and dropped our stick across this first stick. It was a lovely sight. Over 3,000 small fires across the centre of the town. (Fifty-two of the 96 aircraft despatched claimed to have hit Hamburg.) We left the target swiftly in a northerly direction and came home the same way. Navigation was excellent and we altered course on an Astro-fix and came over base on ETA. Load. 14 x 400lb incendiaries. Time 6.10 hrs. Total Time: 24.50 hours. No of Trips. 4. Between 17 January and 8 April No 97 Squadron was re-equipped with Lancaster I aircraft. These gave some trouble and operations recommenced in earnest on April 8th.'

On the night of 8/9 April Darkie Hallows and 23 other aircraft carried out a minelaying operation (while the main Bomber Command thrust, 272 aircraft, was aimed at Hamburg), as he recalls in his diary entry:

'Flight No V, Target: Gardening Heligoland Bight. Date 8.4.42. Night Sortie. Remarks. A.C. R5475 "K". No 5 Crew. We took off at dusk with six mixed mines for target. We flew at 20,000 feet the whole way. Fixes were obtained by TR1335 until it landed. A landfall was made almost on track at Westerhaven and course set for the garden. Veg (mines) were planted at the correct place at asi of 150 and 600 feet. Some flak was seen at Sylt and Heligoland and on the mainland, but none was at us. We arrived home after a completely uneventful trip. Load:- 6 x 1,500 mines (A.V.W. 60,000lb). Time 5.05 hrs. Total Times. 29.55 hrs. No of trips 5.'

The next trip, an experimental raid on a diesel engine manufacturing workshop at the

MAN (Maschinenfabrik Augsburg-Nürnberg Aktiengesellschaft) factory at Augsburg was certainly not uneventful. The raid went ahead despite some opposition from the Ministry of Economic Warfare, who wanted the ball-bearing plant at Schweinfurt attacked instead. Air Marshal Harris wanted the Augsburg plant raided by a small force of Lancasters flying at low level (500 feet) and in daylight. Twelve Lancasters, six each from Nos 44 (Rhodesia) and 97 (Straits Settlements) Squadrons, were specially selected and South African Squadron Leader John Deering Nettleton was chosen to lead the operation. Each Lancaster would carry a 1,000lb bomb load, fused for 11 seconds' delay.

One of the 97 Squadron crews was led, in *B-Baker*, by 'Darkie' Hallows, who wrote:

'Flight No 6. 17 April 1942 (daylight formation) Target: MAN diesel engine factory at Augsburg, Bavaria. After three days of long formation cross-countries, we were briefed for this trip. Plenty was said about how important it was and all that stuff. So we were obviously not intended to come back in any strength. Fighter Command had been on the job for several days, hounding the German fighters, and when we were on the job we saw no fighters at all, all the way. We set course from Woodhall at 1500 hours, crossed the coast at Selsey Bill at 1615, French coast at 1650. (Five minutes after crossing the coast, Nettleton's first two sections were intercepted by fighters and four of the six bombers were shot down in a running fight that lasted an hour.) From there we flew to south of Paris, then down to Lake Constance, which included a good view of Switzerland, thence nearly to Munich and north to the town of Augsburg. On

the way we shot up a passenger train in a large station, and saw an aerodrome crowded with Ju 90s. The target was easily picked out and we bombed the hell out of it.

'Waddington's formation were just ahead of us. The gunners were ready for us, and it was as hot as hell for a few minutes. Our leader (Squadron Leader J. S. Sherwood DFC*) was hit and caught fire in the port inner tank and crashed and blew up about ten miles N of the town. (Sherwood, still strapped to his seat, was thrown from the aircraft and was its only survivor.) One aircraft of 2nd flight also blew up. I led the remaining aircraft back without any opposition. The quintessence of loneliness is to be 500 miles inside Occupied Europe with one serviceable turret!! The second formation lost one aircraft (Warrant Officer Mycock DFC).

Squadron Leader John Deering Nettleton, No 44 Squadron, who led the Augsburg raid, survived, and was awarded the Victoria Cross. As a Wing Commander, he failed to return from a raid on Turin on 12/13 July 1943. (IWM)

A reconnaissance photo taken on 29 April 1942 showing the bomb damage to the MAN diesel engine works at Augsburg. (RAF Museum)

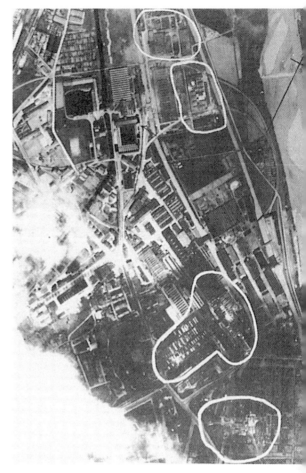

Load. 4 x 1,000 RDX bombs. Full petrol 2,134 gals. Time 8.15 hrs. Total time 38-10 hrs. No of trips 6. Note. Waddington lost five aircraft, one in target area, four shot down by fighters south of Paris whilst outward bound. One crew believed safe.'

Hallows returned safely and was one of eight officers to be awarded the Distinguished Flying Cross for his part in the raid. Winston Churchill sent the following message to Air Marshal Arthur T. Harris: 'We must plainly regard the attack of the Lancasters on the U-boat engine factory at Augsburg as an outstanding achievement of the Royal Air Force. Undeterred by heavy losses at the outset, the bombers pierced in broad daylight into the heart of Germany and struck a vital point with deadly precision. Pray convey my thanks of His Majesty's Government to the officers and men who accomplished this memorable feat of arms in which no life was lost in vain.'

Later, Hallows wrote: 'This is the one event which sticks in my mind. Over half the bombs dropped failed to explode!' Five of the 17 bombs dropped did not explode, and although the others devastated four machine shops, only 3 per cent of the machine tools in the entire plant were wrecked. 'A bad way to spend an afternoon!' Thirty-seven aircrew were lost, of which 12 were made PoW, and 36 returned. Squadron Leader John Nettleton was awarded the VC for his efforts; although also recommended for a VC by Air Marshal Harris, Sherwood was awarded the DSO. Later, as CO of 44 Squadron, Wing Commander Nettleton failed to return from a raid on Turin on 12/13 July 1943.

'Flight No 7. Target: Stuttgart. Bosch Works. Date. 5.5.42. Night Sortie. Remarks. A.C R5537 "B" No 5 Crew. We took off at dusk in hazy weather, expecting haze all the way. This was fulfilled. Course took us down to Selsey Bill and South of Channel ports area. No opposition was encountered all the way. Near target area a large cone of 35 searchlights was seen, but we were not picked up. The town was easily identified in large fires. 14 balloons seen over town. Dummy fires and incendiaries all round the target. As we could not see the target or the river we bombed the centre of the town. The return journey was uneventful, and we landed at dawn. Load. 6 x 1,000lb & 3 x 500lb. S.A.P, Total 7,500 lb. Time 7.05 hrs. Total Time 45.15 hrs. No of Trips. 7. (Four

Some of the 97 Squadron aircrew who returned safely from the Augsburg raid. Flight Lieutenant B. R. W. 'Darkie' Hallows is sitting, fourth from left. To his right is Pilot Officer Friend, his 2nd pilot on the raid, and to Friend's right is Pilot Officer P. M. Cutting, navigator. Second from right, centre row, is Flight Sergeant B. G. Louch, Hallows's wireless operator, and third from left is Sergeant Jones, the second wireless operator. To his left is Sergeant Broomfield, the mid-upper gunner, and Sergeant T. Goacher, rear gunner, is extreme left, back row. On 27 April 1942 Hallows was awarded the DFC, while Goacher and Louch received the DFM. On 2 June Hallows was promoted to Squadron Leader, OC 'A' Flight in 97 Squadron. (IWM)

aircraft – three Wellingtons and one Stirling – from the 77 aircraft despatched were lost.)

'Flight No 8. Target: Gardening. Date. 22.5.42. Remarks. A.C. R5558 "J". Crew No 5. We took off in very poor weather, vis 1,000 yards, clouds at 1,000 feet for the garden in the Baltic. On the way trouble was experienced with the EDGs (compasses) so course was set for alternative area in Heligoland Bight. "Veg" were dropped OK. Convoy of 6 merchant ships seen and reported. Weather was bad for return vis 500 yards, closed in to 100 feet half an hour after landing. Load 5 x 1,500 Veg. Time 4.40 hrs. Total time. 49.55 hrs. Trip no 8.'

'Flight No 9. Target: Destruction of Cologne. Date. 30/31 May 1942. A/C 5502 "M".'

This was the first 1,000 bomber raid. Air Marshal Sir Arthur Harris, Chief of Bomber Command, had for some time wanted to send 1,000 bombers to a German city and destroy it with incendiaries. Although RAF losses would be on a large scale, Churchill approved the plan. Harris gave the order 'Operation Plan Cologne' to his Group Commanders just after midday on 30 May so that 1,000 bombers would be unleashed on the 770,000 inhabitants. All bomber bases throughout England were at a high state of readiness to get all available aircraft airborne for this momentous raid. Many aircraft came from OTUs and were flown by instructors. One-quarter of the 1,046 aircraft despatched came from 3 Group, which operated in a fire-raising capacity, carrying loads of 4lb incendiary canisters. Some 599 Wellingtons made up the bulk of the attacking force, which also included 88 Stirlings, 131 Halifaxes and 73 Lancasters. The rest of the force was made up of Whitleys, Hampdens and Manchesters.

'We took off with over 1,000 others to destroy Cologne. The fires were seen over sixty miles away on our way out. 26 other aircraft were seen; Wellingtons, Stirlings and Lancasters. Fires were tremendous.'

For 98 minutes a procession of bombers passed over Cologne, and stick after stick of incendiaries reigned down from the bomb bays of the 3 Group Wellingtons, adding to the conflagration. Altogether, 898 crews claimed to have hit their targets, but 40 bombers failed to return.

'We hit the town with 1 x 4,000 and eight SBC (small bomb containers). On way back we encountered a Me 109, but he did not open fire. Fires were visible at Dutch coast on return. Load. 1 x 4,000lb R.D.X. 8 x SBC.4lb. Time 3.40. Total Time 53.35. Trip No 9.

'P.S. P/O Friend broadcast his story on 9PM news on 1.6.42. What a line!'

Post-bombing reconnaissance photos certainly showed that more than 600 acres of Cologne had been razed to the ground. The fires burned for days and almost 60,000 people were made homeless.

Meanwhile the squadrons repaired and patched their damaged bombers and within 48 hours were preparing for a second 'Thousand Bomber Raid', this time against

---

H.Q., No. 5 Group,
Royal Air Force,
Grantham,
Lincs.

25th April, 1942.

Dear *Hallows*,

My heartiest congratulations on your award for the fine work you did in the Augsburg raid which was an outstanding feat of gallantry in this Command and in the annals of our Service.

On behalf of the whole Group I would like to thank you for your part in the raid and to say that we look forward to having you with us for many more months, both in the Squadron and later, when duty calls that way, at one of the O.T.U.'s.

Yours *sincerely*

H. a. Haines

Group Captain,
Commanding, No.5 Group,

Flying Officer B. R. W. Hallows, DFC.,
No. 97 Squadron,
Royal Air Force Station,
Coningsby.

Avro Lancaster I R5689 of No 50 Squadron, the type used by Nos 44 and 97 Squadrons on the Augsburg raid. (Flight)

Essen. On the night of 1/2 June a force of some 956 bombers reached the target; 31 were lost. Although seemingly lacking the concentration of the earlier raid on Cologne, the bombing was nevertheless effective enough to saturate the defences. Some bombers returned early with mechanical and engine problems, as Hallows recorded:

'Flight No 10. We went to Essen but due to rear turret failure, bombs were jettisoned and we returned home. Time. 2-25. Total Time. 56-00.'

After an uneventful mining operation on 11 June, Hallows took part in the third 'Millennium' raid, against Bremen on 25/26 June, when 960 aircraft, including 142 from 5 Group, were despatched. No 97 Squadron, and the rest of 5 Group, were given the Focke-Wulf factory as their target. Hallows wrote:

'Flight No 12. Target. Bremen. Date. 25/6/42. A/C R5548 "A". Another 1,000 raid. Well over 1,100 were briefed. We were warned of low cloud and we found it. All the way in over Holland and Germany we were shot at quite heavily. Several fighters seen. Our T.R. went u/s early on and as no holes were visible we bombed a large fire on D.R. after a search. Trip uneventful on way home. Load. 1 x 4,000lb. 8 x SBC 4lb. Time. 4.35. Total Time. 66.50.'

5 Group destroyed an assembly shop at the Focke-Wulf factory when a 4,000lb 'Cookie' scored a direct hit, and six other buildings were seriously damaged. Altogether, a total of 48 aircraft were lost, or 5 per cent of the total force despatched.
    Hallows's tour of operations continued:

'Trip No 13. Target. Gardening near Copenhagen. Date. 1 July. A/C. R5548 "A". As nights are short in Denmark we had to go well north and in daylight to 6°E it was dusk. Then we could easily map read all the way. We had a late start due to a broken rear turret, and a convoy in the Channel was almost on the Garden, causing much alarm by shooting. We were not hit however and dropped the veg at 400 feet and came home uneventfully. Load. 5 x 1,500lb Veg. Time. 5.20. Total Time. 72.10. Later, two small holes in bomb door discovered as result of this trip.'

'Trip 14. Target. Destruction of residential area of Duisburg. 23.7.42. A.C. R5548 "A". After a shaky start, due to intruders etc, we set off loaded with 4lb incendiaries etc. (Altogether, 215 bombers were despatched, including 45 Lancasters.) The attack was to be on T.R. only, with visual if possible. There was very little fire at us on the way in but over the target in spite of 8–10 tenths clouds, things were hot. On the way out of the target we saw an aircraft shot down and also through a hole saw the incendiaries burning well, on the west bank of the Rhine. Nothing much else on the way back. Load. 14 SBC. 4lb incendiaries. Time 3.45. Total Time. 75.55.' (Seven bombers failed to return.)

'Trip No 15. Target. Hamburg town. 26.7.42. A.C. R5548 "A". The take off weather was not very good but over the sea conditions improved. At the mouth of the Elbe we could clearly see twenty miles, with all ground details. We map read our way to Hamburg, and dropped our stick across the aiming point, where we saw them burning. (Some 403 bombers were despatched for the loss of 29 aircraft; 800 fires were started, 823 houses destroyed, and more than 5,000 dwellings damaged.) Flak was very heavy and we got three holes in the aircraft. Trip back was uneventful. Landed first. Load. 14 SBC. 4lb. Time 4.35. Total time. 80.30.'

'Trip No 16. Target. Düsseldorf. 31 July 1942. A.C. R5548 "A" Crew No 1. During the flight to Norfolk coast we flew over radiation fog which we knew would obscure most places by dawn. Off the coast a convoy shot one shell and 27 colours of the day were fired at once. Opposition was quite good over whole Ruhr and we saw aircraft shot down. (Altogether, 630 aircraft were despatched, including, for the first time, in excess of 100 Lancasters, and 484 aircraft claimed to have bombed. Destruction was on a large scale, but 29 aircraft failed to return.) There were good fires in the target area and we helped with our H.E., all fitted with screamers. 150 searchlights all round the town. We were "coned" once but escaped by pelting like hell out of it. Landed base just before the fog closed in. Time. 3.45. Load 1 x 4,000lb. 6 x 500lb, 4 x 250lb. Total Time. 84.15.'

'Trip No 17. (9/10 August 1942) Remarks. A/C "L" 5634. Crew No 1. After being briefed for Osnabruck (the target for 192 aircraft), we set course but had a turret failure fifty miles from target. We accordingly searched and found a lighted aerodrome which we bombed. Time. 3.05 hrs. Total Time. 87.20. Load 1 x 4,000lb 10 SBC. 30lb.'

'Trip No 18. Target Mainz. August 12th. A/c "A" R5548. Crew No 1. After flying over 10/10 cloud the whole way to the target, I tried to get below cloud to attack but got caught by heavy predicted Flak in cloud. We bombed a fire through cloud. (Altogether, 138 bombers attacked for the loss of five aircraft.) Over cloud all the way back. Return was uneventful. Time 5.40 hrs. Total Time. 93.00 hrs. Load 1 x 4,000 lb 12 SBC.'

'Trip No 19. Target. Nuremburg. 28.8.42. A.C R5548 "A" Crew No 1. We took off early and wasted time before setting course. There was little or no cloud to the French coast but 10/10 there, thinning out over Germany. Visibility very good. With good navigation we arrived at the target dead on time, to find things just getting going. (In all, 159 bombers were despatched.) We planted them all (one 4,000lb and ten SBC [30 x 4lb]) well in the middle and came home (although 23 aircraft did not). No great activity but we got one hole from a three gun battery, first round it fired. Time 6.35 hrs. Total Time. 99.35 hrs. Load 1 x 4,000lb 10 SBC. 30 x 4.'

A Lancaster bomber in flight. Flight Lieutenant B. R. W. 'Darkie' Hallows successfully completed 23 trips in Lancs between 8 April 1942 and 9 January 1943.

'Trip No 20. Target. Munich. 19.9.42. a.c R5548 A. Crew No 1. We took off at dusk (in all, 89 Lancasters and Stirlings were despatched), and flew south, near Boulogne and into France to Lake Constance, which we found with no trouble, from there to Munich, which was surrounded by searchlights, about 150, but few guns. After dropping flares, we could clearly see the town so we bombed and came out, getting caught in a cone of thirty lights. On the way back, the fires of Saarbrücken, where the little bombers (118 Wellingtons, Halifaxes and Stirlings) were, were going well. Same route home, with no trouble. Time. 7.15. Total Time. 106.50. Load 1 x 4,000lb H.C. 6 x SBC 90 x 4lb.' (The Saarbrücken force lost five bombers and the Munich force six aircraft.)

'Trip No 21. Target Krefeld. 2–3 October. a/c "A" 5548. Crew No 1. Weather at take off was poor, visibility 2,000 yards with lowering clouds. Diversion was 90% possible. On the way the cloud thinned out and visibility improved but in Germany smoke haze took over and with flares shining on this nothing could be seen. We did a T.R. run and bombed on ETA. Nothing of any event was seen, and we were not shot up at all. Time 3.30. Total Time. 110.20. Load 1 x 4,000lb H.C. 12 SBC. 8 x 30lb.' (Of the 188 aircraft despatched, seven failed to return.)

'Trip No 22. Target. Kiel. Date. 13/14 October. A/C "A" R5548. Weather at take off was very hazy, but it was still light and across the sea it cleared and cloud 5/10 at 5–10,000 feet over Denmark. We map read to the target and bombed visually. (Altogether, 288 bombers were despatched.) On the way out we were caught in 20–30 searchlights and badly shot up. Port outer engine caught fire and was feathered. We returned on three engines (eight aircraft failed to return). It was very dark and hazy for return. Piece of shell found next day in radiator of outer engine. Time 5.30. Total Time. 115.5 hrs. Load. 1 x 4,000lb H.C. 12 SBC 30 x 8lb.'

'Trip No 23. Target. Genoa. 6.11.42. A/C R5548 "A" Crew No 1. A grand trip. Weather was ideal, no moon and little cloud, less than 3/10 at 5,000 feet. (In all, 72 Lancasters from 5 Group and the PFF Force were despatched.) After an uneventful trip across France and the Alps, the Mediterranean was reached, and we flew along the coast from Monaco to the target, which was well lit up by its own very ineffective Flak and searchlights before any bombs or flares were dropped. When the flares went down it was like day. We bombed with no trouble. The photo flash held up, but we got three photos in spite of this!! Nothing was seen on way back. After crossing Channel some very poor weather was encountered to base, which was clear. (Two Lancasters failed to return.) Time. 8.55 hrs. Total Time. 124.45 hrs. Load 10 SBC. (90 x 4lb).'

'Trip No 24. 8 November 1942. Target. Gardening. Gironde River mouth (Bordeaux). A/C "K" 5917. Crew No 1. As "A" was being modified and u/s we set off in "K" in misty weather. In south of England mist cleared and it was fine and clear but very dark. We crossed Brest peninsula at 6,000 feet with no trouble except at St Nazaire, down to the garden, dropped the veg and home. We had a shot at a small ship which blazed away at us. Crossed peninsula at 4,000 to 1,000 feet but saw nothing to shoot at. Time 6.15 hrs. Total Time. 131.00 hrs. Load 5 x 1,500 Veg.'

'Trip No 25. 21/12/42. Target. Munich. A/C A. 5548. Intercom failed over France and we could not get it right, so we came back, to land in bloody weather. Time 4.40 hrs. Total Time. 135.40 hrs. Load. 1 x 4,000 8SBC 90x4.' (Of the 135 aircraft sent, 111 claimed to have bombed the city, and 12 were lost. All or most of the tonnage dropped fell in open fields.)

'Trip No 26. 31/12/42. Target. Gardening. Gironde River. A/C A 5548. Her last operation! We flew over France for this and down thro' cloud to garden. Very dark but quite uneventful. Time 5.45. Total Time. 141.25 hrs. Load 4 x 500 Veg.'

'Trip No 27. 9/1/43. Target. Essen. "Wanganui"! (Target Indicator flares) A/C "C". A lovely night, clear and dark. (The city was bombed by 50 Lancasters in 5 Group and two PFF Mosquitoes for the loss of three Lancasters.) We pranged the flares. Flak very hot and too close too. Bombs seen burning in built up area. Time 4.00. Load 1 x 4,000 12 SBC. Total. 145.25.'

Hallows was now posted to ground duties and non-operational flying – Group HQ, two different Bomber Conversion Units (Stirlings and Lancasters) – instructing again, until, in January 1945, he was posted to command 627 Pathfinder Mosquito Marking Squadron at Woodhall Spa, where he completed four operations. At the end of the war he was told that he was not needed for the Far East because he was on his second tour of operations, and was sent on leave. He was then given a permanent commission in the RAF.

6: Blenheim boy

Flight Lieutenant Charles Patterson DSO, DFC

BY THE TIME I finished OTU on Blenheims early in 1941, I'd acquired quite a considerable degree of confidence in flying. I was still frightened of night flying and instrument flying in cloud, but just flying as such I enjoyed. My fear was that I would never be able to cope with being shot at and that I would fail, turn round and run away. The nearer it got, the stronger the fear of failure became.

Admittedly, Blenheims had had an easier time during the winter of 1940–41 because they had been put on night operations, especially quite a lot of bombing of barges at invasion ports. But by the time I was posted, at the end of April, to 114 Squadron, Blenheims had gone back on daylight again and they were being used on low-level shipping strikes. Blenheims were totally vulnerable once intercepted by fighters but I was incredibly fortunate in that, instead of being thrown straight into the deep end by being posted to Norfolk to do standard, routine daylight bombing operations, I was posted to the one squadron in 2 Group that had been detached to Scotland to cover the North Sea and the Scandinavian coast. Opposition there was on a very much lower scale.

My first operations were low-level daylight and dusk reconnaissance of the Norwegian coast and a few convoy escorts. In June I was sent out to look for the pocket battleship *Lützow*, which was known to be steaming up the Norwegian coast towards Bergen. It was the time of the midnight sun and I was flying down the Norwegian coast virtually within sight of the cliffs. Staring forward into the gloom I thought that I only had another minute of my patrol to go and I had escaped without finding anything. Then suddenly I saw in front of me an enormous area of white. It was

Squadron Leader Charles Patterson DSO DFC.
(Charles Patterson)

the bow wave of the *Lützow*, whose enormous and terrifying looking superstructure suddenly loomed into view, steaming at about 30 knots. I was practically on top of it. This bloody battleship was only 10,000 tons but, when viewed from 300 feet and flying straight at it, looked about 40,000 tons. It was the most terrifying thing I had ever seen.

I gave one horrified glance and swung away to starboard and opened the throttles. Amazingly they never opened fire. I sent my radio message and 114 Squadron and a Beaufort Squadron went out to attack it. (Subsequently, a torpedo from one of the Beauforts hit the *Lützow*; it limped into Bergen and did not come out again for a year.)

In the middle of July, the day of reckoning that I knew must come finally arrived. We had to leave Scotland and the comparative safety of the Norwegian coast and rejoin 2 Group in Norfolk for daylight bomber operations. Virtually every operation from now on meant being shot at in some way or other in broad daylight.

We flew down to West Raynham in formation. Wing Commander 'Bok' Hull DFC, our South African Squadron commander, a veteran from 1940 and the most marvellous CO, was absolutely thrilled that we were going back to 2 Group proper where he would be able to head his squadron into the thick of things. I could not help being caught up in the excitement, even though I was very nervous of what was to come. I was also, in a way, exhilarated.

From the moment we landed the whole tempo became more highly charged. We arrived to find that our station commander was the famous, ineffable and unique Paddy Bandon, Group Captain, the Earl of Bandon, whose personality and achievements were a legend. Behind his always cheerful and friendly exterior was a man of extraordinary sympathy, kindness and tolerance. His task was to maintain morale amongst very young, mostly inexperienced, raw and terrified crews during this period of appalling casualties. He was a teamwork leader, wonderful at getting people of conflicting personalities to work together.

I also had the unexpected and completely new experience of finding myself billeted in Weasenham Hall, which belonged to the Earls of Leicester, the Coke family, which had been turned into a mess for us. To my amazement I found myself a Flight Lieutenant overnight, having only done about 12 operations. A state of affairs had been reached where any officer pilot who completed about ten operations was virtually automatically a Flight Lieutenant. Anyone who could get through 15 was a Squadron Leader. This situation most certainly never existed at any other time during the war.

'Bok' Hull was keen and ready to start operating. The very day after we arrived I had to move the whole of my flight to Bodney, a satellite airfield about 8 miles away, and have it ready for operations the next morning. It was a standard *Circus*, a formation of Blenheims going out with Fighter Command on a fighter sweep across the Channel at medium level, about 10,000 feet. Our target was a power station near Rouen. It was regarded as a fairly safe form of operation, but it was made clear that there would inevitably be a great deal of heavy flak, which is what one encountered from 8,000 feet upwards. I had no idea what it would look like, although I was told there would be a lot of black puffs. The main thing that was impressed upon me was to keep formation, and follow the Squadron commander in his evasive action, which would be gentle weaves and turns towards the target. I must follow him and keep them going straight and level when he said 'straight and level'. The moment bombs were gone the Squadron commander would swing away and resume evasive action.

I led a 'Vic' of three and formated under the Squadron commander's tail. It was a glorious, sunny day, necessary of course for a *Circus* – you could not do it with cloud. The whole thing was a sort of daze. I just did not know what would happen when the flak started. I genuinely had no confidence that I would be able to take it. On the other hand, the thing in my head was that it just had to be done. There was no way out. I suppose my training and instincts were subconsciously operating even though I was not aware of it.

We circled over Dungeness and out of the corner of my eye I saw a sight that raised my spirits to a remarkable degree. Down below, against a bank of cumulus cloud, I could see an enormous swarm of what looked like gnats, silhouetted against this cloud,

Flying Officer Charles Patterson in 114 Squadron flew low-level daylight and dusk reconnaissance operations off the Norwegian coast during the summer of 1941 on Blenheim IVs like this one.

A bomb-aimer in the nose of a Blenheim IV.
(IWM)

racing across and climbing in a great upward sweep. This was 11 Group's Hurricanes coming up to provide our escort. They joined and took up close positions all around us; one could see the pilots in their cockpits. Of course, it gave a wonderful sense of security, although it was no security whatsoever against flak.

I felt quite good but crossing the enemy coast had a sinister connotation, then I seemed to just live from minute to minute, longing for the target to come up, dreading the flak. We carried on straight and level. Still nothing happened, then my navigator said, 'We must be getting to the target fairly soon.' Sure enough, the Squadron commander started gentle evasive action, then the dreaded moment arrived. There was a thud and the aircraft shook. My first sight of the famous black puffs produced an irresistible longing to just turn and run, but I couldn't. I was in the middle of the box. I had my orders. I just had to carry on.

The puffs got nearer. The thuds got more severe. I actually saw the orange flash in the puffs of smoke, but I didn't feel too bad while the Squadron commander was still

A Blenheim IV being bombed up with four 250lb bombs for an anti-shipping strike.

doing this gentle evasive action, weaving slowly and gently to port or starboard with a climb or with a loss of height. Then we had to straighten up and go straight and level. I just sat there, frozen at the controls, waiting for the whole aeroplane to disappear into oblivion, but we went on and on, and still we were surviving. The longer it went on the more I thought with just a bit more to go that'll be when we get it. I don't know how, but I carried on, on this long straight and narrow run, which never seemed to end. At last, the leading navigator gave the signal for 'Bombs gone!'. In a Blenheim the bombs opened the doors with their own weight.

Every now and then some of the thuds were extremely close, but we were still in one piece. Then to my unforgettable relief, Wing Commander Hull turned away and we were all able to swing away. I was so exhilarated that I had got through and done it that I really did not think much about the dangers that might occur on the way back. The fighters were all around us and we returned across the Channel. At the English coast the fighters fell away and we flew on at 8–10,000 feet back to Norfolk. Hull gave the order to break formation, then we all landed. I'd actually done it. I did a few more *Circuses* like that and managed to get through them, but I still had not done a low-level daylight.

On Blenheims we lived day to day, each governed by what the bomb load was, your fate designated on the notice board at Weasenham Hall. If you had instantaneous fuses in the bomb load, it meant that you were going on a *Circus* at medium level. If it was semi-armour-piercing (SAP) 11-second delay, it meant a low-level shipping attack. Then you simply turned away from the notice board and assumed that your own death warrant had been signed.

Ten days after I had arrived, on 2 August, I saw the dreaded SAP. There was nothing

In June 1941 Charles Patterson in a Blenheim spotted the pocket battleship Lützow *steaming up the Norwegian coast towards Bergen, and 114 Squadron Blenheims and some Beauforts, like this one, went out to attack it. Subsequently a torpedo from one of the Beauforts hit the* Lützow *and it limped into Bergen and did not come out again for a year.* (IWM)

I could do about it. Then I got my first experience of flying across the North Sea, at low level, in formation. I was one of a 'Vic' of three going to do a beat along the Frisian Islands. Apart from flying over to Norway, this was the first time I experienced the sensation of flying very low over the sea in broad daylight, little knowing that it was to be an experience that was to become so familiar over the years ahead. It is difficult to describe the sensation, really. You were literally racing across the surface of the sea. The concentration required to do this and formate at the same time kept the mind fully occupied, but still at the back of one's mind was the dread of when one would have to turn on to the actual shipping beat and whether one would actually find a convoy.

We raced on and when we reached the Frisian Islands we turned to port and ran along the northern shores of Ameland towards Borkum. Suddenly, the leader said something on the TR9. Alan Griffith, my gunner, assured me on his intercom that it was a call of 'Snappers', which meant that fighters were coming to intercept us. I looked everywhere and couldn't see any. Suddenly, the leader climbed. Fortunately, there was a thin belt of cloud, enough in the leader's opinion to conceal us. He climbed and I tried to follow, but I soon lost him in the cloud. Now the operation would have to be abandoned, and we would drop down out of the cloud when out of range of the German fighters. I decided to take a peek below: on the port side from a thousand feet, as plain and as clear as anything, was Ameland. I just don't know what came over me, but I was suddenly seized with the idea that to go home without dropping my bombs on anything was wrong. Against all the training and against all my own views and principles, I decided to use the thousand feet to get up speed, charge down, and race across the island at full throttle in the hope of seeing something that might be worth bombing.

So, without consulting my crew, I just told them I was going to do it. I put the Blenheim into a dive, pulled the Plus 9 boost and went down to the sea in a fast shallow dive. I should think that the aeroplane was doing about 260 on the clock when I got down to sea level. The island came racing toward me at an alarming speed and, before I knew were I was, I was racing up over sand dunes. There in front of me were four enormous long barrels, 4.7mm AA guns, pointing to the sky, surrounded by a lot of sand bags and a lot of German soldiers. I pressed the tit and dropped the bombs. I saw a lot of steely blue flashes around the ground, which I realised was machine-gun fire. Turning to starboard I raced down to the beach to get out to sea again. There were a lot of young naked men, presumably German soldiers, having a swim. Alan Griffith raked them left and right with machine-gun fire. As we raced out to sea he told me that there was a great deal of blood and so on. I thought he'd done very well. So did he. (I now look back on it with revulsion). Then he called out that there were terrific flashes and a lot of smoke. Something had been hit.

When I landed Group Captain Bandon was waiting to greet me. His face was wreathed in smiles. Apparently, the Squadron leader had seen me dive down and cross the coast and he saw, following my bombing, a tremendous flash and smoke up to 1,500 feet. It was evident that the detonation of these bombs had touched off their ammunition dump! Being very young and inexperienced this was the first time in my life I'd ever done anything that appeared to be individually rather successful.

Two days later, on 4 August, I was sent out on a shipping beat in the Heligoland Bight. I had to lead two Sergeants who'd never been on operations before. One was only 19, and I don't think the other one was more than about 20. My morale was lifted by the previous attack so I was not quite as frightened as I ought to have been. It was a cloudy day, grey and rather sinister. As we turned south we entered a rain storm and visibility came down. We emerged and quite suddenly, there, 2 miles slap in front, was what looked like an 8,000-ton merchant ship, surrounded, to my horror, by twelve flak ships as escort. And we were racing toward it!

I got very low down on the sea and started to open the throttles. The two Sergeants, whose formation-keeping up to now was poor, weaved around, obviously panic-stricken by the sight of this convoy. One was at about 200 feet and the other at about 100 feet, one each side of me. The whole tactical essence of low-level attack on ships was to keep right down on the sea so that the enemy did not see you until the last minute. If you were over 20 feet you could be seen over the horizon from the deck of the ships. To my final horror, a mile out the leading flak ship flashed an order signal for me to identify myself. There was a lot of cloud above and I made a sudden decision to lead the two Sergeants into it, try to drop out and attack again from about 800 feet.

When we came out all I could see was grey sea. We never found the convoy again. I set course for home, bombing a 'Squealer', a little vessel a few miles out to sea used as an observation post for anti-shipping Blenheims. I was crestfallen because although I could put a perfectly genuine tactical reason forward for having turned away, I knew in my own heart that I'd funked it. I was not so much worried about what the Group Captain and the AOC, 'Butcher' Stevenson, of whom we all lived in dread, would say; I was more worried by the fact that I knew the real reason. However, the explanation was accepted and I heard no more. Then I realised that I had got to try to live with it, and cope next time. All my elation was gone. I went out again two days later, leading another shipping beat up the Dutch coast, low level, but fortunately nothing was sighted.

Then something fundamentally changed my whole operational career, and indeed my whole life. We got wind that there was a major operation to be laid on and as time went by the more alarming became the rumours. We understood that it was to be a major effort involving all the Blenheims in 2 Group. We did a lot of low-level formation practice. We had a new Squadron commander, Wing Commander John Nicol, who arrived with no previous operational experience, to take over from Wing Commander Howe, who fell out of the first floor window of Weasenham Hall after a party, and was in hospital in Cambridge – not a very gallant accident for such a gallant man. The operation was to be led by 114 Squadron, and Nicol had never operated before. This seemed very strange to us, but he had a wonderful navigator to go with him. Flight Lieutenant Tommy Baker DFM, Howe's navigator, was an ex-Halton boy who became a very great friend of mine and whom I admired tremendously.

Meanwhile, low-level practices went on. Then, on Friday 10 August Nicol and I, very inexperienced but one of the most experienced pilots in the Squadron below the rank of Squadron Leader, were taken into the operations room. I was to be deputy leader, and we were to look at the target and see what this operation was to be. It had been rumoured that it was to be a factory outside Paris, which, without fighter escort, sounded terrifying enough. I'll never forget the sight that met my eyes. On a table in the centre of the ops room a huge map had been laid out and there, leading absolutely straight, was a red tape from Orford Ness, across the North Sea, right through Holland and right down to Cologne. At first I just did not believe that this was the target. I assumed it referred to something else. Then I realised it did not. The truth, the reality, dawned on me. I was going to have to take part in a low-level daylight attack on Cologne – with no fighter escort – in Blenheims.

It was no use panicking so I listened to the briefing and the instructions I was given. The target was not Cologne itself, but the Knapsack power station, which the Group Captain said was the biggest in Europe. I was shown a photograph. It had eight chimneys on one side and four on the other (known in Germany as the 'twelve apostles'). We were to fly between these chimneys, then turn round and come back again. Of course I couldn't communicate what the target was to anybody else. I had to carry this secret about with me for two days. The chances of surviving an operation like this were negligible. How could I, a fundamental coward who'd managed to skate past it up to now, make myself do this operation? The next two days were spent wrestling with myself as to how I was to do it. The only thing to do was to stop worrying and to say to myself, 'You're not coming back. You've just got to go. You're caught in this situation.' The alternative was to funk it and not go at all. Of the two this seemed the more impossible, so I just resigned myself to the fact that I was not coming back. Curiously, this rid me of uncertainty and made it easier.

Then came the early morning of 12 August when we were to go. I had a pretty poor night's sleep the night before. When I woke at 6.30 I suddenly remembered that this was the Sunday morning when I was just not going to come back. I was still saying, well, it's got to be. In the operations room all the crews in the Squadron realised what the target was. Hardened though some of them were, there was the gasp of disbelief, even from the most hardened ones. Unlike me, they had not had the opportunity to prepare themselves. It was the only time that I saw some of my fellow aircrew, including my own gunner, who was a pretty imperturbable type, literally grey and shaking. Curiously enough, seeing all the others looking so alarmed rather bolstered me a bit.

The operation was very comprehensively planned. Thirty-six aircraft were to attack Knapsack in six formations of six aircraft each. Everything was being done to mislead and divert the enemy fighter force, with diversionary bombing attacks in France and northern Germany. We took off at about 0800 and I formed up closely on Wing Commander Nicol, setting off for Orford Ness. We rendezvoused on time and came down to low level over the North Sea. Although we thought we were going to certain death, perhaps it was the scale, the element of the adventure, the actual flying, but somehow one was not as panicky as expected. I had always wondered what enemy territory looked like. In fact, everything looked so normal that in some way it was actually reassuring.

We flew down the Schelde estuary, south of Woensdrecht airfield, and into the heathland of Holland, all of it new to me. At any moment we expected enemy fighters. We went on, mile after mile, not a cloud in the sky, and still no fighters.

I asked my navigator, 'How long?'

'Not long now,' he said.

On the R/T Nicol said, 'Turn to starboard.'

As I turned slightly, there, up on top of a long, long slope about 3 miles away was this enormous industrial complex. I realised that this was Knapsack. I thought, well, we've just got to go on now and there'll be a big bang.

We had to climb a bit to avoid the increasing maze of electricity pylons and cables. Then the chimneys came into view, until they were coming right at us. Wing Commander Nicol swung in between the chimneys and I followed him. I became enveloped in mist and steam. I was in it now. There was nothing I could do except concentrate on flying the aeroplane properly. We had been told not to release our bombs on the attractive-looking water coolers but to keep them for the actual power house at the far end. We flew on down between these chimneys. As we did so I saw again a lot of blue flashes, which would be machine-gun fire, but I was past caring about that now. At the far end I could see the great turbine house and the steam and the smoke and everything. I pressed the tit and let the bombs go. As I did so, Nicol, just

ahead of me, swerved sharply to starboard, and I did the same. I realised he was about
to fly into a chimney, which he just missed.

Then, out the other side, a lot more blue flashes and sparks and tracer. We dived
down to the ground. Nicol was there. He'd survived. I formed up on him. We raced
away across the cables again down past the other side of the power station. We started
to turn to starboard to fly on the course for the Dutch coast, then to my amazement all
of the other five members of the formation emerged safely and formed up with us. We
set off on the journey home.

I settled down in formation and another chap formated on me. The whole formation
got together. On to Holland we went. No interception yet. Then we flew into a rain
storm and for a wonderful moment I thought we were going to get cloud cover, but it
was only a shower and we emerged shortly afterwards into the brilliant sun again, and
no cloud above us. On and on, past little villages and hamlets, occasionally an
individual diving into a ditch beneath us. Just before we got to the Dutch border, we
flew over a baronial German mansion. In the garden, beside a cedar tree, I just got a
glimpse of a table with a large white table cloth, all laid out for lunch, and a group of
people standing around it. As we whizzed over the top my gunner let fly and it broke
up the party. He felt that any rich Germans who were living like that while the war was
on deserved it.

On across Holland, now it suddenly seemed to me that we were going to make it.
Nothing was going to happen after all, but it's always when that psychological moment
comes that you're brought down to earth. Ahead of us, just as we were coming up to
the Schelde estuary, black dots appeared. For a moment my navigator thought that they
might be Spitfires that had come out to escort us home, but of course they were not.
They were not Whirlwinds either, which had escorted us out and were due to escort us
back. Nicol called out 'Snappers!' Before I knew where I was, I was flying on straight
into these Messerschmitts, which were circling around about a thousand feet above us.

Nicol told us to close in tight. He led us right down on to the water, sparkling in the
sun, not more than 10, 15, occasionally perhaps 20 feet below. I got as tight into him as
I could, with my wing-tip practically inside his. I knew this was life or death. It took all
the flying concentration and skill I possessed to do it, which drove out most of the fear
of the fighters. The others closed in. Then Nicol handed over to the leading gunner,
Pilot Officer Morton, a very experienced second tour man. He directed the formation
because the gunners, looking back, could all see the fighters coming into attack. He
had to decide when it was the right moment to open fire and when to take evasive
action.

Then I heard the rattle of machine-gun fire and realised that our guns were firing.
Every now and then the water was ripped with white froth, which was of course the
cannon shells of these 109s. On one turn, out of the corner of one eye, I caught a
glimpse of a 109 right in front peeling off from the attack. It was so close that I could
see the pilot in the cockpit, let alone the black crosses and the yellow nose of the 109.
My reaction was simply one of interest in seeing a 109 so close. We all knew that the
only safety was out to sea and out of range of these 109s. Would we make it? After
each attack we just had to crouch down and prepare for the next. This carried on all the
way up the Schelde. Yet we seemed to survive them.

Then, unbelievably, the islands to each side of us suddenly ceased and we were in
the open sea. We'd hardly gone any distance when the leading gunner told us over the
R/T that the fighters had broken off the attack. I suppose they were running out of
ammunition. Still, we didn't feel it was all over yet. The first reaction of realising that
one had survived was a sort of numbness. The leading Blenheim climbed gently to

about 600 feet and I realised that we had survived. We'd made it. It was just marvellous, happy relief, sheer joy, flying back across the North Sea. Then the cliffs came up – England. We were back.

There was a general opinion that we'd all hit the target and reports came in that we'd got away with it, but by the afternoon word got round that we had lost 12 of the 36, and that several others had been badly shot up and crash-landed. Two Blenheims, which had navigated the Whirlwind fighters out to escort us home, had also both been shot down. This was very tragic and a terrible waste.

Then, of course, the inevitable relaxation. We were all to go to Norwich, the whole group, for a party and a beat-up. We all met up and drank away. All great excitement, great fun. We felt very heroic and wonderful. We thought, 'This is it, we've done it.' We forgot there was any future. For the rest of my operational career I found that the way to make myself overcome my fear was to tell myself that I was not coming back and just accept the fact. That is the way I personally conquered fear. I don't think that all my fellow aircrew thought quite as I did. How we conquered our own individual fear was not a thing we ever talked about, however intimate or friendly we were.

Nicol was awarded an immediate DSO for leading the Knapsack raid. However, it had been taken for granted before we took off that if he got back he would get a VC; it caused a considerable disappointment. About a week later (on 19 August) Wing Commander Nicol went out on his next trip and never came back.

In the summer of 1941 the casualty rate on Blenheims in 2 Group was such that statistically you could not survive more than seven to ten ops, but you had to do 30. As already mentioned, anyone who did seven trips was promoted to Flight Lieutenant, and on average anyone who'd done about 15 was a Squadron Leader. Due to the fact that I'd survived for so long, I suddenly found myself made a Squadron Leader, when only six or seven weeks before I'd been a Pilot Officer, and I had a flight to command. The tremendous privilege of commanding these men when I was only 21 seemed to me the most wonderful, worthwhile job in the world. The rest of my tour consisted of one or two shipping beats, and a number of *Circuses*. To be taken off it, to be sent on a rest, on 10 October 1941, came as a terrible blow. It wasn't because I wanted to go on fighting. It was because I wanted to go on commanding the flight.

After a course at Upavon, for the next ten months I was an instructor. Just before Christmas my spirits were suddenly lifted when I was told to my astonishment that a DFC had come through for me, and a DFM for Alan Griffith. I've never been quite sure about whether I deserved the DFC except that I can always say anyone who got through a tour on Blenheims in 1941 could feel that he'd reasonably deserved it for surviving it.

(Charles Patterson went on to complete two tours of daylight operations on Mosquitoes. He was awarded the DSO early in 1944.)

7: 'Sim'

SATURDAY 25/SUNDAY 26 APRIL 1942 was a starry, cold, clear night, with a full moon. At half past one in the morning only the most inquisitive Danes living in southern Jutland felt able to brave the $-3°$ temperature to look out to see the RAF bombers once again headed for Rostock on the Baltic coast. For two nights running, 23/24 and 24/25 April, the town of Rostock, and the Heinkel factory, had been the

'Sim', 1941. (Mike Lewis)

'Sim', 1941. (Mike Lewis)

target for RAF Wellingtons, Stirlings, Whitleys, Hampdens, Manchesters and Lancasters. Crews were in no doubt that the flak defences would have been strengthened considerably, and enemy night fighters would be alerted once more to the possibilities of a 'kill'. Each and every crew member aboard the 128 bombers knew this only too well, including 23-year-old Sergeant Albert Edward Simmans, a 115 Squadron Wellington rear gunner flying only his fifth operation, and his pilot, Sergeant Alfred Fone, a Yorkshireman from Leeds, whose ninth op this was, despite their limited experience. Fone's 'Wimpy' was one of the dozen in 115 Squadron en route from Marham to Rostock.

This was Sim's second crew. He had been forced to part company with the first, in 40 Squadron at Alconbury, when he developed problems with his ears. No doubt this was caused by the combined effect of a swimming accident as a youngster when he had hit his head on the bottom of the pool, exacerbated by the pressure changes associated with flying. After hospitalisation at Halton, Sim was able to resume his flying career, despite a warning that flying could have an adverse effect on his hearing in later life. He crewed up with Fone and an all-Sergeant crew consisting of Irvine Rollinson, second pilot, Alexander Saint, observer, from Bonavista, Newfoundland, and two Scots, William Smith, the wireless operator, and James Small Grieve, the front gunner. Sim had also become engaged to Ann Wynn, a WAAF, and they had made plans for a June wedding.

On his last leave home to Barking, Essex, on 2 April, Sim's aunt had repaired his silk flying gloves, which he was wearing now to help protect his 'trigger' fingers from freezing at altitude over Jutland. Everything seemed to be going well. They had taken off in KO-Y at 2223 and had crossed Norfolk and the North Sea without incident. Any thoughts Sim might have had concerning lingering mess bills and a paltry payslip of only £2 10s had to be put to one side.

As the bomber stream of incoming aircraft approached Sylt at around 0100 hours, Andr Juhl, Alfred and Johannes Lange and Kirsten Goeg living in the Strandhjorn, Jaegerlund and Neder Jerstal area, followed the sounds of the RAF bombers' engines and those of the German night fighters as they tried to seek them out. Bomber after bomber crossed from west to east. North-west of Toftlund at 0200 hours a searchlight suddenly coned Fone's Wellington and machine-gun fire could be heard as a Bf 110 of

Wellington III X3662 KO-P of 115 Squadron, RAF Marham. On 25/26 April 1942 KO-Y from this Squadron, which was flown by Sergeant Alfred Fone, failed to return from the raid on Rostock.

II./NJG3, which arrived from the south-west, made several passes at the aircraft, which caught fire. No one aboard the Wellington bomber stood a chance.

Still carrying its bomb load, *Y-Yorker* crashed and exploded at a crossroads west of Neder Jerstal, a tiny hamlet of 22 houses. Windows and doors of buildings nearby were blown out, including the windows of Inger Friisk's house. The roads surrounding the crash site were immediately blocked off by the German Wehrmacht and Field Gendarmerie and the Danish civil police. Wreckage from the burning Wellington was scattered over a wide area and a large fire started and burned for hours despite attempts by firemen from Toftlund and Agerskov to put it out.

On Thursday 30 April a clearing commando from Aalborg arrived. In the morning

A Bf 110 night fighter of II./NJG2. It was an aircraft similar to this, from II./NJG3, that shot down Wellington KO-Y. (Collection Rob de Visser, via Theo Boiten)

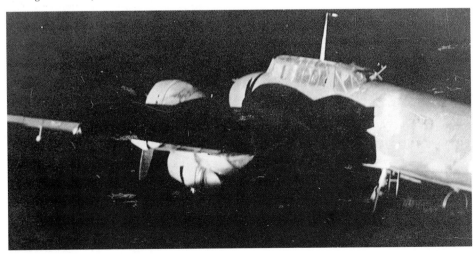

Frederick Thychen, the village schoolmaster, went straight to the commando and asked that they bury the dead airmen. However, an NCO in charge said that he had a direct order that no funeral or ceremony of any kind should take place. Thychen asked what should be done. The NCO said that he was ordered to sprinkle sand over the larger mortal remains and that the rest 'would be eaten by the crows in three days'. Thychen talked to him about soldiers' honour and equality in death. The German asked him what he would do with the corpses. Thychen said he would bury them nearby. The NCO agreed that he could do it 'after sunset', as long as Thychen promised not to involve him or the Danish police. With the help of his two sons, 11-year-old Alfred and 12-year-old Svend, Thychen fetched a sea chest and a big box and he and the NCO collected the mortal remains of the crew. Among the personal belongings was a cigarette case and a ring, engraved 'JSG'. The belongings were handed over to the Wehrmacht.

In the evening Thychen sent for Icvar Gemmer, a 68-year-old bricklayer, Nis Sandtholdt, a 65-year-old coachmaker, and Mr P. Riis, a 47-year-old farmer, who at 11 o'clock dug a grave in the corner of Riis's plantation near the road. Morten Oppel and Mr Ralser, a baker from Rungstrup, came and offered their assistance. Thychen said the Lord's Prayer and undertook the burial.

'We stood at the graves,' he recalls, 'with hats in our hands. I prayed to our Father, and I said, "In this moment the families of these boys do not know anything, but after a few days there will be sorrow in their homes. The fathers and mothers, the sisters and brothers will shed many tears when they know that the boys are not coming back. We cannot help

Aabenraa Cemetery, 6 May 1942. The funeral of the Fone crew was conducted by German chaplain Graumann from Flensburg naval base. (via Mike Lewis)

them, but we will do what we can to honour them." The moon was shining, it was very still, and we all had tears in our eyes. The time now was 12 o'clock and we went home. The next day the farmers and inhabitants from Neder Jerstal laid many hundreds of flowers on the grave and a cross was put on it, and on this you could read, 'Here rest brave Englishmen. They died that we could be free.' Mr Moellet, another teacher, and his wife, from Strandhjorn, helped to decorate the grave with spruce branches and flowers.

On 2 May a German captain and six soldiers from Sonderborg arrived with a team who were to examine the area for unexploded bombs. They found a corpse fairly whole, presumably Sim, lying under heavy aircraft wreckage, which needed 15 men to lift it. On the left arm was a wrist watch that had stopped at 0206 hours. In the pockets Thychen found a tin of toffees and a tiny compass. Furthermore, there was a plastic cover containing about 7,000 francs, Belgian and Dutch money, German marks and a map of northern France. (On 13 April Fone's crew had flown a 'Gardening' sortie and on the 17th had taken part in a raid on Le Havre. On their third operation on 23/24 April they had been part of a bombing raid on Dunkirk.) A coffin was requisitioned and the body was laid inside without any attempt being made by the Germans to find the airman's identity card or anything else. The coffin was driven to a guard post at Laddenhoj and it was the intention to bury it at the Bevtoft cemetery.

On the night of 2/3 May a 106 Squadron Manchester with seven crew aboard crashed near Skrydstrup, killing

The gravestone of Sergeant Albert Edward Simmans in Aabenraa Cemetery. The 25/26 April 1942 operation was only the 23-year-old rear gunner's fifth operation. (Mike Lewis)

five. Early in the morning of 4 May a Wehrmacht corporal came with a message from Kolding saying that Mr Thychen should dig up the buried corpses of the Wellington crew and take them to the guard post at Laddenhoj. Thychen refused, saying he had permission to bury them in the plantation and reminding the German that he did not take orders from a corporal. The corporal became unpleasant and Thychen said that he had served in the German Army in 1914–18 and that he was under the command of the Danish police and not the Wehrmacht! He asked the corporal to take the ring and the cigarette case, and asked for a receipt, which he received.

On 5 May a Wehrmacht truck came with ten soldiers. They dug up the buried remains and put them into a white coffin and drove it to Skrydstrup where it was intended that it would be buried with the five others from the 2/3 May crash. A common grave was dug and finally the two coffins were buried at Aabenraa with five other coffins on the morning of 6 May at 0600 hours. On the grave in Riis's plantation someone put up a cross with the inscription, 'Here are resting five brave British pilots (sic). They fell for the sake of Europe. In honour of their memory.' (The unveiling of the memorial stone of the crew by Mrs Fone, the pilot's mother took place on 12 July 1947.)

That same year Frederick Thychen wrote to Mr and Mrs Simmans, ending his letter with these words: 'I cannot give to you your dear son back again, but I will often go to the grave. I will take care of it; I will plant roses and flowers every year in the spring and I will bring water to the flowers. That I promise you. I hope my letter will bring you comfort. It is difficult for me to convey to you in English all that I feel. God bless you all in the great sorrow of the loss of your dear son. He rests in freedom; he rests in Denmark.'

8: Ijmuiden operation
*Flight Lieutenant George Turner DFC**

NOVEMBER 27, 1942 was a typical November day with grey cloud sheer at about 1,000 feet and visibility of about 3 miles. It started out as a normal one for us Boston crews in 107 Squadron at Great Massingham, Norfolk. The officers had arrived from West Raynham in the crew bus at about 8.30am and the NCO aircrews had walked up from their billets in Massingham to the airfield. As usual we gathered round the stove in the crew room. Some played cards, some chatted and some read. By 9 o'clock normal training was under way.

Some time during the morning, probably about 11 o' clock, the Flight Commander sent for Warrant Officer A. J. 'Tony' Reid and myself to tell me that we had been detailed for a low-level operation that I was to lead. (The squadron was only sending out a pair of aircraft.) We were to tell our crews to have an early lunch and to report for briefing at 1 o'clock.

I was a bit excited (low-level trips in Bostons were exciting) and rather flattered, as this was the first time we had been chosen to lead another aircraft on a raid. Tony Reid was not pleased. He was a much more experienced pilot than me (although his operational experience was about on a par with mine) who had spent nearly a year at Upwood flying observers under training in Ansons, and had thus built up twice as

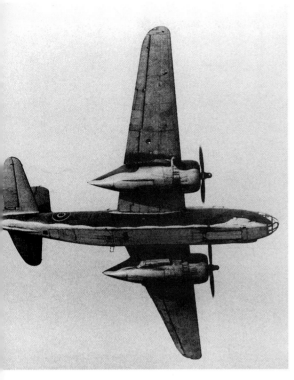

A Douglas Boston of 107 Squadron. (via Nigel Buswell)

many flying hours as I had. With this behind him he felt that he should be the leader and said so to me.

The Royal Dutch Steelworks at Ijmuiden lay behind and slightly to one side of the town, and for some reason we were briefed to come in from the sea, cross the harbour and town, then attack the steelworks. In our ignorance this meant nothing to us (we were still very inexperienced as this was only our fourth low-level trip), but it certainly meant something to the Intelligence Officer, who came out to our aircraft as we were getting in and wished us luck. This was unusual – it had never happened before, nor did it ever happen subsequently!

We took off, flew to the coast at about 100 feet, and set course for the target, dropping down to sea level as we did so. The visibility was not very good and, being very conscious of Tony Reid's displeasure, I flew as low and as accurately as I could. We had no aids so accurate compass courses were essential. We had a full load of fuel and four 500lb bombs fused for 11-second delay. I was flying one of the few aircraft on the squadron (at that time) that incorporated an RAF modification to improve the Boston's range – a 140-gallon fuselage tank fitted over the bomb bay. The normal tankage was one inboard of the engine of 140 gallons, and one

Boston IIIs pictured at Great Massingham in 1942. The nearest aircraft is AL280 and the next is W8373. (via Nigel Buswell)

George Turner and his crew, who took part in the operation to Ijmuiden on 27 November 1942, beside their Boston 'EST MELIOR DARE QUAM ACCIPERE'. Left to right: Arthur Liddle, navigator; George Turner, pilot; George Murray, air gunner; and Ron Chatfield, WOP/AG. (George Turner)

outboard of 60 gallons, in each wing. For some reason I decided to use the outboard tanks first. I don't know why, but it had a bearing on subsequent events.

We did not say much over the sea. We were never a chatty crew, so it was Arthur Liddle, my navigator, warning me that the enemy coast was 5 minutes ahead that broke the silence. I changed tanks to inners, went in to rich mixture, pushed the revs to 2,350 and the boost to 40 inches of mercury (flat out was 2,400rpm and 45 inches of mercury). As the speed built up to about 280mph I re-trimmed the aircraft and gave a quick glance over my shoulder to see Tony Reid nicely in position a little to one side

George Turner and Arthur Liddle in their 107 Squadron Boston. (George Turner)

and behind. Visibility had improved as we neared the coast and we saw Ijmuiden from about 5 miles out.

Impressions now get a little confused. I remember flying between two breakwaters into the harbour and there was tracer flak from all directions criss-crossing in front, at the side and straight at me from ahead. I was flying as low as I could with the prop tips about a foot or so above the water, and most of it seemed to be going over the top of us, then I heard four loud bangs and knew we had been hit. The engine instruments seemed OK, although the starboard engine was a bit down on boost, but the fuel gauge for the starboard inner tank and the fuselage tank gauge were sinking towards zero.

At the time I conned myself that I was trying to check on the damage to the aircraft, but in retrospect I was probably suffering from shock because when I looked out again we were up about 300 feet and a target for every flak gun for miles around, who were having a field day. It seemed to take ages to register that I was the centre of all this attention, but it can only have been a second or two before I pushed the stick forward, shot down to ground level, pushed throttles and pitch levers against the stops and changed to the starboard outer tank, which still had a few gallons in it.

I flew in a wide curve to port well behind the town and turned north for a couple of miles or so before taking up a north-westerly heading that Arthur gave me before passing out. In our sweep round I checked on the crew. The gunners were OK, but Arthur said he had been hit. The starboard engine was making a horrible clanking noise and was down to about 30 inches boost, but it was helping us along at about 270mph so I kept it going.

We crossed some sand dunes and headed out to sea. Heavy guns opened up behind us and great spouts of water rose around, but that did not last long as the chances of us being hit were remote. Ron Chatfield, my WOP/AG, now reported a couple of Me 109s behind us, so I pulled up into cloud. After settling down there I switched off the starboard engine (it had done us proud but it did not sound at all well), transferred the remains of the fuel from the outer tank to the port inner and calculated that we had enough to reach England at our reduced airspeed. From time to time I tried to raise Arthur but with no success.

George Turner's Boston en route to the target. (via Nigel Buswell)

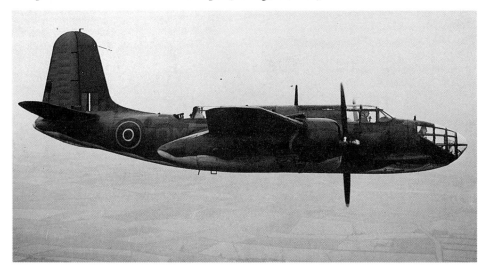

The iron and steel works at Ijmuiden, George Turner's target on 27 November 1942, pictured during an earlier, equally low-level daylight attack, by Blenheim IVs of 139 Squadron at Horsham St Faith on 7 April 1941 (two 500lb bombs are circled). (PRO)

Just short of the English coast we came out of cloud, and as we approached land I fired the colours of the day to identify ourselves. I had decided to land at the nearest airfield to get medical attention for Arthur as soon as possible. I pin-pointed our position near Norwich and headed for Horsham St Faith, the nearest airfield. At that time the only R/T the Boston possessed was a set called a TR9 (the following year we were equipped with VHF radios), a very efficient apparatus with a theoretical range of 5 miles, but which in practice rarely worked, so we tended to ignore it. Thus I just flew over the tower at about 800 feet, did a circuit and landed. As a Boston would taxi on one engine I switched off the good engine on touch-down.

At the end of our landing run we shot out of our cockpits, raced around to the front of the aircraft and started to get Arthur out. He and the nose were a mess. There was blood everywhere and great chunks of the perspex were missing. Arthur was covered in blood, unconscious and very cold. As we were doing this I looked towards the tower but nothing seemed to be happening, so Ron dashed off to wake them up while George and I finished getting Arthur out and laid him on the ground.

At an operational airfield a twin-engined aircraft landing on one engine would have had a fire tender alongside as it stopped, and things would have happened fast. Unknown to us the RAF

A Douglas Boston III of 107 Squadron homeward bound to Great Massingham. George Turner landed at St Faith's following the 27 November 1942 operation to Ijmuiden. (via Nigel Buswell)

had left Horsham, leaving a care and maintenance party to hand over to the Americans, whose advanced party had just arrived, so things were very different.

Ron eventually turned up with a fire truck, having browbeaten the corporal in charge to take action. I went off with Arthur in the truck to SHQ (Station Headquarters) where I made a bit of a nuisance of myself because I thought they were so slow. In fairness to them, we had arrived unannounced and unexpectedly, and they were short of men and vehicles. I was a bit overwrought and rather rude. Although it seemed ages it was probably less than 10 minutes after landing that Arthur was rushed to the Norfolk & Norwich Hospital in the care of a medical orderly.

Having seen Arthur away I went back in a truck to the aircraft to pick up Ron and George. This time I had a good look at the machine, which was a sorry sight. All the shells that had hit her had come from ahead and the right. One had burst on the bombsight, flinging fragments of steel (and perspex) into Arthur's leg, arm and face. A second had entered the fuselage a foot or so behind my head and had burst in the fuselage tank. A third had smashed through the leading edge of the wing inboard of the starboard engine and holed the fuel tank there. The fourth had burst against the bottom two cylinders of the starboard engine, making a mess of the cylinder heads and rocker boxes. These were all 20mm and probably came from one gun.

It was getting dark by now, so we collected up our flying gear and went to the control tower to report to base and arrange transport home. Eventually, an 8cwt van with a WAAF driver came from Massingham to pick us up and we got back to our messes about 10 o'clock. It had been rather a long day.

This operation illustrated the part that luck played in these things. We were lucky that the tanks that were hit were full, otherwise they would most likely have exploded and caught fire. Intelligence had given Ron a 16mm cine camera to take a film of the target. He was using this, not his guns, when 140 gallons of 100 octane swished past his legs and out of the rear hatch. George told me that he was getting ready to fire back when he was soused in petrol and thought it unwise to do so. It was a miracle that we were untouched after bombing when I was stooging along at 300 feet; quite a lot of the stuff was coming from the harbour and town behind us and it was non-deflection shooting for them.

Conversely, it was our bad luck that our very experienced CO, Wing Commander Lynn, had been replaced by Wing Commander P. H. Dutton, who had come from India and had no experience of European operations. No experienced CO would, at that stage of the war, have allowed any of his crews to fly through a heavily defended harbour to attack a target behind it. I suspect that the instructions came from Group. Dutton, a regular officer, would not question it and the Intelligence Officer, who did know the score, was not senior enough to get it altered. Apart from the normal harbour defences, an E-boat squadron was stationed there and those not out on patrol would have joined in the fun. (107 Squadron attacked the steelworks again in 1943. Six aircraft under a very experienced CO, Wing Commander Dickie England, came in from the north and attacked the works, keeping the town between them and the harbour. Although one aircraft was shot down by a fighter, none were hit by flak.) I guess that our attack was to have an element of surprise – straight in from the sea was the shortest way to the target and it might have worked. We didn't surprise them, but they certainly surprised us.

Tony Reid, who was behind us, and theoretically in the more dangerous position, did not get a scratch. (The theory was that gunners aimed at the leading aircraft and did not allow enough deflection to hit the No 2.) However, his luck ran out a week or so later and he was shot down on the Eindhoven operation (on 6 December 1942, as was Wing

Commander Dutton, both crews being lost.) We were on this one too, with a spare observer, but were untouched.

9: It just couldn't have happened
Tom Wingham DFC

DORTMUND, ON 23/24 MAY 1943, was our 20th operation as a Halifax II crew, although it was the first with us for Sergeant Jim Nightingale, who replaced our former wireless operator, Flight Sergeant Norman 'Chiefie' Beale, who had previously done a first tour on Hampdens. After our last operation he had been called to the adjutant's office and told that as he had completed 50 operations he was now 'screened' and would not do any more ops. So we had had to find ourselves another wireless operator. Jim Nightingale was an experienced spare wireless operator on 102 Squadron, having lost his crew one night when he was unable to fly with them. So this was to be his first trip with his new, permanent crew.

We took it rather hard that 'Chiefie' had been taken away from us without a 'by your

leave'. Like most crews who managed to survive, we were very close-knit, very rarely being off the station unless we were all together. Our pilot was Sergeant Dave Hewlett, I was bomb-aimer, and Sergeant Harry Blackallar was navigator. Sergeant Eric 'Joe' Holliday was engineer, and Andy Reilly, rear gunner, and Sergeant Willie Hall, mid-upper gunner, completed the crew. We had our own crew song adapted from that well-known ditty 'Sweet Violets', which had been sung to distraction in pub after pub since we had joined the Squadron at the beginning of the year. Having a rear gunner from Dublin and a mid-upper from Belfast often led to interesting arguments on the Irish question when flying on the long grind to Holland or Denmark over the North Sea when life might have been quiet and otherwise dull.

When we got to the briefing room and the target was revealed, there were the usual curses and trepidation at finding ourselves back on the 'Happy Valley' run but, as a crew, we couldn't complain since we had not operated since April, when we had, admittedly, had a heavy month,

Tom Wingham DFC.

Sergeant Dave Hewlett's crew in 102 Squadron. Left to right, standing: Joe Holliday, flight engineer; Dave Hewlett; Sergeant 'Blackie' Blackallar, navigator; Flight Sergeant Norman 'Chiefie' Beale. Front row: Sergeant Andy Reilly, rear gunner; Sergeant Tom Wingham, bomb-aimer; Sergeant Jim Nightingale, WOP (it is his alsatian in the foreground), who replaced Beale on the 23 May raid; and Sergeant Willie Hall, mid-upper gunner. (Tom Wingham)

visiting Essen both at the beginning and end of the month, with Kiel, Frankfurt, Stuttgart, Pilzen, Stettin and Duisburg sandwiched in between, and a minelaying trip to the Kattegat thrown in for good measure. This was the March/July period that was later to be known as the Battle of the Ruhr.

As the briefing commenced, we quickly found out that this was to be something different. It was to be the heaviest raid of the war. Up to this date, apart from the 1,000 Bomber raids of 1942, which pressed everything into service that could take off without necessarily being able to carry much bomb load, Bomber Command had only been sending between 300 and 580 aircraft on individual raids. Tonight, Dortmund was to suffer the mightiest blow that the Command could administer, with the use of 826 aircraft, the majority being 'heavies' – Lancasters, Halifaxes and Stirlings – with 151 Wellingtons and 13 *Oboe*-marking Mosquitoes. This was presumably why Command had not operated for the previous nine days in order to get as many aircraft as possible serviceable.

The weather forecast was good with no cloud cover over the target, and at the duly appointed time we took off and

On the night of 4/5 February 1943 188 bombers, mostly the four-engined 'heavies', went to Turin, while 128 aircraft, 103 of them Wellingtons, made an all-incendiary attack on Lorient. Two Wellingtons (A) are photographed over the port during the attack. Sticks of incendiary bombs (B) are burning among the port installations at La Perrière and on Ile St Michel. One Wellington was lost.

headed towards Holland. It was usual to expect fighters to begin to meet us some 30 miles off the enemy coast and thereafter continue to make life difficult with the help of various flak and searchlight batteries dotted all over the place until we began to close in on the Ruhr. At that period all the German night fighters were operated in boxes and were directed against individual bombers. This was the reason for the bomber streaming – with so many aircraft flying through a box it was difficult for the ground control to pick out individual aircraft. Hence it was the stragglers and those outside the stream, port or starboard, higher or lower, who could be guaranteed to get most attention.

As the bombers approached the Ruhr the game changed, and masses of searchlights and guns took over. It was estimated at that time that the Ruhr was protected by several thousand AA guns and to meet them on your own was never a pleasant prospect. Again, as with fighters, if within the stream, it was difficult for the guns and searchlights to use radar to predict individual aircraft, so once a raid got into its stride the flak became more of a barrage, which had to be flown through, rather than fire directed at given aircraft.

For Pathfinders and aircraft in the van of the attack those early minutes of the raid were the most dangerous; the guns and searchlights had the opportunity to pick up individual bombers and send up very accurate predicted fire, and always made the most of their chances. Anyone flying straight and level for more than a few seconds on their own could be certain of some near misses, if not direct hits. Because of their role in marking the target, PFF losses of heavies were very high at this stage since they had to follow in the *Oboe* Mosquitoes, which flew very much higher, and put down continuous back-up markers on the Aiming Point; the control stations of *Oboe* could only operate one Mossie at a time, which meant a gap of 10 minutes between *Oboe* markers. By this time there had been another pair of stations installed, which meant that marking by *Oboe* could be carried out every 5 minutes, providing the equipment in the aircraft did not fail. Unfortunately, the equipment was rather temperamental and sometimes, when the first Mossie had failed to mark, there was a long wait for the PFF and Main Force until the next one came along.

Oboe had proved to be the only reliable and extremely accurate marking system to

A Handley Page Halifax bomber, the type that carried Sergeant Dave Hewlett's crew in 102 Squadron to Dortmund on 23/24 May 1943. (via Mike Bailey)

overcome the notorious mist and smoke cover that had for so long prevented the Command from hitting the Ruhr and, therefore, since March it had been a cardinal rule that bombing on the Ruhr only commenced with the laying of an *Oboe* marker. It was then the job of the PFF back-up heavies to maintain continuity of the markers by aiming theirs, of a different colour, at the *Oboe* ones. This ensured that if there was a failure in an *Oboe* Mossie later in the attack, the Aiming Point would still be marked, although not quite so accurately.

On this night, Halifaxes of 4 Group were leading the attack with 102 Squadron in the van. We had an uneventful trip at first, crossing the North Sea and Holland without any problems for ourselves, having as usual observed aircraft falling on either side of us. We continued across Germany before we turned on our final leg, which would bring us to Dortmund from the north. As we started to run down to the Ruhr the flak began to warm up and turned into the usual flashes and thumps so familiar to anyone who has experienced AA fire – quite frightening in its way. I checked the latest wind with Blackie and, after switching on, fed this into the bombsight before checking that all the switches were on to ensure that the bombs were live and that the distributor would function. Taking the bomb tit release button in my hand, I settled down in the prone position over the bombsight ready to carry out my task.

Everything was still dark, although it was a clear starry night with very good visibility. As we neared our target the flak intensified, although there were at this point no searchlights. Quite often the Germans would delay the use of these until the target had been marked in case, one presumes, the searchlights would give them away. Being in the forefront of the attack we kept on course to Dortmund, although we were only a couple of minutes from our ETA and no markers were yet visible. Suddenly a vivid splash of colour appeared ahead and below us, and relief set in that this was the primary *Oboe* marker and we would not have to go round again.

Now I took over and guided Dave through my bombsight. 'Bomb doors open.'

'Bomb doors open,' repeated Dave.

'Left . . . left . . . steady . . . steady.' I pressed the tit. 'Bombs gone!'

The aircraft jumped with the release of the two 1,000lb HEs. At the same time the photoflash left its 'chute at the rear of the aircraft and we now flew straight and level while I counted the 10 seconds. We carried a mixed load of HE and incendiary bombs, which, unfortunately, had different terminal velocities. This meant that the HE bombs had a better forward travel than the smaller incendiaries, which would fall almost vertically. We still, therefore, had six small bomb containers of 30lb incendiaries and seven SBCs of 4lb to be dropped; these would be released in sequence so that the hundreds of incendiaries would cover an area over 100 yards long. The idea was that the HE should open up the buildings, then the incendiaries would follow to set fire to the exposed rubble. In order for this to happen there had to be a time lag between dropping the two types of bombs, hence the 10-second run. The bomb release had also set up the camera ready to record our position at the time of the impact of the bombs. Providing we maintained our run, which went on for a little longer after the release of the incendiaries, the centre of the photograph would indicate the impact point of our bomb load. It was not often that I had a virgin target to aim at with no other bombing except the *Oboe* marker, but of course this also meant that we were way out front, an ideal target for the gunners below and, moreover, making life easy for them with the prolonged straight and level photo run. We had been getting a bumpy ride as the flak intensified almost to the point of realisation of the old line shoot, 'The flak was so heavy you could get out and walk on it.'

With the bomb doors closed we continued to cross the target going south and had

A bombed-out city in Germany. (Graham Jones
Collection via Theo Boiten)

just got our photo and were now free to
jink about a bit to confuse the guns when
there was an almighty bang. The aircraft
almost shuddered to a stop and we
seemed to be dropping out of the sky.
There was confusion on the intercom,
which had gone extremely fuzzy with the
loss of the generator, and for a brief
moment there was a babble of voices as
all the crew were enquiring what had
happened. The rear gunner's voice
continued and Dave cut in to ask, 'Who's
that?'

'It's me, the rear gunner. What's up
Dave?'

The answer was very swift. 'Prepare to
bale out.'

With the loss of power the aircraft had
swung to starboard, and as we rapidly
descended we were heading west along
the Ruhr Valley with all the gunners
turning their fire on us and searchlights
seeking us out for the kill. Meanwhile, in
the nose, Blackie and I clipped on our
'chutes and started to clear the navigator's
chair away from the forward escape
hatch. Ever since the first time I had seen
the Ruhr being bombed I had made up my
mind that I would never bale out over a
German target on the assumption that the
populace would be quite likely to tear
aircrew to bits, and in fact this did happen
in many instances, sometimes observed
by their fellow crew members. And here
we were, falling out of the sky over the
Ruhr of all places.

To this day, I am not sure whether I
would have jumped in those
circumstances. All these thoughts were to
be re-enacted a year later when I did have
to jump, but fortunately not in the target
area. However, Dave was still wrestling
with the controls and attempting to reduce
our rate of descent. In the meantime, Joe
had decided that maybe the petrol tanks

The result of an RAF fire raid.

F/L Bracken's Halifax on fire at 18,750 feet over Gladbeck on 24 March 1945. This was the only aircraft lost from the 175 aircraft (153 Halifaxes, 16 Lancasters and six Mosquitoes) that took part in the raid, one of three that day to marshalling yards and fuel and munitions plants in the Ruhr, now just 15 miles from the front line following the successful Rhine river crossing on the 24th.

had been holed and, although he had, as normal, changed to full tanks before going in to the target, he hurriedly turned the cocks to switch to alternative tanks. By this time we were coned in the searchlights and were down to 7,000 feet with everything that was within reach beginning to bear on us. This now included light ack-ack with the frightening tracer, every one of which seemed to be heading towards the aircraft before it curled away.

While all this was happening, I had looked back towards the cockpit and had been surprised to see a pair of white socked feet dancing by the side of the pilot. At the time I did not question what they were doing there, and it was not until many years later when talking to Dave that I recalled the incident and asked for an explanation. Apparently, on the order 'Prepare to bale out', Andy had shot out of his turret, his boots being ripped off as he scrambled out, and had run up the fuselage to the cockpit, where he had shouted in Dave's ear words to the effect of 'Come on, Dave, this can't happen to us, you can't let it happen to us. Get it flying again. It can't happen to us.' But then so many crews believed that it couldn't happen to them, only to other crews!

At 7,000 feet the miracle occurred, as gradually the engines began to splutter again and Dave began to stabilise the aircraft. With power to our elbow, as it were, we now had a chance against the enemy, weaving to get out of the searchlights and, above all, starting to climb to get some height again, having lost some 10,000 feet in our fall. As we were in the middle of the Ruhr we had no choice but to continue to fly westward through the best-defended area in Germany, but we eventually made our way out and had an uneventful trip back to base.

Arriving back at dispersal we now had the chance to examine the aircraft to see what had happened. We had apparently been hit by shrapnel from a rather near miss, as witnessed by some 20-plus holes in the aircraft, with one large piece slicing through the fire extinguisher buttons, setting them off in three engines, and thus giving them foam rather than fuel to digest. Not taking kindly to this, they had given up. We lost 38 aircraft that night, but it could easily have been 39. That same night, and again just after dropping its bombs, a Wellington of 431 Squadron was also hit and the pilot and rear gunner baled out thinking that the tail had been lost, leaving a friend of mine, with whom I had trained in South Africa, trapped with the navigator and wireless operator in the nose. Sergeant Stu Sloan, an observer-cum-bomb-aimer, like me, regained control of the aircraft with the help of the other two and in spite of two very rough engines, one of which had to be shut down, not only managed to fly the Wellington back to this country, but landed it for good measure. He was given an immediate award of the CGM, commissioned in the field and sent on a pilot's course. Without his efforts it could have been 40 lost that night.

The following morning it was arranged for us to meet up with an Engineering Officer for an inspection of our aircraft. When we got to dispersal we found him already wandering around, poking into holes at various places as engineers are wont to do. For a few minutes we all drifted around surveying the damage before we assembled in front of the Halifax with the Engineer facing us but keeping a few paces distance from us. Then began an encounter that will last in my memory until I die.

The officer concerned had been a regular NCO in the inter-war years when all actions had to be governed by books of rules. He first addressed Dave by asking for an account of the events of the previous night. This Dave gave in full, answering questions as he went. There was a brief pause before the Engineering Officer asked Dave, 'How far can a Halifax fly on one engine?'

Dave replied, 'Not very far.'

'Could you have flown back from the Ruhr on one?'

'That would be impossible.'

'You would agree that three fire extinguishers have been operated?'

'Yes.'

'What are the regulations about using an engine after the fire extinguisher has been used?'

'Normally, shut down the engine, feather the propeller and don't use it again – but this was different. The engines had not been on fire.'

'"The Book" says that an engine must not be used again after the fire extinguisher has been used. Three of your fire extinguishers have been used, therefore you could not have used those engines again. A Halifax could not have flown back from the Ruhr on one engine. It just couldn't have happened, otherwise you wouldn't be here.'

We stood there dumbfounded. Apparently, we were not where we thought we were. There was not the slightest sign of a smile on his face or humour in the situation as he turned away and arranged for our aircraft to have three engines changed and the holes to be patched up. At the tender age of 20 I had learned that, when using a Rule Book, always make sure that it is up to date and applied to the current situation when using it.

When, later that morning, I visited the Photographic Section it was with great satisfaction that I found my developed photo showing a very clear picture of Dortmund with the Aiming Point right bang in the centre.

10: Press on regardless
Bill Reid VC

'Here is the news and this is Frank Phillips reading it. Our home-based bombers were over Germany in great strength last night. The main attack – both concentrated and effective – was on Düsseldorf. Cologne was among the other targets . . . After yesterday's daylight attack on Wilhelmshaven by the largest force of American Fortresses and Liberators ever sent from this country, aircraft of Bomber Command were over Germany in great strength last night. They made a heavy attack on Düsseldorf, and first reports indicate that the bombing was concentrated and effective. A small force attacked Cologne, and Mosquitoes bombed objectives in the Ruhr and Rhineland. Mines were laid in enemy waters. The bombers destroyed at least four enemy aircraft and another was shot down by Fighter Command intruders which attacked targets in France and the Low Countries.

Nineteen of our bombers are missing.

Düsseldorf – one of Germany's most important arms centres – was heavily raided last June when we dropped considerably more than two thousand tons of bombs, devastating an area covering over two square miles.'

AFTER A LAPSE of almost five months, on the night of Wednesday 3/Thursday 4 November 1943, Düsseldorf was again raided in strength by RAF Bomber Command. Air Marshal Sir Arthur Harris was in the midst of a campaign of area bombing German cities at night using Lancasters and Halifaxes, while B-24 Liberators and B-17 Flying Fortresses of the US 8th and 12th Air Forces stoked the fires by day. Three heavy bombing raids in ten days by RAF Bomber Command on Berlin during August had resulted in the loss of 137 aircraft and great loss of life to Berliners in the Siemensstadt and Mariendorf districts, and also to Lichterfelde. It was but a prelude to the Battle of Berlin, which would open with all ferocity in November, but for the time being Harris was obliged to abandon raids on the Reich capital and instead turn his attention to targets at Mannheim (5/6 and 23/24 September), Hanover (four raids in September–October), Kassel (3/4 and 22/23 October) and Düsseldorf.

William Reid VC.

All of these raids involved between 500 and 600 bombers. For the raid on Düsseldorf on 3/4 November, 577 bombers and 12 Mosquito Mk I/IIs, including a special force of Lancasters equipped with G-H, who were to test this precision device for the first time on a considerable scale in a raid on the Mannesmann steelworks, were despatched. Some 52 Lancasters, including 20 blind-markers, and ten Mosquitoes were detailed to carry out a feint attack on Cologne 10 minutes before the start of the main raid on Düsseldorf. Thirteen *Oboe*-equipped Mosquitoes were detailed to hit Rheinhausen, two more, equipped with G-H, went to Dortmund, and 23 Stirlings and Lancasters were detailed to lay mines off the Frisians.

At stations throughout East Anglia, Lincolnshire and the Midlands, the orders for the night's attack were delivered. Together with everyone else, Acting Flight Lieutenant William 'Bill' Reid RAFVR, not quite 22 years old, and his crew of Lancaster Mk III LM360 *O-Oboe* in 61 Squadron, a 5 Group unit based at Syerston, near Nottingham, sat impassively at briefing listening to the intelligence reports and the details of the part their squadron would play in the overall plan. Reid, the son of a Scottish blacksmith, was born at Baillieston, Glasgow. Educated at Coatbridge School, before the war he was a student of metallurgy. In 1941 he enlisted for training as aircrew and trained as a pilot in the United States. Commissioned in 1942, Reid had reached his present rank in 1943 and had been posted to 61 Squadron on 6 September.

Düsseldorf would be his 10th 'op'. The plan of attack and target marking details were read out to the assembled crews. P/O John Jeffreys RAAF, Reid's 30-year-old navigator from Perth, Western Australia, and 22-year-old Wireless Operator Flight

Five of the crew of Lancaster Mk III LM360 O-Oboe *of 61 Squadron, 5 Group, based at Syerston, near Nottingham, who flew the operation to Düsseldorf on 3/4 November 1943. Back row, left to right: Flight Sergeant Les Rolton, bomb-aimer; Flight Sergeant Frank Emerson, gunner. Front row: Flight Sergeant Jim 'Taffy' Norris, flight engineer; Flight Lieutenant Bill Reid, pilot; Flight Sergeant C. Baldwin, gunner. Pilot Officer John Jeffreys RAAF, navigator, was killed on the operation and Wireless Operator Flight Sergeant J. J. Mann died the next day from his wounds. (Bill Reid Collection)*

Sergeant J. J. Mann, a Liverpudlian, jotted down notes. The rest of the seven-man crew was made up of Flight Sergeant L. G. 'Les' Rolton, bomb-aimer, from Romford, Essex; Flight Sergeant A. F. 'Joe' Emerson, rear gunner, from Enfield, North London; Flight Sergeant Jim W. 'Taffy' Norris, flight engineer, from Cardiff; and Flight Sergeant Cyril Baldwin, mid-upper gunner, who was from Nelson, Lancashire.

The same scene was being played out at all other Bomber Command stations, including the 4 Group airfield at Melbourne, near Hull, where the crew of Halifax B.II HX179 ZA-L were among those who listened intently at the 10 Squadron briefing. The crew of seven – average age 23 – consisted of Scotsman Pilot Officer Robert Cameron, the 22-year-old pilot; 21-year-old Londoner Flight Lieutenant Roland Fielder, bomb-aimer; Sergeant Samuel Eyre, the 37-year-old flight engineer from Lancashire; Sergeant John Hutton, WOP/AG, from Buckinghamshire; Flight Sergeant Roy Tann, navigator, from Forncett St Mary, Norfolk; Sergeant Adam Williamson, the 21-year-old mid-upper gunner; and 19-year-old rear gunner, Sergeant Jack Winstanly.

Weather could affect the overall success or failure of an operation. Salient points were noted. A minor front would cause a narrow belt of low cloud which would affect Yorkshire at midnight, keeping visibility from deteriorating until later. Elsewhere, conditions would become difficult after 2200 hours, but East Anglia would 'hold' until midnight. A front over north-west Germany would give a wide belt of medium cloud with tops at 12,000 feet or below, with very patchy cloud above. In met men's vernacular, Düsseldorf would have 'doubtful amounts of strato-cumulus, probably less than 7/10ths (perhaps even less with a risk of 10/10ths in patches). Tops 6–8,000 feet; chance of some medium cloud above. Similar conditions en route.'

Nine *Oboe* Mosquitoes (with three reserves) were to drop red TIs (Target Indicators) on the Aiming Point, together with release-point flares. Lancaster 'backers up' were to maintain the ground-marking with greens aimed to overshoot reds (or the centre of all greens visible) by 1 second. Watches were checked as Zero Hour was announced for 1945 hours. Duration of the attack would be from 1942 to 2005 hours. In that time 93 Lancasters of the Main Force would bomb zero-to-zero + 4, followed by 113 Halifaxes from zero + 4 to zero + 8, then 100 Lancasters from zero + 8 to zero + 12, 100 Lancasters from zero + 12 to zero + 16, and finally 98 Lancasters from zero + 16 to zero + 20. Approaching the target, *Window* was to be dropped at the rate of one bundle every 2 minutes, then within 20 miles of the target in both directions one bundle was to be dropped every 2 minutes.

Main briefing and individual crew briefings over, the RAF crews went out to their waiting Halifaxes and Lancasters at the six Group stations. They began to take off in 10/10ths strato-cumulus at 2–3,000 feet with some haze. There was good visibility in East Anglia, but by 2200 hours visibility in 4 and 6 Groups had fallen to 1–3,000 yards, but remained above 2 miles in 1, 3, 5 and 8 (PFF) Groups, with no cloud below 2,000 feet. Meanwhile, fog had begun to form in the south-east corner of East Anglia, and became widespread after midnight.

Reid's and Cameron's crews took their places in the long bomber stream. A belt of layer cloud extended from the Dutch coast to 90 miles west of Düsseldorf. Contrails extended at all heights above 15,000 feet. The wind at 20,000 feet was 25mph, and 28mph at 28,000 feet. All was going according to plan when suddenly, shortly after crossing the Dutch coast, Reid's windscreen was shattered by fire from an enemy twin-engined night fighter. Joe Emerson in the rear turret was unable to open fire immediately because his hands were frozen owing to a failure in the heating circuit, and he could not operate his microphone for the same reason.

He said later, 'My fingers were frozen when I first saw the Me 110 come in astern, at

250 yards range. At 150 yards I found the energy to pull the trigger, and I am pretty certain that I hit him.'

The rear turret was badly damaged, the communications system and the compasses were put out of action, and the elevator trimming tabs of the Lancaster were damaged. The bomber became difficult to control. Emerson was unaware of the damage that the night fighter had caused to the rest of the aircraft, but it had registered hits in the cockpit area of *O-Oboe*, leaving Reid nursing wounds to the head, shoulders and hands.

He said later, 'I just saw a blinding flash and felt as if my head had been blown off. My shoulder was a bit stiff and it felt as if someone had hit me with a hammer. Blood was pouring down my face and I could feel the taste of it in my mouth. It soon froze up because of the intense cold.'

Reid asked, 'Everybody OK?' Miraculously, the rest of the crew were unscathed and, on receiving answers, he said, 'Resuming course.' He didn't say he was hit, but 'the wind was lashing through the broken windscreen and pieces of the perspex had cut my face.'

Despite his wounds and damage to the aircraft, Reid was determined to carry on to Düsseldorf. 'There were other bombers behind us and if we had turned we might have been a danger to them,' he said.

Flight Sergeant Rolton added later, 'We gave all the oxygen to the pilot, who was navigating by the stars.'

Soon afterwards, however, *O-Oboe* was pounced on again, this time by an Fw 190 *Wilde Sau*. The German raked the Lancaster from nose to tail with cannon fire. Emerson put up a brave resistance, returning fire with his only serviceable machine-gun, but the damaged state of his turret made accurate aiming impossible.

Flight Sergeant Baldwin climbed out of his mid-upper turret, which had been hit, to

In a second attack by an Fw 190 the Luftwaffe pilot raked the Lancaster from nose to tail with cannon fire. Despite the damage to the aircraft and being badly wounded, Reid and his crew managed to nurse O-Oboe *back to England.* (Bill Reid Collection)

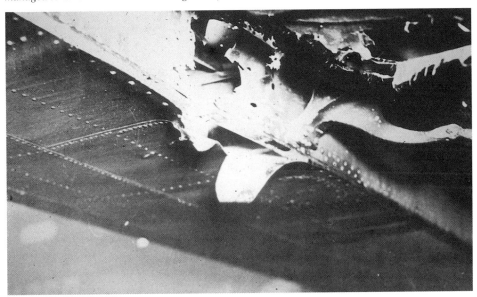

Damage caused by German night fighters to the port elevator of O-Oboe. *In the first of two attacks by night fighters, Emerson's turret was badly damaged, the communications system and the compasses were put out of action and the elevator trimming tabs of the Lancaster were damaged.* (Bill Reid Collection)

see for himself the extent of the damage to the aircraft. He found Flight Sergeant J. J. Mann lying full length over the navigator, Pilot Officer John Jeffreys, who was dead with a bullet through his skull. The oxygen system aboard the aircraft had been put out of action. Baldwin helped the badly wounded wireless operator into his seat and put an oxygen tube from a portable supply into his mouth. Reid had also been hit once again. Though wounded in the forearm, 'Taffy' Norris, the flight engineer, supplied him with oxygen from another portable supply, and Reid was able to carry on.

En route the bombers encountered heavy flak with searchlights from Rotterdam, Antwerp, Krefeld (where one bomber was shot down by flak on the way home), Duisburg, Eindhoven, Tholen and Herenthals (two aircraft were seen shot down by flak on the outward route, one at Tholen and another at Herenthals). Four bombers were shot down by fighters en route to Düsseldorf.

Meanwhile, Halifax B.II HX179 was apparently forced to turn back, possibly after being hit by flak or fighters, or with engine trouble. Robert Cameron crossed over Norfolk and lined up for an emergency landing at Shipdham, an American B-24 Liberator base just west of Norwich, home of the 44th Bomb Group, 8th Air Force. It would appear that at least some of the bomb load was jettisoned, because a few UXHEs were found later in fields. Cameron circled the airfield three times before finally attempting a landing. As he descended, the Halifax struck telephone lines, and crashed and burst into flames at 2115 hours on land farmed by the Patterson family. Cameron, Sergeant Samuel Eyre, Sergeant John Hutton, Roland Fielder, Flight Sergeant Roy Tann, and Sergeant Adam Williamson, the mid-upper gunner, all perished in the fire.

Ernie Bowman, a member of the Home Guard, was sitting with his wife and their newborn child as the Halifax crashed 60 yards from his home. Ernie could see the flames but noticed that the rear of the bomber was not alight, and tried to get Sergeant

The remains of the Halifax B.II of No 10 Squadron that also crashed at Shipdham on 3/4 November 1943. (via Steve Adams)

Jack Winstanly, who was unconscious, out of the rear turret. The latter's parachute was snagged, and Ernie had to rush home and get a knife. On the way he met his brother-in-law, Sergeant Williams Wilkins of Norfolk Police, hiding behind a tree that earlier Ernie had sheltered behind for safety, and they returned to the aircraft. The two men removed Winstanly's parachute and got him out on to the ground. However, he died of his injuries in hospital two days later. Ernie Bowman was awarded the British Empire Medal and two American servicemen were awarded the Soldiers Medal for the rescue.

Reid, meanwhile, had reached the target, 50 minutes after the Fw 190 attack. He had memorised his course to the target and had continued in such a normal manner that the bomb-aimer, Flight Sergeant Rolton, who was cut off by the failure of the communications system, knew nothing of his captain's injuries or the casualties to his comrades. Rolton was to recall, 'He gave me a good bombing run over the centre of the target, and I knew the bombs fell in the right place.'

Some 525 aircraft succeeded in reaching Düsseldorf, where the anti-aircraft guns opened up with a vengeance.

General Leon Johnson, CO, 14th Combat Wing, offers his congratulations to the rescuers in the Halifax tragedy at Shipdham. Ernie Bowman, second from right, was awarded the British Empire Medal for the rescue of Jack Winstanly, the Halifax rear gunner.

Heavy flak reached 15–16,000 feet, occasionally aimed at aircraft held by searchlight cones above this level. Eighty fighters were reported over the city, as many as 55 of these being twin-engined. Fourteen returning bombers were damaged by the fighters, while three enemy fighters were claimed destroyed, two Ju 88s to Halifaxes of 4 Group over Düsseldorf, and an Me 210 to a 5 Group Lancaster near Gilze-Rijen.

The 'heavies' opened their attack with three red TIs dropped in salvo by an *Oboe* Mosquito. The serviceability of *Oboe* on this night was very poor, with the result that only five bundles of sky-markers and three of TI were dropped. However, 72 Main Force aircraft carried H_2S for navigational purposes, and 55 reached the target with their sets in order. There was little cloud, and an accurate ground-marking attack was delivered by the light of a half moon. Decoy fires at Macherscheid, 5 miles south-south-west of Düsseldorf, were started, but the main force dropped their HE in the centre of the city. Their Aiming Point was situated in the extreme north-east of the city but, with the usual undershooting, the RAF attack spread rapidly south-south-westwards. Most of the 2,000 tons of bombs dropped fell within the built-up area.

The G-H trial attack by 38 Lancaster IIs on the Mannesmann Rohrenwerke was successfully carried out at the same time as the main operation. Fifteen aircraft attacked the steel works according to plan, but 126 found their sets unserviceable and bombed the city, five returned early and two were lost. Photographic evidence gathered later showed that the accuracy was such that 50 per cent of their bombs had fallen within half a mile of the works.

Bill Reid flew the course to and from the target by the Pole Star and the moon. He was growing weak from loss of blood, and the emergency oxygen supply had given out. With the windscreen shattered the cold was intense, and he occasionally lapsed into semi-consciousness. Rolton recalled, 'The Lancaster went into a dive, and I saw the engineer pull the pilot off the stick and level the aircraft. That was the first I knew of anyone being wounded. I went back and helped the engineer to control the aircraft.

Shipdham airfield, Norfolk, the USAAF 44th Bomb Group base where Bill Reid put down on the night of 3/4 November 1943. (USAF)

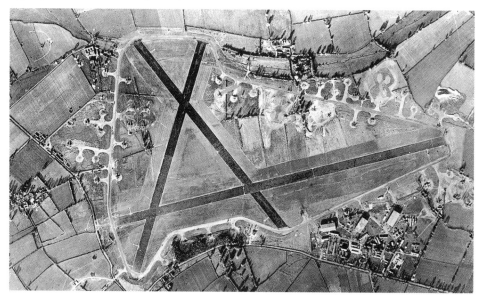

The pilot several times regained consciousness. As one of the elevators had been shot away, the aircraft tended to go into a dive, and both of us had to hold the stick.

Bill Reid confirms: 'Considering that I was in the pilot's seat with my left foot jammed on the rudder because of the effect of the elevator damage and having my hands clasped in front of the stick to hold it back – because of the fact that it acted nose heavy – I did have some effect on the plane's reaction. Les Rolton helped by pushing back on the stick from in front and sighting a beacon flashing, signifying land and asking for the wireless operator's "flimsy" so that we could find out where we were.'

Norris and Rolton braved heavy anti-aircraft fire over the Dutch coast and, clinging to the stick all the way across the North Sea, kept the Lancaster in the air. Bill Reid continues: 'I do remember Jim shaking me, and pointing to the fuel gauges and then downwards, meaning that it was time we landed as we were running out of fuel. I also saw the searchlights to the north of us, for which I headed, and it was en route to them that the layout of Shipdham (where Cameron had crashed 46 minutes earlier) appeared below us.'

Reid resumed control, and made ready to land. Ground mist partially obscured the runway lights and Reid was also much troubled by blood from his head wound getting into his eyes. With the hydraulics shot out, he had no brakes for landing, and the legs of the damaged undercarriage collapsed when the load came on, but he got 'O-Oboe' down safely. The Lancaster skidded to a halt on its belly as ambulances and crash wagons raced over to the unexpected arrival to help get everybody out of the plane.

Flight Sergeant Mann, wounded by shrapnel, died in hospital on Thursday morning; he was buried later in Bootle Cemetery on East Merseyside. John Jeffreys was buried in Cambridge City Cemetery (where Sergeant Adam Williamson from Cameron's crew was also laid to rest). 'Taffy' Norris, who had shrapnel wounds in the shoulder and left arm, did not reveal that he was wounded until he was getting out of the aircraft. (He was awarded the Conspicuous Gallantry Medal for his heroic efforts, while Joe

Lancaster O-Oboe *bellied-in at Shipdham after Reid crash-landed there following the operation to Düsseldorf.* (Bill Reid Collection)

Flight Lieutenant Bill Reid VC and Les Rolton pictured in the grounds of the Petwood Hotel, Woodhall Spa, which at the time was used by 617 Squadron as their officers' mess. Both men joined the squadron after recovering from their ordeal. On 31 July 1943 Reid became a PoW and Rolton was killed when their Lancaster was brought down over France by a 1,000lb bomb dropped by an aircraft overhead. (Bill Reid Collection)

Emerson was awarded the DFM. Flight Sergeant Baldwin went on to complete his tour.) Reid was given a blood transfusion and spent four days at the Norfolk & Norwich Hospital, before being transferred to a military hospital. It was while convalescing that he was told he had been awarded the Victoria Cross.

The citation reads: 'Wounded in two attacks, without oxygen, suffering severely from cold, his navigator dead, his wireless operator fatally wounded, his aircraft crippled and defenceless, Flight Lieutenant Reid showed superb courage and leadership in penetrating a further 200 miles into enemy territory to attack one of the most strongly defended targets in Germany. Every additional mile increased the hazards of the long and perilous journey home. His tenacity and devotion to duty were beyond praise.'

Reid says, 'I nearly fainted. It was like getting 100 per cent in English at school – which I hadn't long left.'

The citation went on, '. . . he showed superb courage and leadership and refused to be turned away from his objective . . .' Reid was to say later, 'My VC is for those who did all the things I did but didn't make it back to tell their stories.'

Altogether, 18 bombers were lost on the night of 3/4 November (3.1 per cent of the attacking force), 37 were damaged, and three enemy fighters were claimed destroyed. Of two Halifaxes that crashed this night – the other came from 6 Group RCAF – only one man was left alive from the two crews.

Bill Reid's Lancaster was repaired and rejoined 61 Squadron on 7 August 1944. Three days later it was transferred to 50 Squadron at Fiskerton and was lost in a crash near the station on 11 November 1944 when Flying Officer Hickling and crew were returning from a raid on Harburg.

Bill Reid, meanwhile, went back on ops in January 1944, this time with 617 Dam Busters Squadron. With him went Les Rolton. On 31 July, during a raid on Rilly La Montagne near Rheims, an RAF bomber put paid to the rest of his tour when an aircraft overhead released its bombs and a 1,000-pounder hurtled through Reid's Lancaster. Five crew, including Les Rolton, were killed. Bill Reid and his wireless operator, Flying Officer David Luker, were thrown clear when the nose of the plane broke off as it spun down. They both spent ten months behind the wire at Stalag Luft III Sagan and Stalag Luft IV Bellaria. Bill Reid left the RAF in 1949 and back in his native Scotland he became a student again. He studied at Glasgow University and the West of Scotland Agricultural College and in April 1949 gained his degree and was awarded a post-graduate travelling scholarship from one of the Lady MacRobert Trust schemes (Lady MacRobert lost two sons in the RAF during the Second World War) to study agricultural methods in India, Australia, New Zealand, Canada and the United States.

11: 'Hellzapoppin'
Pilot Officer Howard 'Tommy' Farmiloe

THE MONTH OF MARCH 1944 was the height of the Bomber Offensive and we at 61 Squadron, Skellingthorpe, in 5 Group, were being very active indeed. Losses were mounting. If a new crew lasted three or so ops we reckoned that they had a reasonable chance of making ten, and then they may possibly complete their first tour (30 ops).

The Lancasters, despite the sterling efforts of the hard-pressed ground crews, always seemed to have 'faults'. Much as we loved her, my aircraft, *H-Hellzapoppin*, gave us problems. We were doing Berlin runs quite often – and on two occasions we had to feather a faulty engine, each time on the way to the target.

On the night of 24 March it was Berlin yet again. Before reaching the enemy coast our port outer had a runaway prop, which created a fearsome noise and sent ice splinters against the fuselage. I tried to feather it but without success, and it was not long before there were indications of fire. I tried diving, etc, but nothing,

Lancs.

Above *Pilot Officer Howard 'Tommy' Farmiloe, 61 Squadron.*

Right *The crew of* H-Hellzapoppin. *Standing, left to right: Sergeant Ken Vowe, bomb-aimer; Pilot Officer Howard 'Tommy' Farmiloe, pilot; Sergeant Ray Noble, mid-upper gunner; with Sergeant 'Wally' Patchett, kneeling.* (Howard Farmiloe)

Results of repeated bombing of Berlin, March 1944.

including the fire extinguisher, solved the problem, and the fire continued on and off all the way. Worse, the port inner also gave problems and had to be feathered, this time fortunately successfully.

Flying just above stalling speed and rapidly losing height, I managed to keep the plane under control and continue towards Berlin. As we were almost on the target I decided to start the run-in and ordered Sergeant Ken Vowe, my bomb-aimer, to take up his position for the bombing run. We would bale out after the bombs were dropped. There was an enormous amount of searchlight, flak and night fighter activity, but we managed to get to the target, if somewhat late and at a much lower height than was comfortable, and made our bombing run. This made the

Two photographs showing the effects of an 8,000lb bomb dropped in a suburb of Berlin during one of RAF Bomber Command's attacks, March 1944. The first photo, taken a month after the bomb was dropped, shows the crater (arrowed) filled in, while the outer dotted line shows the area of about 14 acres over which buildings are seen to have been damaged by blast. The second photo, taken still later, shows the bombed site after considerable clearance. The ends of the damaged buildings have been squared off and the crater surface levelled over.

A photograph taken in March 1944 of damage to the Big City. The Battle of Berlin raged from November 1943 to 31 March 1944, but Harris's Bomber Command and the US Army Air Forces were unable to deliver the decisive blow to the German capital. The Air Ministry can be seen on the right, the largest building in the picture, fronting Wilhelmstrasse.

plane slightly more stable, and my flight engineer, George Gerry, switched the fuel into the starboard side as much as possible. The engine fire must have been a big attraction for night fighters, but we were lucky.

When we left the target I told the crew to stand by for baling out. My wireless operator, Sergeant Eddie Davidson, and the gunners Ray Noble and 'Wally' Patchett, said, 'Let's get away from Berlin as we will be torn to pieces by the Germans.' I asked the navigator for a heading back to the coast and we set course directly for base on 275 degrees. I asked Eddie Davidson to send an SOS, but when he tried he found that the wireless was dead. (The generators in the two port engines, which were not functioning, controlled most of the electrics and in particular the wireless accumulator and the two turrets.) Eddie suggested that all electrical equipment be disconnected to allow the generator in the starboard engine to slowly build up the accumulator. As the gunners could not stay in their turrets or operate their guns and we were still losing height, Eddie suggested that they join him in throwing out the guns, ammunition, Elsan, smoke bombs, the rest bed, and the navigator's *Gee* set.

The homeward journey was extremely perilous. We had lost the main stream and were down to around 7,000 feet and dropping. With two engines gone on one side and the one not feathering, it was very difficult to avoid 'slipping' (and losing even more height). The crew had obviously been told to prepare to jump as the fire may have burned out of the nacelle and into the wing. Also, we were very much 'sitting ducks' and flying at minimum airspeed across very heavily defended country. The 'services' – electric and hydraulic – were now hardly functioning and we first hoped that we were on something like the right course for England. Ken Vowe, hunched in the bomb bay, did a terrific job for something like 2 hours, as he locked his arms round the starboard rudder pedal; without his assistance I almost certainly would not have had the strength to keep such control as I had! Eventually, I saw faint airfield lights below and believing we perhaps had made it to England, I commenced an approach to land. However, when greeted by ground flak, I realised that we had a way to go – and I crawled away from what must have been a German fighter base in Holland!

During a brief period while he was resting his arms, Ken looked down and

Sergeant Eddie Davidson, wireless operator, H-Hellzapoppin, 61 Squadron. (Howard Farmiloe)

recognised a part of the Zuider Zee, which enabled the navigator to direct me towards the coast. Eddie then sent out an SOS in plain language detailing our situation. Eventually he got a reply in code giving us a position as a third class fix, which showed Eddie that we were roughly heading down the coast of Belgium towards France. Ten minutes later Eddie sent out another SOS and this time he received a first class fix, giving him a definite position sufficient to enable me to head for The Wash.

We were struggling to hold 4,000 feet and we were slowly losing height. Once over the coast the order to 'prepare to jump' was changed to 'prepare to ditch'. We got shot at by coastal flak ships (actually a British convoy proceeding up the North Sea), but managed to survive, then my wireless operator got a home bearing in response to his Mayday call. As we neared the East Coast (lucky it was not the South Coast as we would not have got over the cliffs!) a single searchlight came on and pointed us in the direction of Little Snoring, a long-runway emergency aerodrome. Now very low, with the port outer still burning and no 'services', we were unable to signal our approach but struggled in, with no flaps, at 140mph. We did get the wheels down (using the emergency air bottle) and fortunately the gear locked so we made a good landing. (My crew said afterwards that it was the only *good* landing I ever made, but I like to think that there was at least one other!)

We reached the centre of the runway but to my horror, instead of slowing down, we went faster and faster – eventually going off the end of the runway into complete darkness. We shut off everything that could be shut off and rolled through hedges and across several fields until we hit wet ground. The plane stopped and tipped up on its nose with the tail straight up in the air. We got out *fast*, ran away and sat in a group laughing ourselves silly! Then we set off to follow the wheel tracks back to the Little Snoring field and control tower. It was still pitch dark. The control staff were amazed, as we had not been noticed!

I never saw the field again in daylight until years later when I was telephoned by Tom Cushing who kindly invited my wife and I over, and when he drove us along the old runway in his Land Rover it was immediately apparent as to why we accelerated instead of slowing down. The field was like an inverted saucer, and once we had reached the middle it was all downhill!

All I cared about was getting all my crew home safely and that we did! It was a 'team effort', like so many in those days. As a result, I think I was the youngest pilot officer to be awarded a DSO, my navigator, Flight Lieutenant Halliwell, got a bar to his DFC, and my bomb-aimer and wireless operator each got DFMs. I must say that nobody goes for medals – you just want to do the job and get home!

12: Chick's crew
Sergeant C. H. 'Chick' Chandler

IT WAS 0110 HOURS on the morning of 23 April 1944. We were a XV Squadron Lancaster III crew from Mildenhall on our 17th op and we were hit simultaneously by heavy flak and cannon fire from an Me 109 at the precise moment that our bombs were released on Düsseldorf. Being the flight engineer, I was standing on the right-hand side of the cockpit, as was usual during our bombing run, with my head in the blister to watch for any fighter attack that might occur from the starboard side. The bombs were actually dropping from the aircraft when there was a tremendous explosion. For a brief period of time everything seemed to happen in ultra-slow motion. The explosion knocked me on my back; I was aware of falling on to the floor of the aircraft, but it seemed an age before I actually made contact. I distinctly remember 'bouncing'. Probably lots of flying clothing and Mae Wests broke my fall, but under normal circumstances one would not have been aware of 'bouncing'. As I fell I 'saw', in my

mind's eye, very clearly indeed, a telegram boy cycling to my mother's back door. He was whistling very cheerfully and handed her the telegram that informed her of my death. She was very calm and thanked the boy for delivering the message.

As I laid there I saw a stream of sparks pass a few feet above the cockpit, from back to front and going up at a slight angle. This caused me some confusion. If the sparks were from a burning engine they were going the wrong way. It was some little time before I realised that the 'sparks' were in fact tracer shells from a fighter that I did not know was attacking us. The illusion that the tracer shells were going upwards was no doubt caused by the fact that our Lancaster was going into an uncontrolled, screaming dive, but because of the slow-motion effect that I was experiencing, I did not appreciate this fact. This whole episode had taken 2 or 3 seconds at most, then the slow-motion

Lancaster production at Chadderton, 1944.

Sergeant 'Chick' Chandler, flight engineer, XV Squadron. (C. H. Chandler)

effect began to wear off, and I became aware of the screams of the bomb-aimer. Lying in the bomb-aimer's position in the nose of the aircraft, he had caught the full force of the explosion, although this was not immediately apparent.

As the speed of things returned to normal, for some reason I was unable to get to my feet. My assessment of the situation, which was completely wrong, was that a bomb had exploded on leaving the aircraft and that the rear end of the aircraft had been blown off. Therefore, I decided, I should not waste time going to the escape hatch in the nose, but should make my way aft and step out into space, thus saving time fiddling with escape hatches. My frustration was immense, knowing that my very life depended on some quick positive action, but I was unable to get to my feet, let alone clip on my parachute and move quickly to the rear of the aircraft. (It was many years before I realised that, because of the unfortunate position I was in, plus the effect of 'G' when a Lancaster goes into an uncontrolled dive from 22,000 feet, I had very effectively been pinned to the floor of the aircraft.)

Pilot Officer Oliver Brooks, my pilot, regained control at about 14,000 feet, then I was able to get to my feet and clip on my parachute. Here I had another quite ludicrous experience. Always when flying, my parachute harness was tight, even to the extent of being uncomfortable, and my buckles were all done up (some crew members left the bottom buckles undone for comfort and ease of movement). Having clipped on my parachute the harness felt very loose and generally slack. *Knowing* that mine was always tight, I put this slackness down to imagination and convinced myself that it was all a nervous reaction. There is no doubt that given the order to 'bale out' I would have jumped. What I didn't know, and it wasn't discovered until later, was that a lump of shrapnel, or possibly a cannon shell, had passed through the back of my harness, cutting the straps and leaving them hanging by a few threads. Had I jumped, my 'chute and I would have parted company!

A few seconds later the aircraft went into another uncontrolled dive and was recovered at about 7,000 feet. Only a very short period of time covered these incidents. The pilot really had his work cut out trying to control a very heavily damaged aircraft and had feathered the port inner engine, which had caught fire. He gave the order to prepare to bale out.

By now the crew were beginning to sort themselves out. When the aircraft recovered from its first dive, Ron Wilson, the mid-upper gunner, vacated his turret to find that his flying boots and the H_2S were on fire. Unfortunately, the three parachutes had been stowed on this piece of equipment and were destroyed. In order to extinguish the fire it

Chick's crew, XV Squadron, Mildenhall. Left to right: Sergeant Ken Pincott, navigator; Sergeant 'Whacker' Marr, rear gunner; Sergeant Oliver Brooks, pilot; Sergeant C. H. 'Chick' Chandler, flight engineer; Sergeant Les Pollard, WOP/AG; Sergeant Ron Wilson, mid-upper gunner (partly obscured); and Sergeant Alan Gerrard, bomb-aimer. (C. H. Chandler)

was necessary for him to disconnect himself from the intercom, so he was unable to relay this information to the rest of the crew. Baling out was not now an option, and after hasty consultation it was decided to set course for the emergency landing strip at Woodbridge. If we could at least make the coast we might be able to 'ditch'.

My task now was to check the aircraft for damage and casualties. My checks started at the front of the aircraft, in the bomb-aimer's compartment. I am afraid to say that my sheltered life had not prepared me for the terrible sight that met my eyes. It was obvious that this area had caught the full blast of the flak, and Alan Gerrard had suffered the most appalling injuries. At least he would have died almost instantaneously. Suffice to say that I was sick. At this stage I risked using my torch to shine along the bomb bay to make sure that all our bombs were gone. My report simply was that the bomb-aimer had been killed and that all bombs had left the aircraft.

Next stop was the cockpit. The pilot had really worked wonders in controlling the aircraft and successfully feathering the engine that had been on fire. Then on to the navigator's department; on peering round the blackout screen I saw that Ken Pincott was busy working over his charts, but that Flight Lieutenant John Fabian DFC, the H$_2$S operator (the Squadron navigation leader), appeared to be in shock. However, once I established that there appeared to be no serious damage, I moved on. The wireless operator's position was empty because his task during the bombing run was to go to the rear of the aircraft and ensure that the photo flash left at the same time as the bombs. Next, down to the mid-upper turret, where Ron Wilson had re-occupied his position, albeit only temporarily. (Unknown to me, he had suffered a wound to his ear that, although not too serious, would keep him off flying for a few weeks.) On reaching the next checkpoint I was again totally unprepared for the dreadful sight that confronted me. Our wireless operator, Flight Sergeant L. Barnes, had sustained, in my opinion, fatal chest injuries and had mercifully lost consciousness. It was found later that he had further very serious injuries to his lower body and legs. He died of his wounds before we reached England. From the rear turret I got a 'thumbs up' sign from 'Whacker' Marr, so I rightly concluded that he was OK.

As well as having to report the death of our bomb-aimer, and the fatal injuries to the wireless operator, I had to report the complete failure of the hydraulic system. The pilot was already aware of the fact that we had lost our port inner engine through fire, and that our starboard outer was giving only partial power. The bomb doors were stuck in the open position, and the gun turrets had been rendered inoperative because of the hydraulic failure.

Next I carried out a check on our fuel. From the gauges it looked as though we had not sustained any major damage to any of our main tanks, but I thought it prudent to carry out a visual check on the outside. Any fluid coming from the mainplane would almost certainly indicate at least one tank holed. It was then that I discovered that where our dinghy should have been, there was a gaping hole in the mainplane. The dinghy had been shot away. Our alternative possible escape route through ditching was now also out of the question.

I sat down to work out how much fuel we had left, and at what rate it was being used. This was not easy given the fact that we had two engines at full bore, one feathered, and one not giving much power but still churning round a propeller that was stuck in coarse pitch. These figures would give me the length of time that we could keep the aircraft flying. When I arrived at the figure and was in the process of double-checking, the navigator asked me what my figures were. I stalled for time, saying that I had not quite finished. I asked him how much time we required. He gave me his figure and I felt a flood of relief as my figures gave us 20 minutes in hand. After a few seconds I told him that we had at least 10 minutes and possibly a little more.

We now had, in effect, two spare crewmen. Only one of our two navigators was needed since the H_2s was destroyed, and the gunners' positions could not be operated because of the hydraulic failure. The many tasks, such as tending the wounded and throwing overboard as much equipment as possible, was left to them. (Fabian took over the navigation while Ken Pincott took the dead wireless operator's position and radioed SOS messages repeatedly to England, but to no avail because the aircraft was too low for the calls to be received.) The rear gunner remained in his turret. I was able to concentrate on our critical fuel condition. Gradually I became more confident as each check and cross-check bore out my original figure of 20 minutes to spare.

It was at this stage, sitting on my toolbox in front of the engineer's panel, that I became very aware of the red warning lights indicating the loss of our port inner engine. They appeared to be glowing like beacons (quite wrongly I am sure, but I thought that they could be seen from miles away by any fighter that happened to pass overhead – my remedy was to chew some chewing gum and stick it over the lights). Many thoughts now

The Frazer Nash tail turret of a Lancaster bomber. (via Mike Bailey)

struck me. We were struggling along on two engines with a third giving only partial power. We had no gun turrets working. We had started our journey at about 7,000 feet and because of the damaged state of the aircraft we could not maintain height. Should we be attacked, any sort of evasive action was out of the question. In our very badly crippled state any violent manoeuvre would have resulted in complete loss of control and certain disaster. We were well within range of even the lightest ack-ack, and our predicament obliged us to make a direct route from Düsseldorf to Woodbridge; there was no question of avoiding heavily defended areas. There was also a distinct possibility that through miscalculation or mismanagement we could run out of fuel.

In spite of all this I can remember very little of the actual trip. Certainly we were heavily coned by enemy searchlights at between 3,000 and 4,000 feet, but for some unaccountable reason we were not engaged. Again, quite without reasonable explanation, I cannot recall being unduly alarmed, possibly because I had by now resigned myself to my fate, or because I was so aware of our critical fuel situation that I had pushed all other problems to one side. There was one 'silver lining' to the problems. We had steadily lost height from the moment we had headed towards Woodbridge, in spite of the fact that we had jettisoned all possible equipment, including guns and ammunition. Because our bomb doors were stuck open and there was a gaping great hole in our starboard wing, with other smaller holes all over the aircraft, our engines were using fuel at an alarming rate trying to pull our very unstable aircraft through the air. Just when it seemed that all was lost, the fact that we had used so much fuel, and consequently weight, meant that the pilot was able to coax the aircraft from just above the sea to 500 feet on crossing the coast.

Almost as we reached Woodbridge I was faced with another problem. I had no means of testing the emergency system that should enable the undercarriage to be lowered pneumatically. We would have to wait until the aircraft was actually over the runway on our final approach. There was no way that we could go round again – it would either work or it wouldn't. Since I was the flight engineer, it was my task to attempt to lower the wheels, so that instead of sitting in my crash position (the other crew members sat with their backs to the main spar, feet braced against a part of the aircraft in front of them, hands clasped behind their heads), I was standing next to the pilot as we came over the end of the runway. Ron Wilson, instead of taking up the recommended crash position braced against the main spar (and so increasing his chance of survival), had opted to stay at the rear of the aircraft and cradle the wireless operator (who, unbeknown to him, had already died).

As we passed over the threshold lights (the Emergency Landing Strip at Woodbridge was 250 yards wide and 2½ miles long, or about twice as long as a normal runway) I yanked on the toggle that should have lowered the undercarriage. To my horror, there was no response. At this stage the dreadful 'slow-motion' effect returned. We were crabbing very slowly from left to right. I saw very clearly every runway light as we passed it. The ground appeared to come very slowly towards me. I thought, 'How stupid to have survived the many problems of the past couple of hours only to be catapulted through the windscreen on arriving!' I made a very conscious effort to hang on to the pilot's seat and waited for the crash.

As we hit the runway I saw very clearly and distinctly the perspex blister on the starboard side break away and 'float' towards the rear of the aircraft. To my utter amazement I found myself still standing as we careered down the runway. By now the slow-motion effect had left me again, and I was fully aware that we were careering down the runway at 120mph on our belly. When the aircraft eventually came to rest I was still standing and clinging to the pilot's seat. Our crash-landing must have been perfect, and my theory is that because the bomb doors were stuck in the open position, they gave a slight cushioning effect and softened the initial impact. Almost before the aircraft had ground to a halt I was through the top escape hatch situated immediately above the flight engineer's position.

Since I had experienced the 'slow-motion' effect on a few occasions, I was in a state of near terror, probably due to an excess of adrenalin, something that most of us were not aware of in those days. I really did feel so relieved that I got to my knees and kissed the ground. Almost immediately someone thrust an incident report into my hand asking details of damage and fuel states, etc. In my intense anger, I am afraid that my remarks were very blunt and would not have been appreciated in the least!

13: Invasion day
Flight Sergeant Jack Parker

ON 5 JUNE 1944 at Hartford Bridge there began to develop, by mid-afternoon, some sort of a 'flap'. We had been up in 'our' Mitchell II, FV900 in 'C' Flight, 226 Squadron, on an exercise involving air-to-sea firing at patches of aluminium powder in the sea just off the Isle of Wight. I was the navigator/bomb-aimer. On looking back, the mentality of those responsible for sending us off on such an exercise in *that* area at *that* time must seriously be called into question. However, possibly even they may have

Mitchells taxiing out on Invasion Day, 6 June 1944. (IWM)

been having second thoughts, for it was just after George 'Junior' Kozoriz, our Canadian mid-upper gunner, remarked, 'Jeez, look at all them ships out there', that we had a very panicky 'Return to base' message sent to us personally on VHF. We returned . . .

On our return we were amazed to find all and sundry being press-ganged into grabbing cans of paint and suitable brushes and painting broad black and white stripes, later to be known as 'invasion stripes', on the wings and fuselages of our Mitchells. Being now somewhat experienced, we ourselves, by methods known only to professional aircrew, managed to skive out of this. However, we did not think of invasion, but rumour-spreaders had been at work, and had accounted for the stripes by saying that we were going to Iceland to protect the Atlantic convoys and the stripes were to help our shipping identify us (partly right, anyway, but hadn't they heard of Coastal Command?). Another faction had us going to the Middle East, but this did seem a bit unlikely in spite of a claim to have seen 'a hangar full of tropical kit'.

I had just finished an early supper, unwisely as it proved, washing it down with several cups of strong tea, when my Aussie skipper, Flying Officer Grant Crawford Suttie, a pre-war regular RAAF, appeared on the scene. Old 'Sut' told me with some

Flight Sergeant Jack Parker, navigator, 226 Squadron. (Jack Parker)

George 'Junior' Kozoriz, mid-upper gunner, 226 Squadron. (Jack Parker)

urgency to report to the Operations Room for briefing, as we were to be 'on' that night. I grabbed my kit, mounted my squadron bike and on the 1½-mile ride to the 'Ops' Room, visualised a course either to Prestwick, Reykjavik or St Eval, and ditching in the Bay of Biscay if Gib' didn't come up on ETA. Or were we to bomb Berlin, Berchtesgaden or whatever? No, that's the heavies' job, thank God.

With such thoughts I entered the Ops Room, having saluted as was *de rigueur*, and was there amazed to see our route already displayed – 'from HARTFORD to POINT OF AIR to POINT OF AYRE, Isle of Man, to TREVOSE HEAD to STURMINSTER NEWTON to BASINGSTOKE' – thence back to base. I asked, as respectfully as I could, 'What the hell . . .?' The Briefing Officer told me that, as far as I was concerned, it was a VHF calibration trip. What it was as far as he was concerned he didn't say, nor did I press the point, being much too relieved by this 'non-op' operational route being presented.

(Our flight was, in fact, to test specialist communications equipment, although we did not know this at the time. 'C' Flight was code-named the 'Ginger' Mitchell Flight, a very special and secret Flight under the direct operational orders of SHAEF. From early summer, Mitchells were sent out at night over France, ostensibly on 'Nickelling' – leaflet dropping sorties – but really as a cover for picking up transmissions from agents. To the normal Mitchell crews were added a number of French radio operators. Later, ours was André Bernheim, who had been a French film producer and was a personal friend of Charles Boyer. Another was Joseph Kassel, the writer. The special operators' task was to receive transmissions on the 'quarter wave' voice system from agents in Occupied France who were equipped with special radio equipment for the purpose. The normal slow Morse transmission was too dangerous because it could easily be picked up and 'homed' on to by Gestapo direction-finding vans. Quarter wave transmissions, on the other hand, were very difficult to detect at ground level, but

Left to right: Jack Parker, navigator; George Kozoriz, gunner; Flying Officer Grant Crawford Suttie RAAF, pilot; French radio operator André Bernheim; Cecil Ray RNZAF, WOP/AG; all of 226 Squadron. (Jack Parker)

they could easily be picked up by an aircraft at 20,000 feet or above by a special operator using 'Ginger' equipment.)

I prepared the flight plan with some trepidation, for the met forecast was terrible. Cloud base was 1,000 feet, tops 2,000 or above, Icing Index high. I therefore spent more time than usual on the flight plan. I was to be glad of this. At about 2230 we clambered into dear old FV900, by then fully refuelled, but without stripes as I recall. We had not been airborne long before the forecast proved only too accurate. We climbed up through ever-thickening cloud and at one stage, when lumps of ice hurled off the prop were striking the fuselage, I suggested the possibility of a return to base. Young George – he was all of 18 – made the same suggestion, but in more forceful terms. 'Sut', however, was the 'press on' type, so we pressed on. In fact, old 'Sut' really deserved a medal for this trip, for he was on instruments all the way round.

We saw neither the Point of Air, nor of Ayre. We passed our VHF messages, but got no reply. All I do recall was a broad North Country voice from time to time saying 'Turret to turret, over'. This meant nothing to us. We were now at 20,000 feet, oxygen full on. The oxygen did make one feel just a little intoxicated, at any rate sufficient to take the rough edges off. The cold was fearful. Cabin heating? Don't make me laugh. I was, in fact, far from laughing, for about half-way between Point of Ayre and Trevose Head my excessive tea-drinking earlier now led to an anti-social accident, the stuff freezing on the floor of the kite and costing me a quid later that day to have the long-suffering ground crew mop up.

No sign of Trevose Head. We were in and out of solid cotton wool cloud. No *Gee* – that packed up very early on, so we had to rely solely on the flight plan. We got no messages, and no response to our transmissions. We were now heading in the general direction, hopefully, of Basingstoke, and I felt that we were at least sufficiently clear of the hills – we were in awe of these – to start our let-down. I informed 'Sut' accordingly, so down we let through the clag. As the altimeter unwound, I recalled the old joke about 'If this altimeter's correct, we're in a ruddy submarine', and as it went off the scale at zero, I prepared for one big bang and oblivion – I had a ring-side seat in the nose of the Mitch. But just then the cloud mercifully broke and there, below,

Three Mitchell IIs of 226 Squadron in flight, the nearest being FV905 MQ- S for Stalingrad. (via A. S. Thomas)

perhaps 200 feet, perhaps more, was a broad, winding river meandering through a built-up area. It couldn't be the Rhine, nor the Seine, but . . .

'OK, Sut, two-six-zero Magnetic – sharpish!'

I think 'Sut' put our port wing tip into the Thames somewhere east of Putney Bridge. We whipped round in a split-arse turn – to quote the jargon of the day – and headed in the general direction of Hartford. Continuing our previous course might have led to an even greater anti-social accident, costing more than a quid to clear up, for we were headed for Big Ben and the Houses of Parliament!

Ten minutes or so later, we were thankfully in the good old Hartford circuit, 'Downwind, cleared to finals'. We landed, cleared the runway, and finally got back to dispersal. We did our post-flight checks – 'IFF off, Petrol off, Switches off' – and went off to debriefing. In the mess later we were able to obtain our 'operational' eggs and bacon. The kitchen staff believed that we had been on some daring mission over the invasion beaches. We did not disillusion them, but ate to a background of 'Mairzy Doats' alternating with 'Lili Marlene'. It was only at about 05.30 on 6 June that we even *heard* of the invasion.

Now, if anyone mentions D-Day to me, I cannot help laughing. Privately, I picture myself in a pool of urine trying to avoid a too-close encounter with the Mother of Parliaments. A strange sequel to this was that, on 28 July 1945, a USAAF B-25 Mitchell similar to ours did collide with the Empire State Building in New York. We might have made a similar spectacular impact.

14: D-Day in a Stirling
Flying Officer Gerry F. McMahon DFM

THE ATMOSPHERE AT FAIRFORD was electric. 620 Squadron had just been briefed that we (33 Stirlings in No 38 Group) were to spearhead the main force of the D-Day attack, which was to take place the following day. Our first task was to drop (north of the village of Ranville) a force of paratroopers (of the 7th Light Infantry Battalion, 5th Parachute Brigade, 6th Airborne Division) who were to hold one of the main bridges (the Orne River bridge), which would form part of the supply route for the defending German forces. (The paratroopers were to reinforce the *coup de main* party of the 2nd Battalion of the Oxfordshire & Buckinghamshire Light Infantry and a detachment of Royal Engineers, all under the command of Major R. J. Howard, who had landed earlier in six gliders to seize the Orne and Canal de Caen bridges). It was necessary to get this force into position before the Germans knew that the actual invasion was under way.

We took off at 2230 hours on the night of 5 June with a full complement of paratroopers on board our Stirling IV, LJ849 *E-Easy*. Our pilot was Flight Lieutenant G. H. Thring, a Canadian. We had a quiet flight until we crossed the French coast, when we were hit by a considerable amount of light flak and suffered some minor injuries amongst the paratroopers. Shortly afterwards the flak thinned out and we were on an immaculate run to the dropping zone. All the paratroopers left the aircraft in their original order, including those who had suffered slight injury and who had refused to return to the UK with us for treatment. We learned later that they landed bang on target and held their position, as had been planned. (Fifty years later, in the Tower Hotel,

Gerry McMahon and Richard Todd meet in 1994, 50 years after they parted at Pegasus Bridge. (Wing Commander Gerry McMahon DFM)

London, my wife and I met Richard Todd. We were both guests of the *News of the World* and on our way to a reunion in Caen. In conversation it was discovered that I had actually flown Lieutenant Richard Todd, as he then was, the night before D-Day and dropped him and his paratroopers at Pegasus Bridge. Richard's comment was that our drop wasn't so close, as he had a long way to walk to the bridge. My comment was that you can't please everyone all the time, and why had it taken him 50 years to make the complaint! Several large whiskies resolved the situation.)

We returned to England, being hit again by flak over the French coast, and landed back at Fairford at 0145 hours on the morning of 6 June. It had been our intention to sleep before the next trip, but this proved impossible. The excitement that brewed when it was learned that it would be announced to the world that we had invaded the continent was a little too great. Later, our aircraft was in position, ready to head the 620 Squadron invasion fleet of glider-towers. The scene on the airfield was one that I shall always remember. On the grass beside the aircraft were several large gatherings of soldiers in camouflaged dress, armed to the teeth, all kneeling at their respective religious services, the padres in their white cassocks and regalia standing out very clearly amongst the men. Also intermingled with the soldiers were a great number of the aircrew.

We took off in the afternoon. Although we had originally set off leading our squadron in what appeared to be clear sky, as we arrived at our rendezvous on time we soon became a little cog in a very big

Paratroopers synchronise their watches before departure.

Stirlings of 620 Squadron en route to their drop zone. (Sevenside Collection via Carl Bartram)

wheel, and the surrounding air, in front, beside and behind us, was just a solid mass of aircraft and gliders. On crossing the English Channel, the sight in the air appeared to be reflected in the sea, in that as far as the eye could see shipping of all sizes was heading in the same direction. As we approached the coast of France we witnessed several lines of heavy naval ships bombarding the French coast.

Our job was to drop the glider in an area between the French coast and the city of Caen. On the way to the dropping zone I noticed on our starboard some very accurate gunfire coming from a wood, which had picked off a number of aircraft and gliders as they were coming in. I gave the skipper a fix on this position with the intention of putting it out of action after we had dropped the glider.

Richard Todd, pictured in 1993 at the Derwent Dam celebrations held to commemorate the 50th anniversary of the Dams raid. On the eve of D-Day Lieutenant Todd was a member of the 7th Light Infantry Battalion party dropped near Ranville from Stirling IV LJ849 to reinforce the coup de main *party landed in six gliders to seize the Orne and Canal de Caen bridges. After the war Todd starred in the epic films* The Dam Busters *and* The Longest Day, *in which he played Major R. J. Howard, commander of the* coup de main *party that took Pegasus Bridge.* (Author)

Pegasus Bridge pictured in the mid-1970s. The bridge was unceremoniously replaced just prior to the D-Day 50th anniversary celebrations in June 1994. (Author)

We duly released the glider in the dropping zone and headed for the wood at low level. Regrettably, the gun position saw us coming and hit us first. The first thing to blow was the petrol tank in the port wing, which blew up the wing and turned the aircraft on to its back. As rear gunner, my first indication that there was something wrong was when my ammunition came up out of the 'chutes and hit me in the face.

Flying Officer Gerry McMahon, standing, on the left. In the centre is Flight Lieutenant Gordon H. Thring RCAF, pilot of Stirling IV LJ849 E-Easy *on the 5/6 June 1944 operation.*

Because of the 'G' pressure, we were in absolutely no position to do anything.

However, my skipper had given up trying to fly the aircraft through normal elevators, etc, and had his feet up on the dashboard pulling back on the stick in the fond hope that we would pull out of the dive. It was then that one of the miracles of the war happened. The aircraft came over off its back, and we made a most beautiful belly-landing in a ploughed field that would have done justice to any pilot under normal conditions.

The whole crew left the aircraft completely uninjured and we were able to run some 25 yards into a wheat field before the remainder of the aircraft exploded and burned furiously. Within minutes the aircraft was surrounded by German troops and, from the gist of their shouts, we realised that they thought we were still in the aircraft. We therefore stayed where we were in the wheat field for some time. Once all the Germans had left the scene, we had a crew conference as to what action we should now take, the position being, of course, that we had an invasion going on some miles behind us and odd pockets of paratroopers could be on either side of us. All we knew of our flight position was that after we had been hit we had about-turned and headed back over enemy territory and, from where we were, it was impossible to accurately pin-point our position.

One of the crew felt that we should walk about unarmed and hope to find our own kith and kin. This I disagreed with. As a result he handed over to me his revolver and ammunition, and this I placed in the top of my battledress, together with my escape kit and money wallet. It was then decided to wait until dark and walk in the general direction of the French coast. We hid out until dusk and just as the light was falling, along came two figures that at first glance appeared to be wearing American helmets. One of the crew in his excitement even thought the men were whistling 'Lili Marlene' and cried, 'The Americans are with us!' He leapt out to greet them. I think it was sheer reaction that made us stand up. By this time the two so-called 'Americans' had leapt off their bicycles and were covering us with machine-guns. They were German! Never has one felt so small. We were marched to a nearby German army camp where we were locked in a room, still wearing our guns, to await the arrival of a German officer. He very quickly put a stop to the nonsense, and we were immediately disarmed of all visible weapons.

As I was the only member of the crew wearing a decoration, they presumed I was the captain and I was called forward to meet the Army captain. He proudly announced that he was educated in England and that he would interrogate me in English, but he must first search me. As his hands were about to search, starting under my armpits, I reached into my battledress and withdrew my escape kit in its plastic container and wallet of foreign money, and handed them to him quite openly. He said, 'What are these?' I replied that the escape kit was my ration for three days and the wallet of money contained personal papers to be opened only by the Gestapo, to which he replied, 'Ja, ja, I understand', and handed them back to me. I put these back into my battledress and was horrified to hear the clunk as the escape kit hit my hidden revolver. However, by this time I was already stepping backwards and the German captain did not appear to hear. He seemed satisfied with his search so I continued to walk backwards and Flight Lieutenant Thring stepped up as next in line to be searched. Each member of the crew adopted the same 'patter' as I did, and we were all left with our escape kits and money.

We were then ushered into another room and locked up until later that night. Time did not seem to mean very much, as we were all so desperately tired and hungry, having been up all the night before and throughout this day without a drink or a meal.

Some time during the night the German army captain came to us with the news that he had been ordered to retreat to a position nearer Caen and that we were to accompany him. We started off, surrounded by what appeared to be a couple of hundred German soldiers, and began to march. We then came across another small company of soldiers, some of whom had seen battle, and one of whom had a badly broken leg with a protruding bone. Two of us were instructed to support him by crossing our hands so that he could sit on them. He was only about 16 years old. I was selected as one of the first 'chair bearers', an honour I did not appreciate at all.

One of the German soldiers eventually found a stretcher that enabled the four of us to carry a corner apiece. In our weary state this lad weighed the proverbial ton and we resorted to a ruse whereby every few yards one of us took a turn to shout 'Holtz!', which not only stopped us but brought the whole company to a halt as well. Each time the captain had to return to our position to find out why the company had halted. En route we also watched, against the night sky, large fires in some town or other that was being bombed. The general consensus of opinion throughout the German company was that we should be tied to stakes and left to burn with it.

On one of our stops, while sitting at the road side, I suggested to Gordon Thring that we might take advantage of the thick black night and make a run for it – some of us might get away. Gordon was of the opinion that two of the crew were not capable and that if others of us managed to escape those remaining would be shot. I agreed, seeing that the noise of battle all around us was making the Germans very touchy, but said that when I got the opportunity to escape without endangering the crew I was going to at least make an attempt.

After a while we managed to find a motorcycle by the side of the road, which had been abandoned with no petrol, so we sat the wounded soldier on this and pushed him to the top of a hill. On reaching the top, and seeing that there was a steep descent on the other side, we accidentally let go and the soldier disappeared into the dark. He was later found in a ditch at the bottom of the hill and his language was not appreciative of the help we had given him. The German captain then decided that it would be safer for him to look after his own wounded, and we did not see the wounded man again after this.

We marched all night and as dawn approached we arrived at a chateau that had obviously been used for some considerable time as a German headquarters. Listening to the conversation on arrival, we understood that all staff officers of the headquarters had withdrawn and now this was to be a fighting garrison. We were shown into a barn and a guard was placed at the door. I quickly removed the gun and ammunition from my battledress and hid it between some bales of straw. Although we were desperately tired, the skipper and I made a quick reconnaissance of the barn, finding that on the first floor there were wooden hayloft doors that, if pushed open, would give us access into the grounds. There was also a hoist and pulley and it was felt that we could probably swing over the chateau wall on to the road on the other side. Having agreed on this possibility, we gave up and fell asleep in a pile of hay.

After I do not know how many hours, the German captain appeared with several bottles of champagne and some sauerkraut sausage and what appeared to be a type of brown bread. This was devoured with relish, even though the sauerkraut and bread had been 'off' for some time. The captain explained that the champagne was the only drink they had as the water was polluted. Later he brought a bottle of port and some cigarettes. Best of all was when an NCO brought us a pot of coffee!

As night approached again, I began thinking of the hayloft doors and the possibility of escape. Two of our crew were not in good fettle and the skipper, quite rightly, decided against a mass escape. However, I said I proposed to go it alone and take my chance. As soon as it was dark I recovered my revolver and ammunition from the hay and climbed into the loft.

I gently eased open the doors and noted with pleasure that there were no sentries in sight at this end of the barn. Also, there appeared to be just the right length of rope on the hoist and pulley for me to swing over the chateau wall, but I would have to take my chance on what was on the other side. I took hold of the hook and jumped for the wall, but instead of completing the swing I plunged violently downwards, ending up in a tangled mess at the base of the barn wall. After rubbing my various sore spots, I discovered that the reason was a simple one – the other end of the hoist rope had not been secured to the wall!

I made a reconnaissance of the grounds and noted the positions of the German sentries, after which I headed back to the barn, securing the hoist rope to the wall and climbing back up and through the hayloft doors. All the crew were sound asleep, so I hid my revolver and ammunition back in the bales of hay and settled down. In the morning I explained to Gordon Thring that I had done a reconnaissance of the grounds and had decided against escaping. By this time there was a considerable amount of activity outside, and on two occasions the Germans entered the barn to count that we were all still present.

During the day the chateau suffered numerous rocket attacks by hedge-hopping Typhoon fighters and shells from the army. Gradually, it was being reduced from its three storeys in height to a load of ground rubble, and the morale of the German troops was equally low. Talk between the soldiers indicated that they believed they were surrounded, but they no longer had R/T communication and, apart from the captain, no one to advise them as to what was the state of the war.

Early the next morning Typhoon fighters again carried out rocket attacks backed up by mortars. The German soldiers moved out into a slit trench dug in the grounds. The captain asked us to leave the barn for our own safety. I collected my gun and ammunition and hid them again in my battledress, and we then joined the Germans in the trenches. This was most fortuitous, because a few minutes later the barn was struck by two rockets and went up in a flash of fire and smoke. There was some talk amongst the Germans about sentries being killed during the night on the chateau wall opposite that from whence the invasion was coming, and they were convinced that they were surrounded.

One of the most amazing things to happen was that as we sat in the slit trench and as the Germans had to pass backwards and forwards, they would say 'Excuse British soldier!' and give a little bow, with old world courtesy. It got crazier and crazier, but we were pleased enough to share their protection.

During the afternoon the German captain sent for me and for the skipper. We found him in a room in the basement of the chateau, admiring his stubbled face in a mirror. As we entered he turned around, obviously embarrassed, and said, 'Me no English gentleman.' He then uttered the most surprising thing by saying, 'I wish to surrender to you myself and 40 men.' This came completely out of the blue as far as we were concerned because, although we had caused the rumours, we had no idea how far behind enemy lines we were. However, we decided to take a chance and said to the captain that we would only accept his surrender if he did so in the proper military fashion and marched with the men fully armed to give themselves up. He agreed, and to show faith he handed me his own revolver.

This was how a queer little party of armed Germans and ourselves set off from the chateau in the general direction of the coast. Just before we started, the German captain produced another bottle of champagne. He handed it to me measuring little sections of it with his finger and pointing around to the six of us. To make sure what he meant, he said, 'Too much for one drink', and rolled his eyes. The NCO shook hands with us all, with tears rolling down his face. I carried that bottle of champagne all the way back home to RAF Fairford.

I also insisted that no matter what happened en route there was to be strict discipline and no talking in the ranks. This was also fortuitous in that on the march another 21 fully armed Germans joined us, thinking that we were going to reinforce the German front! These 21 were hand-picked snipers who had been left behind to cause havoc during the Allied advance. We marched for over 3 miles and were suddenly surrounded by Canadian soldiers. We shouted that the Germans were our prisoners and were coming in to surrender. After seeing them safely into a prisoner of war cage the army captain gave me a receipt for one German officer and 61 other ranks.

The Canadians supplied us with jeeps to get us back to the coast and we had only one incident en route. We were stopped in one French village and told that a catholic priest and a girl were up in the belfry of the church sniping at our troops. They had sent for an 'artillery piece', and we watched the Canadians put this gun in place and take aim. Only one round was fired and it blew a hole right through the steeple, removing the opposition from inside.

On arriving at the coast a beach marshal had us put aboard a ship, where we had our first meal for three days – and a safe passage home. Our encounter with the beach marshal was another strange coincidence, as he turned out to be a naval officer who not only came from the home town of our stalwart flight engineer Sergeant Bill Buchan of Galashiels, but also lived across the road from him! This strange reunion was conducted in Scottish and well beyond our multi-national comprehension. The amazing thing was that we were standing on a beach with the war going on all around us and we had two Scots passing the time of day as if they were on a peacetime day out to Berwick-upon-Tweed. We could not have asked to have been sent on our way home by a more friendly face.

Our return to RAF Fairford caused quite a stir. Letters had been sent already by the commanding officer to our parents and families saying we were 'Missing, believed killed' because eye-witnesses of our crash thought the aircraft had blown up on hitting the ground. Over the next few days many VIPs came to talk to us and Gordon Thring was awarded the DFC for his crash-landing of the aircraft.

We were all sent on seven days' leave and I headed for my home in Newcastle-upon-Tyne. As I opened the garden gate my mother and father were just coming to the front door and going to church for my requiem mass. My mother took one look at me and fainted. The original commanding officer's letter had not been cancelled, and I was very lax in my own writing at any time, and telephoning was just not a habit. My parents were not fully au fait with my flying habits as I told them very little about flying in those days so as not to worry them. All in all it was a colossal cock-up, and the only one to blame was myself.

On our return from leave we were despatched to be interrogated by MI9 in St John's Wood, London. I was not impressed by the quality of the interviews/interviewers, both of which reminded me of 'jobs for the boys'. After sitting for what seemed an endless time I was interviewed by a Squadron Leader 'penguin' who seemed to be a typical 'pen-pusher' – probably a very good administrator, but lacking any idea of what to do in actual war conditions. He accused me of endangering the lives of my crew members because I had tried to escape on my own. The interview was abruptly terminated when I told him what I thought of him!

15: Nearly a nasty accident (1)

Squadron Leader Bob Davies AFC

I JOINED THE TERRITORIAL ARMY at the time of the Munich Crisis in 1938 (my mother was half-German). I enlisted in a searchlight unit that until 1942 was part of the British Army, the Royal Engineers. Believe it or not the anti-aircraft guns were also in the British Army, but in the Royal Artillery. In retrospect it is so easy to argue that, like the Luftwaffe, *all* the UK air defences should have been an integral part of the RAF. Knowing the mentality of the Army top brass they would have never surrendered any of their units to the RAF, the junior service. Nevertheless, there was no excuse for me and my fellow soldiers trying to find a German aircraft flying at 16,000 feet at night with a 1918 sound locator. Thank God all the radar early warning chains were manned and operated by RAF personnel!

In 1942 I transferred to the RAF. I received my wings (Class 42H) in the USA, followed by one year's instructing the Americans to fly BT-13 Vibrators at Shaw Field, South Carolina. My flight commander was a Captain Murray. When I said goodbye to

him I thought the chances of our meeting again were remote to say the least. On my return to the UK I went through the usual 'sausage machine', converted on to Oxfords, Whitleys and Halifax IIs, and ended up on No 578 Squadron, No 4 Group, at Burn, flying Halifaxes.

It was the policy of Bomber Command to fly mainly at night. However, at this period of the war the ever-cautious General Montgomery asked Bomber Command to abandon temporarily its night role and bomb tactical targets in daylight. This is how I came to be, on 3 September 1944, at 17,500 feet in MZ559 on the bombing run for Venlo airfield in Holland. The weather was good, there was light flak and, so far as I could see, no fighter opposition.

At 1730 hours I remember my bomb-aimer, Sergeant P. E. Wells, saying 'Bombs gone!', when there was an almighty crash. My first thought was that we had taken a direct hit by flak, which was supported by the top gunner saying, 'There's a f—— big hole in the top of the fuselage about 10 feet aft of my turret!' However, when the first moments of panic had died down a bit, I found that the aircraft was behaving normally – despite

'Nearly a nasty accident.'

The crew of Halifax II MZ559 of No 578 Squadron, No 4 Group, taken at Riccall in 1944. Left to right: Flight Sergeant R. E. 'Bob' Burn RCAF, navigator; Sergeant R. G. 'Sam' Browne, rear gunner; Flying Officer B. D. 'Bob' Davies, pilot; Sergeant F. E. 'Wally' Scarth, flight engineer; Sergeant M. U. Hayward, top turret gunner; Flying Officer B. A. 'Ron' Corbett RCAF, bomb-aimer; Sergeant Tither, radio operator. (Squadron Leader Bob Davies AFC)

the news that there was an equally big hole in the floor of the fuselage and that the Elsan chemical closet and the flare 'chute had disappeared!

A quick crew check revealed that the rear gunner was beginning to suffer from lack of oxygen. I told him to leave his turret and plug into the emergency bottle. He declined my suggestion that he jump over the 'hole' and take up his crash position near the main spar.

The nature of the damage to our aircraft dictated what we should do next – initiate SOS, set course for Woodbridge, the emergency airfield on the Suffolk coast, and slowly lose height to 10,000 feet. As we approached Woodbridge it was the decision of the whole crew (we were going on leave the next day) to cancel landing there and proceed to base (Selby in Yorkshire). However, deteriorating weather forced us to fly lower and lower and at 800 feet in moderate turbulence some 15 minutes from base we were diverted to the (American Liberator [453rd Bomb Group]) base at Old Buckenham in Norfolk (12 of the original 18 aircraft that took off landed away from base). So back we went virtually on a reciprocal course. The circuit and landing were an anti-climax – everything came down that should come down. We taxied to a halt and a very relieved crew went to debriefing and to their respective messes for a much-needed drink!

However, for me fate still had two more cards to play. At the bar I was approached by a young officer who asked whether he could buy me a drink as 'he was the bomb-aimer of a diverted Lancaster who had watched one of his 1,000lb bombs go through

A captain in the 453rd Bomb Group inspects the damage to Halifax II MZ559 after it landed at Old Buckenham on 3 September 1944 after sustaining a direct hit from a 1,000lb bomb dropped from a Lancaster overhead during the bombing run on Venlo airfield. (Squadron Leader Bob Davies AFC)

my Halifax'. I accepted his drink and we shook hands. I wonder if he remembers the incident, which for both of us could have gone so terribly wrong. (Why didn't the Lanc's bomb go off when it hit the aircraft? Was it a dud or was there another reason? I think I know the answer. RAF bombs had a wind-driven propeller that spun off, and then and only then was the bomb fully armed – the Lanc's bomb had not fallen far enough for it to be armed.)

As I was finishing my drink I was tapped on the shoulder and a voice said, 'What are you doing here, Bob?' It was my captain from Shaw Field, South Carolina, now a major and an operational pilot of a B-24 Liberator. It was and still is a small world.

(Bob Davies flew 16 ops on Halifaxes before being posted to 100 Group and serving with 171 Squadron [no aircraft] before taking command of 'A' Flight, 214 Squadron, flying ten ops on Fortresses.)

The wrecked fuselage of the Halifax replaced after the accident. (Squadron Leader Bob Davies AFC)

16: Into battle with 57 Squadron

Flight Sergeant Roland A. Hammersley DFM

IT WAS ALWAYS A STRUGGLE carrying two kit bags and other equipment when moving from one unit to another, and my trip from home to East Kirkby was no different from my other moves. I left home early on 17 March 1944 so that I would be able to reach my new unit in time for the evening meal and be settled into the camp before dark. This time it was different. I was now to take my full part in a squadron of Bomber Command. The training we had received was second to none and I was confident in each member of our crew on whom so much depended.

Lincolnshire, 'The Garden of England', was now a massive area of bomber stations – more than 50. East Kirkby, half-way between Spilsby and Coningsby on the A155, was just one of the wartime airfields and on it was based No 57 Squadron, which I was joining, and 630 Squadron, both equipped with Lancaster bombers. The whole crew arrived at about the same time, and after booking into the camp we were shown to our Nissen huts. Our crew consisted of Pilot Officer Ron Walker, pilot; Flying Officer H.

B. 'Mack' MacKinnon, navigator; Sergeant Esmond Chung, flight engineer; Sergeant Bill Carver, rear gunner; Flying Officer Ken Bly, air bomber; Flying Officer Tom Quayle, mid-upper gunner; and myself, 'Ginger', as WOP/AG.

With the crew I met the Squadron Commanding Officer, Wing Commander W. H. Fisher DFC. We were informed that we would be flying with 'B' Flight. After operations had been cancelled on 20 March we were briefed to fly on a local exercise of circuits and landings. At 1430 hours the following day we took part in a fighter affiliation exercise. The 24th was a memorable day. On arrival at the Flight Office we found our names on the battle order for that night's operations. The aircraft we were to fly was ND405 *T-Tommy*. We set off on bicycles, which had been issued to each one of us, to look the aircraft over and check the equipment. The ground crew were a fine bunch and gave us as much information as was possible about the aircraft as we went through the checking procedure. The bomb load was one 4,000lb, 48 30lb and 600 5lb bombs.

Later we were fully briefed both as individual crew members, then all the

'Bombs away!' (K. Percival-Barker)

crews together. We soon learned that the target was Berlin – the Big City. At the briefing we were told at what time there would be signals broadcast from Bomber Command; when we would receive the weather reports; where the searchlight belt and anti-aircraft guns were known to be; and also the positions of known German night fighter units and airfields en route. A weather report was given by the Station Met Officer, the indications being that the weather conditions were not too good and we would be meeting quite strong winds at 18,000 to 20,000 feet. We were issued with amphetamine tablets, which were taken just prior to take-off and would keep the crews wide awake and on a 'high' for the duration of the flight. If the operation was cancelled, it meant a sleepless night, which, for most of the crews, meant that a wild night of drinking would take place in both the officers' and sergeants' mess until the effects of the drug wore off and sleep would take over.

It was customary for a meal to be prepared for the crews before we flew. We were then issued with a flask of tea or coffee, with chocolate, sandwiches and an apple; a .38 revolver and parachute; and Codes and a Very Pistol with cartridges, which when fired would give the coded colours of the day. We were even given what were understood to be those in use by the German forces that day. After emptying my pockets and locking my personal items into my cage-type locker, I joined the crew in the crew bus with

WAAF Connie Mills at the wheel; she often drove the bus that collected the crews from near the control tower. We were then taken out to *T-Tommy*. We had another look around the aircraft with the ground crew, and about an hour before we were due to take off we settled into our places to await the take-off order.

When the first part of the take-off procedure commenced, we were lined up on the airfield perimeter with 17 other Lancasters from the Squadron. All crews would by now have taken their amphetamines and would be wide awake. The first Lancaster was given the 'Green Light' from the Mobile Watch Tower and we watched as it slowly climbed away. The remainder all slowly moved around the perimeter track towards the runway, then it was their turn for Destination Berlin! The smoke from the engines and the smell of burning high octane fuel eddied across the airfield. Some 60 tons of explosives and incendiaries were to be dropped by 57 Squadron that night, and the sight of 17 Lancasters, each under full throttle roaring away into the evening sky, was an awesome spectacle. Sergeants Frank Beasley and Leslie Wakerell with

Flight Sergeant Roland 'Ginger' Hammersley DFM. (Roland Hammersley)

the ground crews and a number of other well-wishers watched us away before retiring to while away the long hours before our return. The smoke and smell slowly thinned and drifted away over the silent airfield, and we were on our way to our first bombing operation with the Squadron.

We were airborne at 1845 hours. This was to be the order of things for some time to come. As the weather reports came in and I decoded them, it became apparent from Mack's findings that they were not as he expected them. We were faced with greater wind speeds than those indicated in the signals being sent out to us from Command, so we used our own. We were late arriving over the target and we could see that there were great fires as the run-in towards the target commenced.

Having bombed successfully, we headed back towards home, only to be told that we would have to land away, so we spent the night at RAF Coltishall, an airfield in Norfolk where fighter squadrons were based. The time we had spent flying the operation was 7 hours 30 minutes. We were debriefed and fed, then shown to our sleeping quarters. We made the 35-minute flight back to East Kirkby the following afternoon, leaving at 1500 hours, by which time the fog that had prevented our landing the previous night had cleared. Of the 17 Lancasters from the Squadron that flew the operation, one made an early return and two others failed to return. We made our reports at the Squadron office before leaving for our huts to await the evening meal.

The morning of the 26th found us on the battle order again. The aircraft we would be flying was ND560-N. Again a thorough check was made of the aircraft and its equipment, and later there was a full briefing on similar lines to that for the Berlin operation. The target was to be Essen, and our bomb load was one 4,000lb, 85 30lb and 1,500 4lb bombs. Twelve crews were briefed for the operation. We took off at 1924 hours, bombing the target in spite of a heavy barrage by AA guns. It was 0055 hours when we landed back at base. All our colleagues arrived safely after making their attack and we suffered no losses. We then went for the debriefing where coffee and rum was served to us while we waited for our turn.

Now there were two days off from flying, which gave us time to take stock of what we had so far achieved, then, on the morning of the 29th, our crew was on the battle order again. We were to fly the same aircraft used on the Essen raid, but the whole thing was cancelled before take-off. Fortunately, we had not taken any amphetamines. On 30 March, again we were on the battle order. Like the flight to Berlin, it looked as if we were set for a long trip this night, and this proved correct when it came to the briefing. The target was Nüremburg. Eighteen crews were briefed and we were airborne in *N-Nan* at 2211 hours. Our crew were in the first wave after the Pathfinders. On this occasion these were hardly required as the moon was brilliant and other aircraft were plainly visible. This was also, of course, a bonus for the German night fighters, and they were soon in action. Although our wave received little attention during the attacks, we could see the battles taking place around us and there were a considerable number of aircraft being shot down as we flew on deeper into Germany. The Pathfinder aircraft were about 5 minutes late on target and their marking was rather scattered; however, my crew bombed from 21,000 feet and Mack informed me later that we had hit our target. The flight home was a long haul south of Stuttgart, north of Strasbourg and Nancy, heading towards the French coast. We crossed the coast near Dieppe and so back to Lincolnshire and base. At debriefing we told of the aircraft that we observed being shot down. One of our own crews was missing, while another crew claimed to have shot down a Ju 88 night fighter. The losses suffered by Command that night turned out to be the highest during the whole of the war. With three operations flown I had seen the loss of 176 crews from Bomber Command.

We were now granted leave and I took the opportunity to relax and meet family and friends. I told Dad for the first time that I was serving on a bomber squadron and flying operations. The news was out that there had been considerable casualties on the Nüremburg raid and I had told him that I had flown that operation, asking him not to tell Mum. However, he could not keep the news to himself and I found him telling all and sundry in the pub – 'My boy was on that raid last night!' The news soon filtered through to Mum, and then the tears flowed. I felt sorry that I had said anything, but by then it was too late. Leave over, it was back to the war and life on the Squadron. I missed the operation on 9 April, my crew not being on the battle order. This was a mission to drop sea mines, code name 'Gardening'. Twelve crews had flown and one, piloted by Pilot Officer J. Finch, failed to return.

The following day, 10 April, my name, together with the rest of the crew, was on the battle order. The aircraft we would fly was ND468, carrying a bomb load of 13,000lb. Fourteen crews were briefed for the attack, which was to be on the railway marshalling yards at Tours in France. Take-off time was 2238 hours, but there was a snag. ND468 was found to be unserviceable and a switch of aircraft had to be made to ND560 'N' for the raid. Along with the other 13 crews, it was necessary for us to make two bombing runs over the target before we were certain that we would hit it and not the French people living in the vicinity of the yards. The time spent airborne was 5 hours 55 minutes.

On 11 April, after our early return on the 10th, it again proved necessary to prepare to fly to war. The battle order showed our crew with ten other crews listed to fly that night. We were to fly in Lancaster ND475, but later that day this was changed to ND954 'Q'. The bomb load was 12 1,000lb MC and 300 4lb bombs, the target was Aachen, and take-off was to be at 2025 hours. It was a successful trip, and in spite of the enemy defences shooting down nine of the attacking aircraft, fortunately none were from my own Squadron and my own crew were not troubled that night. One of the Squadron Lancasters made an early return due to technical problems, but the rest completed the operation.

A number of the attacks that were now taking place were in preparation for the invasion of France by the Allied forces, and the operation I next flew was in that category. The target was the railway marshalling yards at Juvisy, Paris. It was the night of 18/19th and the aircraft we would fly was one allocated to the crew for our regular use – Lancaster Mk III JB318 'O', called variously *Battling Oboe* or *Olive Oyl*. The bomb load was 13 1,000lb. Just about every other crew on the Squadron was to fly this operation, 18 in all. We were away at 2055 hours and all went well until we made our attack on the target. The bombs were dropped, then there was a failure of the hydraulics; in addition, one of the 1,000lb bombs refused to release. Instead of returning to East Kirkby, we set course for RAF Woodbridge, an airfield that had an extra-long runway. This we required as our brakes might not work. The bomb bay was open with the 1,000lb bomb still inside and likely to drop out on landing, so, using my radio, I advised base of our predicament and Woodbridge of our impending arrival.

The whole crew were involved in a discussion over the intercom regarding our serious plight. Should we parachute out? Would it be fair to leave Ron and possibly Essie to try a landing? As a crew we all agreed to sit it out and pray that the bomb stayed locked in place, for we knew that if it released when the wheels touched down we would all perish. Ron eased the Lancaster down to effect a gentle landing and the bomb held fast. Our hearts were pounding, as we all admitted later.

We were instructed to park the aircraft at a point as far away as possible from buildings. We were then collected by lorry and taken to the control tower to learn that the whole area had been cleared of personnel just in case there had been an almighty explosion if the bomb had dropped out of the bomb bay. We heaved a sigh of relief together with the staff on duty. The target had been attacked from low level (the height from which we bombed varied according to the type of target. The attack on Tours took place from 6,600 feet, on Aachen from 17,200 feet and this latest attack from approximately 5,000 feet.) We were well looked after that night after being debriefed, at which time we were given rum, coffee and sandwiches. We were taken to the accommodation, which had been set aside for us for the night. The fortunes of the Squadron crews on the Juvisy raid had been varied. Of the 18 that had taken off, two had made an early return and brought their bombs home, one had crashed near Peterborough, and my own crew had landed at Woodbridge. This left 14 to make the journey back to base.

There was no let-up in the flying. As on the 18th, the battle order for the 20th showed my crew listed, and we would be using JB318 'O' with the same weight and type of bombs as dropped at Juvisy. The target, in Paris, was the marshalling yards at La Chapelle. At the briefing all crews were instructed not to bomb unless there was a certainty of hitting the target. It was policy not to hit the areas surrounding the marshalling yards as these generally contained buildings occupied by French citizens. Well fed, well briefed and wide awake, at 2145 hours we took off for the second visit to Paris in as many days. There was considerable opposition from anti-aircraft guns as we once again dropped our bombs from low level. This time we made it back to base without any problems, although two of the crews from the Squadron were missing.

With further operations on 22/23 April, my name was again on the battle order together with the rest of the crew. Our Lancaster, JB318 'O', was loaded with a 2,000lb MC bomb together with 6,700lb of incendiaries, including a new type, code-named the 'J' Type cluster. It was a late take-off, so after ensuring that the equipment in the aircraft was in satisfactory order, I retired to my bed for a rest and a well-earned sleep. The target was Brunswick. At the briefing we were given details of the 'J' Type clusters. It was some years later that I learned that they were not as effective as had been hoped, and many failed to explode; they were recovered by the Germans and their content – petrol – was used to fuel their own vehicles.

The take-off at 2345 hours was smooth and the flight went without any mishap. The flight to and from Brunswick took 6 hours. Losses from the force that night were light, with just four aircraft failing to return, 57 Squadron not being affected. We made our attack from 20,200 feet, and as we headed away the fires from the target could be seen from a considerable distance; the attack had served its purpose. Two crews from the Squadron had made early returns, turning back for base with technical problems. The rest of us, 14 crews, all bombed the target, then made a safe return home. That I might survive the full tour of 30 operations was becoming a real possibility, and my confidence was high.

On 24 April we were briefed to fly operations to Munich together with 15 other crews. The bomb bay was filled with incendiaries. Taking off at 2050 hours, we headed south, crossing the Sussex coast near Selsey Bill. The Dutch coast was identified on the H_2S radar, then we headed deep into southern Germany before turning in a north-easterly direction towards Munich. There was a long wait as the target was identified and the markers, bright-coloured flares, were dropped. Those carrying out this work were Wing Commander Leonard Cheshire, Squadron Leader Dave Shannon, and Flight Lieutenant R. S. Kearns, all from 617 Squadron and flying the Mosquito. Looking down at them from our higher altitude, I wondered at the time who on earth I was watching flying so close to the ground, as just about every gun available to the defence force was firing at them. (Later in the year Leonard Cheshire, then a Group Captain, was awarded the VC, and the Munich raid featured largely in the citation.)

Although at 20,000 feet, we were getting our share of intense gun-fire, so we decided to fly away from the area on a 5 minute 'dog-leg' before joining in the mass of aircraft awaiting the order to 'Bomb'. When the order came, we made our bombing run and dropped them successfully from 19,700 feet, only to find that there was a hydraulic failure and we were again in trouble.

Leaving Munich in a south-westerly direction towards Austria and the Swiss border, we crossed the Rhine and headed first south of, then north and west of Paris, towards the English Channel and the comparative safety of England. (Two night intruders shot down a Lancaster returning from a separate raid over the East Coast.)

Later, I read the official report of the Munich raid. It read: '. . . NJG6 German Night Fighter Force was operating in the Munich area. The RAF force attacking Munich met with very little trouble except from fighters and flak at Munich and in the withdrawal south of Augsburg, in which neighbourhood extension of defences was suggested. It is probable that three aircraft fell through flak over Munich, one to flak when coned in searchlights on the south-west outskirts and three to fighters near Munich, Ulm and Strasbourg, a total of four to flak, three to fighters and two to unknown sources.'

I sent a radio signal to base advising them of our hydraulic problem and that we would be landing at Hartford Bridge, not far from Basingstoke. I was becoming quite an expert at signalling base to report our problems! By now the crew was listed as a 'Windfinder'; that is, the navigator and crew up front would prepare a weather report, then it would be my job to code it and transmit it to base, a task we continued to carry out until the end of our tour of operations. It was 9 hours 35 minutes after take-off at East Kirkby when we landed at Hartford Bridge. The reception was good, in particular as the bomb bay was empty! However, it was necessary to leave JB318 behind and we were collected from Hartford by Wing Commander Fisher and his crew.

For the next operation in which I took part, on 26 April, 14 crews were briefed to bomb Schweinfurt. We would be carrying different bomb loads, some with a mixture of high explosive and incendiaries, while others, including my own crew, carried incendiaries and no explosives. Our load was 1,860 4lb inflammable material, which meant that there would be very little chance of survival if we were to crash or if a fire started on board, as would surely happen if we were to be hit by a night fighter or anti-aircraft fire. Sergeant John B. Johnson, on his first day at East Kirkby, flew as our mid-upper gunner. He did not have time to unpack his kit before meeting my crew. His pilot, Pilot Officer G. J. L. Smith, flew as 'second dickie' with the 'B' Flight Commander, Squadron Leader Boyle.

One of our engines was put out of action about 60 miles west of Paris and we were 2 hours late in arriving back at base. By then we had just about been given up as missing. Johnson was absolutely exhausted and was picked up from the aircraft by the Gunnery Leader in his own car. The Squadron had taken quite a hammering on this raid. Squadron Leader Boyle had not returned and was posted as missing. Flying Officer R. A. Beaumont's Lancaster was attacked by a Ju 88 as they were making their way back towards the French coast. The aircraft was struck by a hail of cannon shells and bullets; Sergeant R. I. 'Allen' Hudson, the mid-upper gunner, was seriously wounded and the rear gunner was killed. It was only with great difficulty that the pilot was able to bring the Lancaster back across the English Channel and land at RAF Tangmere. (It was September before Allen was fit for further flying duties. He flew 12 operations with a new crew before being sent off for a well-earned rest.)

That same night, under similar circumstances, the Lancaster piloted by Pilot Officer

A. Nicklin was attacked and the rear gunner so severely wounded that he lost a leg. The mid-upper gunner, in the belief that the aircraft was going to crash, baled out over Germany. Nicklin made a safe landing alongside Flying Officer Beaumont at Tangmere, a station that coped well with the casualties from 57 Squadron that night. It would appear that I was flying at an interesting period in the history of Bomber Command! Schweinfurt was to see the award of the Victoria Cross to flight engineer Sergeant Norman Jackson. He failed to extinguish a fire that broke out in an engine, and climbed out of the aircraft on to the wing with a hand-held extinguisher. Despite the cold and wind, he succeeded in putting out the flames and returned safely to the aircraft.

Following another night in my bed, it was back in action again on the night of 29/30 April. The attack this time was against the airfield at Clermont Farrand Aulnat. I added another 6 hours 45 minutes to my operations flying time and 1,220 miles to the distance travelled.

The air battles continued apace and 1/2 May saw the Squadron joining in the attack on an aircraft repair depot at Tours, France. Operations were also on for the 3rd, an attack upon military barracks at Mailly-Le-Camp. On approaching the target area in bright moonlight there were delays with the marking and with the communications from the controller of the force. This caused the bombers to have to wait and circle the area in most cases. The German night fighters started to attack in force and began to pick off the bombers quickly. I counted at least 12 aircraft go down, and recorded this in my log before I was instructed to act as an additional pair of eyes by looking out

On the night of 29/30 April 1944 Flight Sergeant Roland Hammersley added another 6 hours 45 minutes to his operations flying time and 1,220 miles to the distance travelled since starting his tour, when Bomber Command visited the airfield at Clermont Farrand Aulnat.

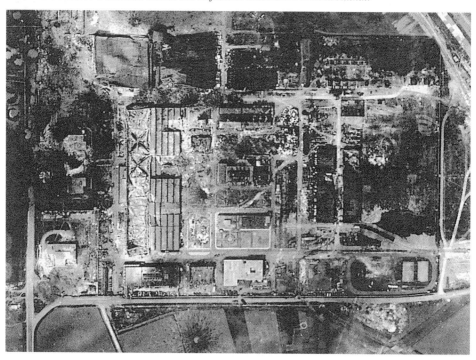

from the astrodome for any possible attack by a night fighter. We avoided combat and dropped our bombs on the target indicators from 5,500 feet as instructed. The defences were very strong and we faced fierce fire from anti-aircraft guns, which when combined with the night fighters made the bombing run at such a low level a positively dangerous manoeuvre. We headed for home, as did the other Squadron aircraft, with the exception of Flying Officer R. A. F. Scrivener, who failed to return. The talk at debriefing was of the many aircraft that were seen to be shot down. In total, 42 failed to return to their bases from the attack.

On 7/8 May operations were again shown as 'on' for the night, and were to provide my third visit to the airfield at Tours. We had real problems after a fairly uneventful flight out into France; when running up to the target at 8,000 feet we were ordered by the controller to orbit it as we had arrived a little before the TIs had been dropped. Next the controller said that the TIs were 'bang on', and we were given the order to bomb. We went through the bombing run, and Ken at the bombsight called 'Bombs away!'. Just before this Ken had warned of horizontal tracer on our starboard side, and Bill of a fighter attacking someone on the port quarter. While Bill kept an eye on this action from the rear turret, Tom was searching above and to the rear from his mid-upper turret. Then things happened quickly.

Tom called, 'Fighter! Fighter! Corkscrew port! Go!'

Ron needed no second telling, and we went down to port in the first move of the corkscrew. The remaining bombs sprayed out from the bomb bay in all directions. I could hear Tom and Bill's guns firing and the crash of cannon shells and bullets from the fighter hitting our aircraft.

Pulling out of this initial dive, I heard Bill call, 'Are you all right up front?' Ron hastened to assure him.

In the meantime Tom had seen a fighter about 400 yards astern and just above us, identified as a Ju 88; he opened fire simultaneously with the Ju 88. Bill quickly joined in. We were doing some 250mph on the first dive, yet the Ju 88 passed us in a vertical dive – we hoped that his dive terminated on the ground and not before. Ron completed two cycles of the corkscrew, and although Ken yelled to keep weaving, Ron decided to turn on to a course 323 degrees true. Already deep into France there was no desire to go any deeper.

On turning on to our course and clearing the defences, Bill was heard to call, 'Skipper, I've had it.'

I immediately left my wireless set and went back to the rear turret, letting Bill know that I was with him on arrival. He was in a sad state, with his face, arms and legs simply streaming with blood. I helped him out of the turret, and with some difficulty managed to get him along the fuselage to the rest bed. Up front Ken had clipped on his parachute in case we had to abandon the aircraft. On hearing the news of Bill he came back to help me for a few minutes, then checked the rear turret, only to find it was too badly damaged to be used. We were without any defence for the rear end! Ken rejoined me at the rest bed and we set about caring for Bill.

Meanwhile, Esmond had completed an engine check and discovered that the port outer engine had no oil pressure and had to be switched off and the propeller feathered. This put the power for the *Gee* navigation equipment out of action. To counter-balance the loss of the engine, Ron began to wind the rudder trim only to find that it went round and round and did little more, so he had to jam the rudder over to starboard. Esmond went down into the nose and hung on to the rudder bar to ease the strain from Ron – really a rope was needed, but that had to wait while Bill's wounds were dressed. It was necessary to cut away clothing from his arms and legs. There were several nasty wounds bleeding profusely in both legs, which Ken covered with wound dressing pads, applying a tourniquet for a short while to each leg. Bill's face wounds were bleeding and Ken slapped a wound dressing straight on to his face. I had to remind him that it was necessary to uncover his nose, as it would help Bill breathe that much better. Having dealt with Bill's wounds I now found the rope that was required up front, so Ron and Esmond were able to have some of the strain of holding a straight course removed. Mack told us that we were about 50 miles from the French coast. This also reminded us of the briefing before the operation when we were told of the heavy coastal defences, in particular the light anti-aircraft batteries.

After injecting pain-killing drugs into Bill's arms, I acted as another pair of eyes from the astrodome. By now Ron had decided to take the aircraft down as close to the ground as possible, and we literally hedge-hopped across France with the three engines giving us some 180mph. Ron's skill as a pilot now came to the fore. It was agreed that we should get up to 10,000 feet to cross the French coast so as to avoid the light flak guns. We were nearly too late – as we commenced the climb one battery opened fire at us. Ron immediately put the Lancaster into a dive straight at the guns. I watched in amazement from the astrodome as the coloured tracer fire came flashing by my head and to each side of the aircraft. Later I discovered that we had been hit along the length of the bomb bay doors in that incident. We pulled up out of the dive and were away into the darkness as the gun-fire stopped. We crossed the coast at 10,000 feet as intended, avoiding the Channel Islands. Bill was now feeling the strain, being semi-conscious much of the time. He was not plugged into the intercom at this stage, and in one of his brighter moments he indicated that he wished to talk, so he was switched into the circuit.

After clearing the Channel Islands, Tom said that there was another aircraft approaching, which he identified as a fighter. Ron was asked to turn a little to starboard and Tom opened fire with the four guns in his turret. It was a long burst. Ron then put the aircraft into a corkscrew. The night fighter appeared not to appreciate our gun-fire and dived away to port and was not seen again. We passed over St Alban's Head and sent out a Mayday distress call; Hurn answered faintly but did not light up. However, ahead there was another aerodrome, Tarrant Rushton, which did light up, so we went in there, other aircraft preparing to land being instructed to wait until we were down. Ron made a good landing on three engines and called for an ambulance, which pulled alongside us as we came to a stop near the control tower.

Bill was helped from the rest bed, out of the aircraft and into the ambulance by several willing hands, and went off to the Station sick quarters while the rest of us were taken off for debriefing and breakfast. After breakfast we made our way to sick quarters only to find that Bill had already been taken to the Military Hospital in Shaftesbury. We all admired his fortitude and courage in the somewhat harassing circumstances. The flying time had been 4 hours 15 minutes. Later, when looking at the aircraft, we saw that it was a mess. The rear turret was sheeted over and the signs of battle damage were all too obvious.

Ron Walker was recommended for an immediate award of the DFC following the events of the night of 7/8 May and the award was confirmed on 9 June. I had now completed 14 operations, had flown 14,795 miles in a flying time of 90 hours 30 minutes, and had carried a total of 161,948lb of bombs over Germany and Occupied Europe to their designated targets.

The world and the war moved on. By 31 May/1 June I had flown 17,455 miles in 105 hours 15 minutes on operations, carrying 185,948lb of bombs plus six sea mines over enemy territory. On 2 June I was promoted to Flight Sergeant.

On 6 June we were on the battle order for an early morning attack. The briefing took place late in the afternoon of the 5th, the only information being that we would be attacking enemy heavy gun positions at La Pernelle on the French coast. It was at 0140 hours in JB318 'O' with a bomb load of 11 1,000lb AN-M and four 500lb GP bombs that we took off with the other 15 crews for the attack. The navigator was Flying Officer M. A. Crombie, Sergeant G. Jennings serving in the rear turret. As we were crossing the English Channel it was apparent that there was either a huge flock of birds, thousands of aircraft or a vast fleet on the sea immediately below our Lancaster – my 'fishpond' was swamped with blips. Banking the aircraft to port and starboard, we could see a huge fleet of vessels heading towards the French coast. The expected 'D-Day' had arrived, and I was there to the fore. Later the figures showed that the number of aircraft that took part in the operations against the different targets totalled 1,136. The Squadron made its attack; one of the crews had to make an early return, but the others, after their attacks, all returned safely to base. The flying time for my crew was 4 hours 30 minutes.

After debriefing and a brief rest period, we found that we were again on the battle order with another evening briefing. The RAF was to be thrown into the battle to establish the beachheads on the Normandy coast, and our part was to prevent movement of enemy reinforcements from the rear of their defences through into the battle area. The flight out to the target (bridges in Caen) was uneventful, and we made our attack from 5,000 feet as briefed. Then, without any warning, our Lancaster was raked with cannon and machine-gun fire, with a short reply from the rear gunner. Ron put the aircraft into a dive to starboard and commenced to corkscrew away from the area. There was no more fire from the enemy aircraft, identified from the astrodome by Crombie, the navigator, as a Ju 88. Ron called all the members of the crew to check if all was well. There was no reply from Tom Quayle in the mid-upper gun turret, so I went back along the fuselage to see what the problem was, only to find that he had been killed in the action. His wounds were such that he must have died instantly.

I told Ron of Tom's fate. Ken came back from his place in the nose, but believing what I had said and obviously taken aback by the event. I persuaded him to return to his place in the nose position and, with Ron's permission, advised East Kirkby of the attack made upon us by the enemy fighter and the death of the gunner. From the inside of the fuselage, it was obvious that we had sustained a lot of damage from the cannon fire from the fighter, and care in landing would be required, particularly as the aircraft was not handling too well. The reply from base said that an ambulance would be ready to receive us. It was nearly 5am as we circled the airfield, and headed down wind when we were given permission to land. Although we made a not too bumpy landing, a tyre burst, the starboard wing broke open and out came the dinghy, which inflated and was dragged along the runway. We headed towards the waiting ambulance and the medical team led by the station Medical Officer.

On entering the aircraft they looked at Tom and quickly confirmed my original diagnosis that he had lost his life when we were hit by the cannon and gun fire from the enemy fighter. Furthermore the Lancaster was in a mess. Both gun turrets were damaged, the bomb bay had been hit, there were many cannon and machine-gun bullet holes in the fuselage and the port, tail and mainplane were damaged – a sad sight indeed. After the debriefing, we met the Medical Officer who prescribed drugs to get us all off to sleep for the day. I slept well into the next day and felt much rested when I awoke. With the rest of the crew, I was stood down from flying for a few days, although the Squadron was still active with attacks on the enemy in support of our land forces in Normandy.

By 10 July I had flown 26 operations. I began to feel that Lady Luck was with me, and that the 30 flying operations it was necessary to complete would be achieved. Still, it was going to take a great deal of skill and care to survive, and as a crew we were well aware of that. (Pilot Officer W. H. 'Goldie' Golding, an RCAF man flying his second tour of operations, took over from the wounded Bill Carver, and on 17 June we were joined by Flight Sergeant Alan F. 'Red' Brown, as mid-upper turret gunner.) We had frequent discussions during the flight and when making our attack at the target.

On the 12th we were briefed for an attack on the railway junction at Culment Chalindrey. This looked like being a reasonably easy operation, with 12 crews from the Squadron taking part. The route took us close to the Channel Islands. Way up ahead of us, two aircraft were seen to be approaching and they were immediately identified as German night fighters. Ken quickly manned his front gun turret and opened fire at one of the fighters, a Ju 88, which turned over on its side and went down in a dive with smoke coming from it. The other Ju 88 veered away and did not return when the mid-upper gunner fired his guns at him. Unfortunately, in the mêlée the bombsight was damaged. Our briefing for attacks on French railway marshalling yards was that we had to be able to guarantee to hit rails and not the surrounding buildings. With a damaged bombsight this could not be guaranteed, so we headed back towards base after part of the bomb load had been jettisoned into the English Channel.

On 16 July we attacked German forces in the vicinity of Caen. Bombing took place 2,000 yards in front of the Allied ground forces and aimed at the Monteville steel works where the German ground forces were strongly entrenched. Later, I learned that Wally, my older brother, was down below watching and guessing, correctly, that I was taking part in helping him and his fellows in their struggle to move forward against a very stubborn enemy. Our next target, on 18/19 July, was a night attack on the railway yards at Revigny. We took off at 2300 hours and all went well until we were about 50 miles from the target, when simultaneously we heard the rear gunner open fire as we were struck by bullets and cannon fire from a German night fighter, of which we had received no warning. I heard Mack, usually a very placid person, say, 'What the hell's that?'

Ron reacted immediately and commenced evasive action. The enemy gun and cannon fire had set the tail end of the fuselage on fire and we lost a great deal of height, dropping from 19,000 feet to about 12,000 feet, before control was regained. We were followed down by a Ju 88 and as we levelled out he came over the top of our aircraft. 'Red', in his mid-upper gun turret, was alert and watching him. He opened fire and hit the Ju 88 with the full fire power from his guns and the enemy aircraft went down. At this moment, in the organised mêlée, Mack went to the rear of the aircraft carrying a fire extinguisher. As he went past me, I pulled at his right arm and told him to take his parachute, but he failed to hear me. I followed him and helped Goldie out of the turret and along the fuselage to the rest bed. His turret was badly damaged and unserviceable. He had suffered bullet wounds as well as serious burns to his feet and legs so that the full extent of the damage to him could be seen.

While this was going on, Mack and Esmond were trying to put out the internal and external lights, all of which had switched on. They were fortunate and most of them were extinguished. The intercom had failed and we were only able to contact each other with written notes. Mack gave Ron a course to fly, as it was essential to return to base as soon as possible. I gave Goldie an injection of pain-killing drugs and dressed his burns with the burn-dressing gel from the First Aid kit. Once I had made him comfortable, I returned to my post at the wireless set, which was still functioning, and with Ron's permission called up the base and gave them details of our predicament, and of the need for the Medical Officer and an ambulance to be ready to receive us on arrival. The bombs we carried were jettisoned into the English Channel.

On our landing at base the doctors were pleased with the care we had taken of Goldie, but were concerned about my use of the gel burn dressing, being unaware of its existence in the First Aid kit. They found it difficult to remove, and later it was withdrawn from all aircraft First Aid kits. Goldie later had three toes removed that were severely damaged.

The rest of us were debriefed. (Mack said, 'Apart from us, Revigny was a dicey do as they lost 24 out of 110 aircraft.') Knowing of the damage we had sustained, the station and base commanders were at the debriefing. A long discussion took place and the operation was declared our last. I had completed the tour, having flown 29 operations. The last had seen us land at 0325 hours after a most exciting but exhausting flight of 4 hours 30 minutes.

The tour was completed just two days before my 22nd birthday. The past five months had seen me grow from a young excited Sergeant WOP/AG into a man matured by his experiences of the violence of war, with all its suffering, for those in the air and on the ground. The crew was granted leave, but before leaving for our various homes we had a discussion as to whether or not we should seek to join 617 Squadron. Two of the crew were not too keen, so the idea was abandoned.

17: Diary of a Pathfinder
Larry Melling

ON 14 JANUARY 1943 I did my last flight at the Advanced Flying School based at Turner Field, Albany, Georgia, USA, so completing my pilot training. I was awarded my 'wings' but, unknown to me at the time, it was to be four months before the RAF allowed me to fly again. We returned to England via Moncton, New Brunswick, arriving in Gourock, Scotland, on 9 February 1943, and from there went to Harrogate in Yorkshire. On returning to Harrogate after two weeks' leave, the powers that be decided that as we had been living in the lap of luxury in the USA for the past nine months, something had to be done to get us back into shape. We therefore found ourselves posted to Whitley Bay in Northumberland for the RAF Regiment battle course! The first few days nearly killed us – but after route marches in full kit, throwing hand grenades, and various other infantry exercises, we were fighting fit at the end of three weeks! We were then shipped to Bournemouth to await space at an Advanced Flying Unit.

I was assigned to the AFU at Little Rissington, Gloucestershire, and there, on 11 May, finally got back into the air, in an Airspeed Oxford. This was to introduce us to flying conditions in England, which were vastly different from what we had been used to in the USA. After completing the six-week course it was on to an Operational Training Unit and, for the first time, we pilots came into contact with the other aircrew trades. My rank at this time was Flight Sergeant. We were all thrown together in a large room and told to sort ourselves out into crews! It was a question of walking around looking at different flying badges, and asking various navigators, bomb-aimers, wireless operators and air gunners if they would like to fly with you. It has always amazed me that this hit-and-miss way of making up crews seemed to work out so well.

A German city burns from incendiaries, HE and markers dropped by the Pathfinders.

Cases where some crew members were found to be incompatible were very few. I was very lucky in my crew as we stuck together throughout the two tours that we eventually completed. Flying Officer R. F. Watkins was the navigator, Flight Sergeant L. Bell the bomb-aimer, Warrant Officer H. R. S. Sullivan RAAF the WOP/AG, and Sergeant W. H. Hitchcock the rear gunner.

From 21 July to 5 September we flew around in Whitley aircraft and slowly melded ourselves into an operational crew. Once I had become familiar with flying the Whitley, it was mainly a case of cross-country exercises for the navigator to prove his worth, and also some bombing exercises at various ranges for the bomb-aimer to do his stuff.

Having completed the OTU course satisfactorily, it was on to bigger and better things – especially bigger. We found ourselves at 1658 Heavy Conversion Unit at Riccall, Yorkshire, and were introduced to the Halifax. Here, two additional members were added to the crew – Sergeant J. E. Blyth as flight engineer, and Sergeant E. G. Ostime as mid-upper gunner. There was no selection this time, just two bods who came and introduced themselves as being assigned to fly with us. So we were now seven and, as mentioned earlier, we fitted together perfectly and very quickly became a unit. For reasons I cannot recall, we then spent three months at the Conversion Unit doing cross-country exercises and fighter affiliation for the benefit of the gunners, and finally, on 26 January 1944, we were assigned to 102 Squadron at Pocklington, Yorkshire, part of No 4 Group.

February 15/16 1944 was the day that I was first supposed to get into action. I had been detailed to do my 'second dickie' trip with a Flight Lieutenant Walmsley, the target being, of all places, Berlin! (A total of 891 aircraft were despatched, in what effectively was the last operation in the 'Battle of Berlin'.) The aircraft was one of the few on the Squadron fitted with H_2S at that time, and shortly after crossing the Dutch coast the set packed up. As a result the captain elected to return to base, so that next morning I was unable to answer the questions from the rest of the crew as what it was like 'on ops'. (Forty-three aircraft – 26 Lancasters and 17 Halifaxes – failed to return.)

On the night of 19/20 February I did indeed complete my 'second dickie' trip, this time to Leipzig. Being a second pilot on an operational trip was not a popular position. The crew with whom you were flying resented having an extra body along, and there was really no place where you would not get in the way of the crew carrying out their normal duties. In this regard the Halifax was not as cramped as the Lancaster, and I spent the 7^1/2 hours of the trip standing behind the flight engineer. Of the trip itself I have no recollection.

(The raid was a disaster. Leipzig was cloud-covered and the Pathfinders had to use sky-marking. Bombing results were unobserved. Of the 823 aircraft despatched, 78 (44 of the 561 Lancasters and 34 of the 255 Halifaxes) failed to return. After this raid the Halifax IIs and Vs were never used on operations again.)

Two days later we were advised that we had been transferred to 51 Squadron, also part of 4 Group, based at Snaith, Yorkshire. There, after a few training flights, on 13/14 March we finally did our own first 'op' as a crew (when 213 Halifaxes and nine Mosquitoes of 4, 6 and 8 Groups were despatched to the railway marshalling yards at Le Mans). There followed – in rapid succession – trips to Stuttgart, Frankfurt twice, Berlin and Essen, all before the end of the month.

A trip to Berlin on 24/25 March (when 811 aircraft, including 577 Lancasters and 216 Halifaxes were despatched) stands out in my memory due to the fact that the forecast winds were far from what we actually encountered. I suspect that we probably never came near to Berlin, and on the way home found ourselves far to the south of where we were supposed to be. Directly ahead of us was the Ruhr Valley with its heavy defences, and we elected to head to the north and pass between Hamburg and Hanover on our way to the North Sea. We were lucky enough to get to the coast without any trouble, but by now we were running considerably late because of the extra distance we had flown. Fuel became a major concern as we crossed the North Sea, and at one point Blyth, my flight engineer, when asked, reported that all gauges were reading zero; however, according to his calculations we had about 30 minutes' of fuel left! His calculations proved correct and we landed at Coltishall, Norfolk, whereupon all four engines quit and we had to be towed off the runway! (Forty-four Lancasters and 28 Halifaxes, 8.9 per cent of the total force, were lost.)

At this time the Squadron was visited by Group Captain Hamish Mahaddie, who was looking for volunteers for a new Pathfinder Squadron just being formed. After discussing the possibility with the rest of the crew, I decided to volunteer. Something in my record must have been all right, as we were accepted, so, after one more 'op', we were posted to the Pathfinder Navigation Training Unit at Warboys. There we found ourselves back in ground school, primarily for the benefit of the navigator, doing complicated navigation exercises and problems. On successfully completing that course we were introduced to the Lancaster and, after a 45-minute familiarisation flight, I was sent off on my own. The following evening I was given a 25-minute night circuit and again turned loose on my own. There followed mock operations to check the accuracy of my flying and the navigator's performance, and to assess the bomb-aimer's accuracy. Finally, on 27 May, we were posted to 'B' Flight, 635 Squadron, based at Downham Market in Norfolk. This was to be our home for the next 12 months.

On arrival at a Pathfinder Squadron new crews were first given a 'Support' role until they proved that they were able to meet the stringent requirements of accurate navigation to ensure arriving at the target within plus or minus 30 seconds of the assigned time. The accuracy of the bomb-aimer was also assessed, based on the bombing photos taken automatically when the bombs were dropped. Crews were divided into 'visual markers' and 'blind markers', the latter relying mainly on H_2S to identify and mark the target. We were assigned as a 'blind' crew and, as a result, the bomb-aimer had to do additional training in reading the H_2S screen; he became known as Nav2.

On the night of 11/12 June 1944, in ND811 (F2-T), we attacked the railway yards at Tours in order to disrupt the transport of German army reinforcements to the front in Normandy. When we arrived at the target the area was covered in solid cloud and we were instructed by the Master Bomber to descend below cloud for our bombing run. I do not know what the altimeter setting was in the target area, but when we dropped our bomb load my altimeter was reading 1,500 feet. Hitchcock, my tail gunner, shot at and extinguished a searchlight, and I can still recall seeing the wet cobblestones on the streets of the town! Further operations to disrupt enemy lines of communication to the Normandy area continued during the rest of June, with a couple of trips to attack V1 launching sites.

July started out with a continuation of trips in support of the invasion forces, and I did my first daylight operation, to Caen, on the 7th. Much has been written about the effectiveness of this raid, but I believe that it certainly resulted in saving many lives of the ground forces who had been held up in that area for some considerable time. (The Master Bomber, Wing Commander S. P. 'Pat' Daniels of 635 Squadron, orchestrated a highly accurate raid, and 2,276 tons of bombs were dropped. Only three aircraft were lost of the 447 'heavies' and 20 *Oboe*-equipped Mosquitoes despatched.)

Two days later we were detailed to attack a V1 launching site at L'Hey near Paris (when 347 aircraft bombed six launching sites). We made our bombing run at 15,000 feet amid a few black puffs of flak and made a long slow turn to starboard to begin the trip back home to Downham. Just as we completed the turn the aircraft lurched suddenly, the port wing came up and there was a rattling of shrapnel against the fuselage. A glance out of the port cockpit window showed white smoke coming from the port inner, meaning that we were losing coolant, but of the port outer there was no sign at all – just the bare firewall with some cables dangling loose. Blyth, the flight engineer, had already started the feathering procedure for the port inner and I immediately shut off the fuel cock to the port outer. Then began the struggle to trim the aircraft to fly on only two starboard engines. Full right rudder trim and full aileron trim were not sufficient to accomplish this; it took full right rudder and a somewhat starboard-wing-down attitude to maintain anything like a semblance of a straight course. Having checked that all crew members were unhurt, the decision was made in concert with my flight engineer to head for Manston, the emergency airfield in Kent, rather than return to Downham Market, as we had no way of being certain that we had not sustained any further damage from the shrapnel.

During the flight to Manston, which took about an hour, Bell, my bomb-aimer, suggested that he could relieve the pressure on my right leg by using the long bar of the control lock as a lever by putting it in front of the rudder pedal and across, behind the throttle control pedestal. Unfortunately the bar proved to be too short and all that was achieved was a slight bend in it. By placing both feet on the right rudder pedal I was able to relieve the strain to some extent. Thus we flew back to England in a slow descent, crossing the Kent coast at some 5,000 feet.

At this time I had a total of some 450 flying hours as a pilot, of which only 45 were on Lancasters, with a grand total of 21 landings! Accordingly, as we approached Manston I informed my crew that I was going to land the aircraft, but that if they

Squadron Leader Ian Bazalgette (seated, far left, second row) of 635 Squadron based at Downham Market, Norfolk, lost his life in Lancaster ND811 (F2-T) when it was shot down on 4 August 1944 at Trossy St Maximin, and was awarded a posthumous VC. Larry Melling, in 'B' Flight, 635 Squadron, flew this aircraft back to Manston after a raid on a V1 site at L'Hey near Paris on 9 July 1944 after it was hit over the target. (via Tom Cushing)

wanted to bale out I would not hold it against them. They all decided that they would stay with me, which gave me a much-needed boost of confidence. I instructed them to take up their crash positions behind the main spar, with the exception of my flight engineer, whom I asked to remain with me to handle flaps until I was committed to the landing.

When I got down to about 800 feet on the approach I realised that I was lined up on a railway track, and the runway itself was about a mile off to port. With only the two starboard engines operating there was no way I was going to attempt a turn to port, so I had no choice but to do a 360 turn to starboard! This resulted in my being correctly lined up, but when I gave the order for full flap at some 500 feet on final, my flight engineer had already taken off for his crash position! He later told me that when I had to make the turn around to get lined up with the runway, he was convinced that I wasn't going to make it!

We did, however, land quite safely and there was no further damage to the aircraft; after the two engines were changed it was returned to Downham and continued to fly until it was shot down on 4 August at Trossy St Maximin. (The pilot, Squadron Leader Ian Bazalgette, was to lose his life and win the VC.) During my career I have landed many times on three engines, but this was the only occasion when I had to land a four-engined aircraft with only two engines operating, and two on the same side at that! Speaking with my tail gunner a couple of years ago, he assured me that it was the smoothest landing I had ever made!

Another first for me occurred on 22 July. We were assigned to attack a V1 launching site at Linzeaux in France (four such sites were bombed, by 48 Lancasters and 12 *Oboe* Mosquitoes), but this was a totally different kind of operation. Eight Lancasters were sent in formation with an *Oboe*-equipped Mosquito, and the Mosquito captain instructed us when to drop the bombs. Never having flown anything larger than a Harvard in formation, the 3-hour flight, keeping station with the other aircraft, was a major effort and I am sure that I also lost at least 10lb in perspiration juggling the controls to stay in position. The raid was apparently a success because the same tactics were repeated five days later. In the meantime, we had completed night raids to Kiel and Stuttgart.

August 1944 saw us involved in several support operations, including the 'Falaise Gap' and, among other operations, our first daylight trip to a target in the Ruhr – Homberg (on 27 August, when 243 aircraft were despatched in the first Bomber Command daylight raid to be flown since 12 August 1941, when 54 Blenheims of 2 Group attacked the power stations at Cologne for the loss of ten aircraft). The month also saw me having a test exercise as a 'blind-marker' with the Squadron Navigation Officer. At this time I had completed 26 operations and was presumably now considered safe enough to be entrusted with the job of actually marking a target for the Main Force, although some considerable time was to elapse before I was given that job.

September seems to have been a rather quiet month as I had only three daylight trips and not one night flight. It was also the month in which I was given leave.

October started with a raid on the 4th to the German naval base at Bergen in Norway, an 8-hour trip that commenced just before dawn and was carried out in clear weather conditions over the whole route. We flew up the east coast of England and Scotland, then crossed the North Sea at 50 feet or less to sneak under the radar. We climbed to 18,000 feet just before the Norwegian coast and descended again immediately after the bombing run. Flying a Lancaster at low level like that was an unusual thrill.

The following night (5/6 October, when 531 Lancasters and 20 Mosquitoes of 1, 3 and 8 Groups were despatched) we were detailed to attack Saarbrucken, taking off just before sunset. On returning to base I was a little apprehensive about landing in the dark as my last flight had been some six weeks earlier. I was, therefore, really on my toes for the approach and touch-down, which was just as well because immediately after touch-down the aircraft swung to starboard and off the runway. Subsequent investigation showed that the starboard tyre had been punctured by flak shrapnel and was completely flat.

The night of October 19/20 saw us being given our first official task as 'blind-marker' when we were 'blind illuminators' to mark the Stuttgart railway yards for the visual crews. (In all, 565 Lancasters and 18 Mosquitoes of 1, 3, 6 and 8 Groups in two forces, 4½ hours apart, were despatched. Not many bombs fell on the yards, the most serious damage being caused to the central and eastern districts of Stuttgart and in some of the suburban towns. Six Lancasters were lost.) From here on in we acted as 'blind-markers' on almost all occasions.

During November and December 1944 and January 1945 we were again operating exclusively at night and our targets were chosen to hinder the ability of the enemy to resist the advance of the ground forces. They consisted of attacks on railway networks, oil refineries and industrial plants producing specialised items such as ball bearings.

During the latter part of January and into February the weather conditions in England, especially in the eastern areas, were very poor for flying, with dense fog causing many diversions on the return from 'ops'. This added to the stress as, when

The automatic camera aboard Larry Melling's Lancaster catches Bremen during a daylight morning raid on 21 March 1945. The bomb load was eight medium capacity 1,000-pounders dropped from 18,500 feet. (Larry Melling)

landing away from base, the aircraft had to be ferried back home after the fog cleared, thus interrupting the time available for sleep. We were lucky that our field was equipped with FIDO and, on 23 February (returning from a raid on Essen that involved 342 Halifaxes, Lancasters and Mosquitoes of 4, 6 and 8 Groups), I made my first landing using this facility. It was quite an experience as, on final approach, all that was visible was a red glow ahead that gradually grew brighter and brighter as the threshold was approached and then, with a bump, you were in the clear with flames 20 to 25 feet high on either side of the runway – a rather scary experience for the first time!

Backtracking a little, 1 November 1944 was a big day for me personally as on that date I was given my commission and the rank of Acting Flying Officer. It was a big promotion to go from the sergeants' mess to the officers' mess! Watkins, my navigator, who was commissioned before he joined our crew, welcomed me with open arms and free beer. Now there were two officers in the crew! By the time we had finished our operational flying, Bell, Sullivan and Ostime had also been commissioned, and Hitchcock had attained the rank of Warrant Officer.

During March and April 1945 we were kept busy with both day and night operations, some of which were the longest flights I made during my stay on the Squadron. Targets included Chemnitz, Dessau and Potsdam, all of which were

Pilots of the Pathfinder Force were entitled to wear the PFF Badge after having proven their expertise in operational target-marking techniques. Pathfinders were required to complete 65 operations for a tour. (Larry Melling)

ROYAL AIR FORCE

PATH FINDER FORCE

Award of
Path Finder Force Badge

This is to certify that
ACTING FLIGHT LIEUTENANT
L. J. MELLING. D.F.C. 188615
having qualified for the award of the Path Finder Force Badge, and having now completed satisfactorily the requisite conditions of operational duty in the Path Finder Force, is hereby

Permanently awarded the Path Finder Force Badge

Issued this **30th** day of **APRIL** in the year 19**45**

Air Officer Commanding, Path Finder Force.

flights of more than 8 hours. My last operational flight, which was my 61st, and also the last operational flight carried out by Bomber Command before the end of the war, was to Berchtesgaden on 25 April (when 359 Lancasters and 16 Mosquitoes of 1, 5 and 8 Groups were despatched). That flight stands out in my memory as, in addition to being my last, we took off just before dawn, and flying over the Alps in the early morning sunlight was a sight never to be forgotten. Unfortunately, little or no damage was done to the Eagle's Nest, which survives to this day and has now become a tourist attraction. Nor was Hitler in residence at the time!

Another very important day for me personally was 27 March 1945, as on that day the award of my DFC was promulgated in the *London Gazette*. According to my postwar research, this decoration was recommended by the Squadron Commander on 1 January but only got through all the paperwork some 11 weeks later. I cannot relate the award to any specific incident, and efforts to obtain more detailed information have drawn a complete blank. My navigator, bomb-aimer and wireless operator were also awarded the DFC, while my two gunners and flight engineer received the DFM. Again, efforts to obtain details have drawn a complete blank.

My double tour of 61 operational sorties was accomplished without any crew change. All the individuals who came together as a complete crew in October 1943 were still together on the flight to Berchtesgaden 1½ years later. With the end of hostilities my wireless operator was repatriated to Australia and the rest of the crew were scattered to various parts of the RAF. I myself became an instructor at a Beam Approach Training Flight, teaching pilots to make instrument approaches using a radio beam system called SCS51, the predecessor of the present-day ILS. My final time in the service was taken up by flying Dakotas in Transport Command.

18: Nearly a nasty accident (2)
Flying Officer Elwyn D. Fieldson DFC

ALL WAS PRETTY ROUTINE on the outward trip, to Düsseldorf on the night of 3/4 November 1944. Frequent turbulence from the wash of aircraft ahead gave a comforting reassurance that we were nicely in the stream, although only rarely was another aircraft sighted. I was the pilot of *Clueless 1,* a 76 Squadron Halifax. We arrived over the target on time to find the city well ablaze and made our run. The call of 'Bombs gone!' from the bomb-aimer Flight Sergeant Gerry Tierney was immediately followed by 'Dive starboard!', which I did. Another aircraft, perhaps a Halifax, was turning towards us, not waiting for those critical 2 miles beyond the target. Then there was a God-awful thump on our rear end, which knocked us into a near vertical dive with the whole aircraft vibrating madly. A propeller had sliced through our fuselage, leaving the tail unit attached by the top half only. The gun rams were bent into hair-pins and the tail surface considerably damaged. Remarkably, Flight Sergeant Jimmy 'Junior' Ross, the rear gunner, was not even scratched.

After we had lost about 2,000 feet I seemed to be getting some control back, only to find that the aircraft was now becoming increasingly tail heavy. Obviously the tailplane was no longer supplying its share of lift and I was soon having to push hard on the stick even with full forward elevator trim. Pilot Officer Frank Newland, the engineer, having surveyed the damage, suggested that he try to tie the dinghy mooring

The crew of Halifax LW639 Clueless 1, *of 76 Squadron, which came to grief on the operation to Düsseldorf on the night of 3/4 November 1944: Left to right: Flight Sergeant Jenman, mid-upper gunner; Pilot Officer Frank Newland, engineer; Flight Sergeant Gerry Tierney, bomb-aimer; Flying Officer Elwyn D. Fieldson DFC, pilot; Pilot Officer (formerly Flight Sergeant) Malcolm 'Mac' McLeod, navigator; Flight Sergeant Jimmy 'Junior' Ross, rear gunner.* (Captain E. D. Fieldson DFC)

rope and the escape rope across the gap to try and prevent further opening, and this he did. After a quick conference with Flight Sergeant Malcolm 'Mac' McLeod, the navigator, we decided to try to follow the planned route as far as the French coast in order not to become easy prey for a fighter, then dodge across to Manston, which had a nice long runway.

By this time I had my elbows locked in a straight line trying to hold the stick forward enough to keep descending to the

The badly damaged tailplane of Halifax LW639 and the gashed fuselage. (Captain E. D. Fieldson DFC)

planned 8,000 feet. After a time my arms were getting very tired and the rest of the crew took turns to come and stand alongside me and help push the controls forward. Thus we arrived at Manston, where I planned a flapless landing as I did not think there was enough control left to cope with the flap extension. But it wasn't quite over yet. On final, up went the red Very lights (we had no radio as the aerials had been carried away), so I overshot and went round again ('staggered round' might be a better description) at about 500 feet and, coming in very fast at 160mph, this time I was allowed to land, only to end ignominiously in the mud at the end of the runway (the Halifax always had lousy brakes). But at least the tail didn't break off as I had feared it might. Three days later we were back on ops.

19: The Heimbach Dam raid
Sergeant Bill Hough

THERE ARE MANY PEOPLE who believe in predestination. To support this belief I shall report an event that happened on the day prior to the raid, 3 December 1944. I was the wireless operator in Flight Lieutenant Art Green's crew in Lancaster PB629/J of 582 Squadron. Bad weather had prevented any flying for a day or two, and on the afternoon of 2 December Warrant Officer Johnny Campbell, the rear gunner, 'Mac' McKeon, the mid-upper gunner, and myself were occupying ourselves in the billet at Little Staughton in different ways. McKeon decided to clean his pistol and in the process put the muzzle into the palm of his hand and pulled the trigger. I do not think he was playing Russian roulette, but there was one up the spout and it went clean through his palm, ricocheted off the floor and out through the wall of the hut. The hand

A Lancaster at rest waits to be loaded up with 1,000lb bombs in 1944. (Maurice F. Paff Collection via Theo Boiten)

Sergeant Bill Hough, wireless operator (second from left) in Flight Lieutenant Art Green's crew in Lancaster PB629 J-Johnny *of 582 Squadron at Little Staughton, which took part in the Heimbach Dam raid on 3 December 1944. Warrant Officer Johnny Campbell, rear gunner, is second from right. Far right is 'Mac' McKeon, mid-upper gunner, who missed the raid with an injured hand. Flying Officer Ed Dalik, navigator 2, is third from left and Sergeant Denny Naylor, flight engineer, is far left.*

started to swell immediately and Campbell and I rushed him down to the MO where he received treatment and was put to bed; no flying for him for a while.

We checked in the mess and our crew was down for flying on the following day, with a 5am call. Obviously there was a daylight on. The next morning we arrived at briefing and on checking the crew list we saw that Mac's replacement was to be the Gunnery Leader, Squadron Leader F. G. Grillage. The target was to be a dam at Heimbach on the River Roer, 15 to 20 miles inside Germany from its border with Belgium, and only some 25 miles or so ahead of the front line at the time. This was to be very much a 582 show with 16 of our aircraft marking, including the Master Bomber, Squadron Leader Mingard, and his deputy, Lieutenant Edwin Swales SAAF (who as Captain Swales, DFC Master Bomber at Pforzheim on 23/24 February 1945, was to win a posthumous VC). There was to be additional marking by 109 Squadron, and a main force of about a hundred. The met forecast was not too good with some thunder showers in the area and 5–6/10ths cloud cover.

We were first off at 0805 hours carrying TIs and some bombs. The route took us across the French coast at Dunkirk with about 160 miles to run from there, mostly over Belgium, and an ETA over the target at 0945 hours. No need to worry about Flak now as most of this formerly occupied territory had been retaken by the Allies. We were now flying above almost 10/10ths cloud, but the horizontal visibility was good. Other aircraft were in sight and we seemed to be on the starboard edge of the stream. Tension heightened as we skirted Brussels with about 80 miles and 30 minutes to run. We were not quite sure where the front line was and it tended to be rather fluid anyway.

With some 40 miles to run, it happened. Johnny Campbell burst in on the intercom, 'Unidentified aircraft starboard quarter, level (14,000 feet). Range, 3 miles.'

I fancied myself at aircraft recognition and immediately stood up under the astrodome. The aircraft was closing very quickly and I identified it almost immediately as an Me 262 (which was only just coming into service in its originally intended role as a fighter – the few that had gone into service from June 1944 had been used as fighter-bombers). Before I could regain my seat Johnny again burst in.

'Another enemy aircraft dead astern – up, corkscrew starb . . .'

His words were lost in an almighty clatter and bang, the second aircraft firing its four 30mm cannon from a range of about 500 yards, the rear gunner firing back, and hits being registered on our port wing and engines. We had fallen victim to some very clever tactics using a decoy. The first aircraft went underneath us and the second over the top at a tremendous speed (this was our first encounter with a jet of any kind and their speed of over 500mph certainly showed up against the Lanc's 170 or so).

Black smoke, presumably from the fuel tanks, poured from the wing and the port outer was quickly enveloped in flames. Fire extinguishers were operated up front and we went into a shallow dive, but the fire only seemed to intensify, although the aircraft was still being held steady. Art obviously realised he would not be able to hold her much longer and the order came, 'Abandon aircraft – abandon aircraft'.

Time was obviously short, so the two gunners and myself were told to use the rear exit. One moves pretty quickly in these circumstances and I grabbed the parachute pack and made my way to the rear exit. As I passed the mid-upper gunner I gave him a bang on the legs with my hand in case he had not got the message. Johnny Campbell had the turret centred and was just climbing out as I reached the exit. He indicated that I should go first and while I clipped on my 'chute, he opened the exit door and immediately there was a tremendous roar from the slipstream air. As I stood in the doorway preparing to dive out, my 'chute suddenly burst open and the canopy deployed outside the aircraft, billowing above the fuselage with the lines bearing on the rear edge of the door. I seemed to be snagged against the fuselage side unable to move. I do not know to this day what happened. I can only conjecture that either the 'chute handle caught on something, or the force of the slipstream somehow sucked on the pack and pulled out the 'chute. Anyhow, at this time no one was theorising and Johnny Campbell quickly sized up the situation, got hold of me bodily and with some assistance from the billowing canopy, pushed me out of the door. Once free I was pulled by the 'chute *over* the top of the tailplane, banging my head on the top of the exit as I went out and hitting an ankle on the front edge of the tailplane, then between the fins, free of the aircraft.

My first sensation was a feeling of peace and quiet after the last hectic 3 or 4 minutes, for that is all it was. Peace after the roar of the engines and the howling slipstream. But I quickly realised that I had another problem. My harness had not been as tight as it should have been (I think it was a common practice to slacken them off a little while sitting for hours), and instead of being tight up in the crotch, it had slipped along the right leg towards the knee so that I was in imminent danger of parting company from the 'chute. I therefore held on grimly to the lines with both hands and began to enjoy the ride down. 'J-Johnny' had disappeared from sight, but one Me 262 did pass close enough to be recognised.

As I neared the ground, still hanging on tightly, I could see that I was going to land in a field on the outskirts of a village, and I could see people making towards the area. I did not make a copy-book landing due to the loose harness and a fairly strong breeze, but I was OK and the villagers soon grabbed my 'chute and held on to me. After some

15 minutes or so two Yanks, for we were in the American sector, appeared in a jeep and took me off to hospital nearby. I learned later that I had landed at Juprelle near Tongres, and the hospital was at Hasselt.

I was kept in hospital for about four days and spent a further night at an American base in a nearby chateau. I was not aware at the time of the fate of the rest of the crew, nor was I aware that I had been posted missing and my family informed. On 9 December I was again taken in a jeep to Brussels airport where I was able to hitch a lift in an RAF Dakota calling first at Northolt, then finally to Down Ampney. From Down Ampney I made my own way towards base, by train, arriving in the square at St Neots late in the afternoon. I still had on the clothes and flying boots, but not my helmet and parachute harness, that I had set out in six days earlier. A telephone call to Little Staughton secured me transport and I finally arrived back at base somewhat behind schedule. That was the longest op I did, No 13.

Art Green, Flying Officer Ed Dalik, navigator 2, Willie Mood, navigator 1, and Johnny Campbell had returned to the base before me. Although he had baled out safely, Sergeant Denny Naylor, the flight engineer, never did return to the Squadron and I believe he had some medical problem. Squadron Leader Grillage unfortunately did not survive. He was probably hit by gunfire as he was in line between the Me 262 and the port outer engine.

Possibly we achieved a double first in this trip; the first aircraft of Bomber Command to be shot down by an Me 262, and the first airman to bale out safely *over* the tailplane of a Lancaster.

Our flight had terminated at 0925 hours. The Master Bomber was unable to locate the target, although both he and the deputy went down to 4,000 feet, so the raid was abandoned at 0951 hours. The next day a further force, which included some 562 and 109 Squadron aircraft, went back and destroyed the dam.

20: Friday the 13th

SOMEWHERE ON A DISTANT AIRFIELD stood a neglected 1934 Standard 10 motor car, much used, even ill-used, in the past, but nobody cared. The three men from the aircrew that drove it had gone missing together with four additional crew members of Lancaster 'Y' PB842, on an operation to an oil plant at Pölitz, near Stettin, on 13/14 January 1945.

A few weeks before, in December 1944, Flight Sergeant Frederick Woodger Roots, air gunner, Brian Curran, his Australian pilot, and Bob Wilson, the Scottish navigator, had visited the Roots in Cockfosters, London, and had acquired the car. Mr Roots, a newspaperman on the *Daily Mail*, spent a lot of time helping them patch it. They froze as they grovelled beneath it, tracing broken circuits and tightening loose controls, for garage staff were short. In RAF parlance, there was no 'joy' in the battery, no 'joy' in the self-starter. Eventually they drove it off on the way back to more bombing operations with 619 Squadron from Strubby, Lincolnshire, a 5 Group Lancaster station near Alford, not far from Skegness and Mablethorpe.

Twenty-one-year-old Fred Roots was formerly on the staff of the Press Association, Fleet Street, and had joined the RAF in 1942. He spent his period of training in Canada and the Bahamas, passing his Elementary Flying Training School final air and ground examinations for pilot on 29 September 1942. He was then posted to 38 EFTS at

RAF airmen internees at Falun, Sweden, in January 1945. Fred Roots is at the rear, marked with a cross. (Fred Roots)

Estevan where he soloed on an Anson 11 and continued flying Ansons until 3 January 1943, when he was taken off the course; it was thought that he would not make a service pilot in the required time! Roots then underwent gunnery training in Canada, eventually receiving his air-gunner brevet. Coastal Command training in Nassau in the Bahamas followed, and he was allotted to a crew that flew Mitchells and Liberators. However, the crew was disbanded and they returned to the United Kingdom to be retrained on Wellingtons, Stirlings and Lancasters for 5 Group Bomber Command.

Roots's crew started bombing operations early in October 1944. All went well until 13/14 January 1945. One morning soon after, the Roots received a telegram. It did not 'stun' – it was less merciful. It admitted them to a vast community that mourned in every country or grimly and bleakly fought for hope. Their air gunner son was reported missing on a bombing trip over Germany. Friends and neighbours are very kind at such times. Some came bravely in to help, others as kindly stayed away. Two pressed whisky into their hands. 'Give her a drop tonight,' they said. 'It'll help a bit.' The RAF was kind too. The Wing Commander wrote in practical, encouraging terms, stressing the sound experience of the crew, the qualities of the pilot.

Their grey sojourn was mercifully brief. On the third day came another wire: 'Safe but interned'. The speed of it shook them. How the neighbourhood leapt with them! Even the telephone girls, whom they never saw, rejoiced as the calls sped in and out. The butcher and the baker, the parson and the milk girl heard the news. Everyone called. Someone brought more whisky. 'For a toast to your boy and his pals – and all the others too.' (The giver's son-in-law was home with her, with his legs shot off.)

Friday the 13th had begun like most other nights on operations for Fred and the rest of his crew, as he recalls:

We set off in the usual way from Strubby, having gone through the usual preliminaries, including briefing, inspection of our aircraft, guns and turrets, etc, and of course our special egg, chips and bacon meal as always. We climbed into 'Y-Yoke' PB842 and settled down into our respective positions in the aircraft. As always I was in the rear turret, with its four Browning .303 machine-guns. Our usual bomb-aimer, Sergeant Charlie Lockton, was sick and his place was taken by Flight Sergeant M. P. Quigley. He and Sergeant Johnny Haigh, the wireless operator, and Sergeant David Drew, the flight engineer, all came from Huddersfield. The mid-upper gunner, Flight Sergeant F. A. M. 'Abdullah' Blakeley, completed the crew.

As usual, the commanding officer, padre, and many of the station personnel were facing the runway to wave us off with the 'thumbs up' sign as we took off. We were routed over Sweden, and the flight was comparatively quiet with only the occasional anti-aircraft activity. Over Sweden the Swedish anti-aircraft gunners opened up, to comply with international requirements from a neutral country. However, the aiming was intentionally 'friendly' and we had no need to take evasive action. Closer to the target was a quite well-defended area because of the oil refineries at Pölitz and the number of warships with anti-aircraft guns, and the flak became more intense. However, we flew safely on until we reached our bombing run to the target.

I was obviously keeping an alert look-out for enemy night fighters. It was during the last few minutes of our run-in that I saw the Me 410 night fighter. Because he was sufficiently distant and flying a parallel course to us, I knew at that time that there could be no immediate danger and it was better that the bombing run continued so that we could get rid of our bombs.

However, immediately I saw the Me 410 turn towards us – the pilot had to turn his aircraft towards us in order to sight his guns – I opened fire with my four guns at the same time, giving the order to Brian to corkscrew to port – the evasive action devised by Bomber Command. The Me 410 continued to close in until he was within point blank range and I continued to shoot. Just before the German night fighter came in, our bomb-aimer had released the bombs on to the target. I imagine the enemy pilot had been waiting to see the bombs released, knowing of the danger to himself if they were to explode!

By this time I imagine that the Me 410 must have been extensively damaged, for he fell away from us and the fight came to an end. I claimed the enemy aircraft to be damaged, as I did not actually see it fall to the ground. David, our flight engineer, later my brother-in-law, claimed that he definitely saw the Me 410 fall away to earth. Just before this we felt a judder in the aircraft and a few minutes later our engineer noted that the fuel indicator for the port inner tank registered empty. A shell from the enemy fighter's cannon had entered the tank, causing a hole and the fuel to leak out. The miracle was that it did not burst into fire. By this time we had left the target area and were starting our return journey home again across Sweden.

Discussion then took place on the intercom and estimates were made as to how much fuel we had left and how far we could reach. The progress of the Allies in France was by now well advanced and we wondered whether we could fly back, away from the main stream of bombers and alone across enemy territory, in the hope of reaching Allied lines and baling out. It was doubtful whether we would even reach our own lines; it was also more likely that our lone aircraft would be attacked and shot out of the sky. The only reasonable alternative was to make for Sweden and either bale out or land the aircraft. The machine was flying well so it was decided to make for Rinkaby satellite airfield of the Swedish Air Force.

As we approached the airfield we shot off emergency cartridges from our Very pistol. The airfield, apparently, was not equipped with night flying equipment, so all available cars and lorries were driven on to the runway, and we landed by their lights, finishing very close to the boundary fence. We destroyed all our secret radar equipment, and one of the lorries with armed guards led us to the administrative buildings. We were interrogated very briefly and, of course, revealed only our names, ranks and numbers. We were then fed and entertained with beer in the officers' mess. We had a very friendly evening with the officers and were supplied with sleeping accommodation.

Next day we were taken for a walk, under armed guard, along one of the snow-covered country roads, and were put on the train at the local station. We travelled to Stockholm and on to the office of the Air Attaché at the British Embassy. We were told not to make any attempt to escape as the Air Attaché would do his very best to get us home. There was nowhere to escape to and the attaché's office would be much

Lancaster PB842 PG Y-Yoke *of 619 Squadron at Rinkaby, Sweden, in January–February 1945.*
(Rolph Wegmann via Fred Roots)

speedier. We were then put on a train and transported to Falun for another brief interrogation and a medical examination. I believe arrangements were made for us to cable home so that we could reassure our families that all was well. We were taken by army coach to our 'internment camp' (Internezingsager IV Korsnas) where we were to spend our internment. Here we were given a warm welcome by the proprietress and her staff. The cook, a plump motherly lady, described herself, in what little English she knew, as our 'Swedish mother'. They all became our good friends. Our internment camp was a small hotel and we were waited on with good food and comfortable surroundings.

During my stay at Korsnas there were 13 British internees. We were the only crew who had been able to land our aircraft; the others had parachuted out, one member being badly burned, while another was the only survivor of his crew. We had nothing to do but enjoy ourselves. It was an enforced holiday. We were allowed into the village and into the town of Falun, and were advanced some of our pay by the Swedish Army and the Air Attaché's office in Stockholm. We were taught to ski by an instructor from the Swedish Army, and we met local people, who were very friendly. Our stay was all too short, however. The Air Attaché, true to his word, made arrangements for our pilot, navigator, mid-upper gunner and myself to be flown home on 27 February 1945, as special envoys aboard a Dakota of BEA. We were debriefed at the Air Ministry by senior officials on our return to London.

In Cockfosters, North London, Mr and Mrs Roots awaited the return of their son. The post office had looked up the Roots's telephone number to get the telegram from Stockholm to them more swiftly. The girl who dictated the telegram said, 'Is it the good news we thought?' and they heard her call to other girls – 'It is – it is!'

At the Air Ministry a pleasant WAAF Corporal said, 'I wish we had thousands more cases as happy as this.'

They make them feel comfortable and easy in little rooms with deep chairs. They sent an officer with a file of signals. Yes, there were ways to write, wire and send parcels. So who cared about an old, battered treasure of a car standing idle on an airfield? The Roots could only wish that other parents might have the same comforting news. But how did it happen that days after all this the airfield chaplain sent a long, hand-written letter of consolation, encouragement and hope in their grief and anxiety? Did no one tell the padre anything but the bad news?

21: 'Aircraft of Bomber Command last night raided Dresden'

A. J. Stanley Harrison RAAF

AS I PEDALLED on my bike up to 460 Lancaster Squadron 'B' Flight office at the front of one of the large hangars at Binbrook on the morning of 13 February 1945, I could not know that I would be part of the BBC news the next morning! I was unaware that it was the 13th of the month, and would not worry about it in any case as I was not superstitious, at least not about that date, but as I rode up from the officers' mess I realised that the weather was fine and that meant that we would be operating over Germany that night. Having checked that all my crew were fit for flying at 9.15 I reported this to Squadron Leader Bob Henderson DFC, 'B' Flight Commander. All the aircraft captains, or 'skippers', were sitting round in the Flight Office talking shop or any interesting happenings, personal or otherwise, in which Bob Henderson joined every now and then when something concerning the Flight, operations, the performance or operation of the aircraft was being discussed.

At 10 o'clock Henderson went to the daily conference in the Squadron Commander's office. The three flight commanders, the navigation, bombing, wireless and gunnery leaders, were all

Dresden pictured on 22 March 1945. On 13/14 February 1945, Dresden was bombed by 796 Lancasters and nine Mosquitoes in two separate attacks; 1,478 tons of HE and 1,182 tons of incendiaries were dropped creating a firestorm similar to the one at Hamburg in July 1943. Another 311 bombers of the 8th Air Force followed with a raid the next day. (Geoff Liles)

present, and while they reported their state of readiness, details of the 'Operations for Tonight' came through from Bomber Command via Group and base headquarters. At lunch in the mess, Bob Henderson told me that we were flying that night in our usual kite, 'T-Tommy', and that, as briefing was not until later in the afternoon, we would have time to run-up the engines and check the aircraft. I contacted the crew in the sergeants' mess and told them to be at the locker room at 2pm to take our gear out to the aircraft, to run it up and check it over. There we collected our Mae Wests. Jack Peacock, the wireless operator, took the kit bag of our leather flying helmets, Peter Squires, the flight engineer, took his bag of tools, and on the way out to the aircraft we collected the eight .303 Browning machine-guns for the turrets.

After the crew bus had taken us to our aircraft dispersal area on the perimeter of the airfield, Peter and I gave it a thorough check over externally and internally, including starting up the four engines with a complete test in all phases of operation for each. When the starboard outer engine was run up, 'Curly', officially Flight Sergeant Tony Walker, tested his mid-upper gun turret for smooth, efficient rotation, elevation and depression of the guns, and counted into his intercom microphone as he did so, to test that the intercom was OK in all positions of the turret. Maurice Bellis, the bomb-aimer, tested the H_2S radar transmitter, as Max Spence, our navigator, was still at Navigation Section waiting for any 'gen' that may have come through concerning times for navigators' briefing, etc. When the port outer engine was being run up, Jock Gilhooly, the rear gunner, tested his turret in the same way as the mid-upper, while Jack tested the *Gee* radar receiver.

After a thorough check of the cockpit controls and instruments, compasses, transmitters and intercom at all points, we left the bomb doors open ready for loading from the bomb trolleys, and switched off the motors. Leaving our gear in the aircraft we returned to the Flight Office to learn that briefing was at 1800, with a meal at 1700, but the navigators' briefing was at 1645. This was unusual as the navigators were normally briefed after the meal, before the main briefing, so I thought that maybe it was a very long trip, or a very involved route. The fuel load was 2,154 gallons – maximum load.

While sitting in the anteroom of the mess after our meal, a few whispers were going around about our target for tonight. The Russians were pushing westwards in the southern sector of the Eastern Front, so we looked at the map in the newspapers and my tip was Dresden. I mentioned this to one of the navigators and he blurted out, 'Who told you?' The cat was out of the bag now, but naturally I kept it quiet, sitting there thinking of the route we might fly and the heavily defended areas along the way.

At about 5.40 I went over to the briefing room and drew the Aids Boxes, for use if we were shot down, and our flying rations. There was the usual moan when we had 'Empire' chocolate, as it was the worst grade of chocolate available, but it was remarkable how good it would taste after we left the target and settled down to the long tiring trip back. Then we would be trying to stay alert, when a natural winding down from the tension of the bombing run and general fatigue set in. We each received two small threepenny bars of chocolate, half a box of barley sugar sweets, or about six sweets each, and two packets of chewing gum. Our Aids Boxes contained concentrated foods, a compass, rubber water bottle, some water purifying tablets, and some benzedrine tablets, which bucked you up if you needed a little extra to make a break for it, etc.

We emptied our pockets, then put back only handkerchiefs, about £1 in money, an identity card and an Aids Box. The rest of the contents of our pockets – keys, letters, bus tickets and anything else – was placed in the bag that had contained our Aids Boxes with a label for each crew member. Then all individual bags went into the big crew bag and the intelligence clerks locked this in a safe. This ensured that if we were shot down, there was nothing to tell the Germans where we came from, so they would be unable to identify our squadron and its location. At least, this was the theory, but some of our Squadron who were shot down and interrogated, and later escaped back to England, said that the first thing the German interrogator said to them, after hearing that the crashed aircraft had our Squadron letters 'AK' on it, was, 'How is your commanding officer, *Hewgie* Edwards VC?'. (The Germans never could get their tongues around 'Hughie'!)

Maurie had his target map and we looked at the route on the big map at the front of the Briefing Room and the photos of the target area, its defences and known searchlight areas, as well as the heavily defended areas on or near our route. Times for sunrise, moonrise and moonset, as well as the phases of the moon, were all on the board. So were 'phase of attack' times, 'H' hour (the actual time of the start of the attack when the first phase commenced dropping their bombs), take-off time, total distance, bomb loads, and ETA back at base. On another board was all the signals gen: the Master Bomber's call sign, together with those of the Deputy Master Bomber, radio link, and the VHF radio channel on which to receive them. Shortly before briefing was due to start, Max came in with his navigator's bag crammed full with maps, charts and instruments, and in reply to my query of 'What do you think of it Max?', he made the dry wisecrack, 'I wish Joe Stalin would get an air force of his own or come and fight on the Western Front if he wants our help like this!'

The corniest crack of all was overheard from behind. 'I guess there won't be many Jerries left in Dresden after tonight!'

Similar wisecracks were being passed and general back-chat was being indulged in around the room while the crews all waited. Max told me that we were in the second phase, 'H+2' to H+4', and that we were on the lowest bombing height again! (There were four bombing heights, each 500 feet above the next, starting from our height and going up.) Then everyone was on their feet as the Squadron Commanding Officer entered, followed by the station CO and the base commander. We waited until they were all seated then we all sat down again, but there was no talking now, and the room was suddenly quiet as the Squadron CO, Squadron Leader 'Mick' Cowan, walked to the front and started the briefing proper.

'Your target tonight is Dresden. The attack is divided into three phases. Here are your aircraft letters, phase times and bombing heights. First phase on target from "H" to "H+2 minutes". *"B-Beer"*, Flight Lieutenant Marks.'

Flight Lieutenant Marks stood up. 'All correct sir!' (indicating that all his crew were present and ready to fly).

'18,000 feet.'

This checking of the crews and allocation of the heights was repeated until all the aircraft in the first phase had been detailed.

'Second Phase on target from "H+2" to "H+4".'

'"O-Oboe", Flying Officer Whitmarsh.'

'All correct sir!'

'19,000 feet.'

'"T-Tommy", Flying Officer Harrison.'

I was on my feet. 'All correct sir!'

'18,000 feet.'

As I sat down there was a whispered comment from my friend Doug Creeper, who was sitting behind me.

'Can't that kite of yours get any higher than that, Stan?'

I did not bother to reply. Our aircraft, *T-Tommy*, was certainly not new, had completed more than 30 raids on Germany, and was not the fastest in the Squadron, but as I had pointed out to my crew, 'Tommy' had developed a very good habit of coming back at the end of each trip.

After all the crews had been allocated their bombing heights, the CO called for the various specialist leaders to give their briefing.

The Flying Control Officer produced his blackboard. 'The runway for take-off is "22" (ie, the compass bearing was 220 degrees). "A" and "B" Flight aircraft will taxi round the perimeter track behind the control tower to this side of the runway, whilst "C" Flight aircraft will turn left from their dispersal areas and taxi to the other side of the runway. On a "green", taxi on to the runway and take off on the second "green". Watch the corner of the runway. It's soft on the grass there, so taxi slowly and keep on the asphalt!'

We had heard most of this at every briefing since we joined the Squadron, but there were some new crews and repetition did no harm considering the speed at which some clots taxied. A fully loaded Lanc had a maximum overall take-off weight of 84,000lb, so it took some distance to stop and this could lead to trouble when 23 aircraft had to taxi to the end of the runway, and even with 'C' Flight coming round from the other side, there would still be 15 of us following one another along that side.

'Foggo', as the Control Officer was affectionately known, then had his little joke. 'The runway for return will be the long one (2,000 yards), but I cannot tell you at this stage from which end we will be landing you!' This raised a small laugh, and we were thankful that the forecast was not for strong winds.

'The beacon will be flashing the usual "BK". Join the circuit at 2,000 feet and do not call up (for permission to land) until you are over the airfield! All three emergency airfields are fully serviceable.'

This was a very comforting thought in case we lost engines, brakes or the undercarriage would not lock down.

'When coming back over the East Coast, you must be at 6,000 feet, as the Dover belt of ack-ack guns are still in operation to guard against flying bombs. Do not exceed 250mph.' (This caused general laughter as the Lanc cruised at 180mph.)

'Burn only your navigation lights and *not* your downward recognition light! Any questions?'

As there were none, the CO called the 'Met bloke' who had charts drawn showing where the weather fronts were located and another giving cloud amounts, heights of bases and tops for the whole of the route to the target and home again. He gave us the gen on the weather to be expected during the whole flight. Cloud was expected from the French coast in to the target, hopefully with some breaks near the target, to give a clear view on the bombing run.

'Weather here "mainly clearing", with no cloud over England on return.' (I hoped he was right this time, for we did not want another cloud base of 150 feet after a long trip like this one, with everyone tired and 23 aircraft having to find their way down through it to our airfield. One of these recently was enough for a very long time to come!)

'Icing level 3,000 feet, with Icing Index "Moderate" to "High" in cloud. Any questions?'

'How about contrails?'

'Only above 20,000 feet, so they won't worry you! Anything else?'

The CO called on the Bombing Leader. 'All aircraft are carrying the same load, one 2,000lb, and 11 containers of incendiaries.' (Each container held 150 4lb incendiary bombs.)

'Bomb-aimers select and fuse bombs when the bomb line is crossed. After bombing check *immediately* that all bombs have gone, and if unable to get rid of any hang-ups there, do *not* jettison them on the track out of the target, but keep them until you cross the jettison area in The Wash on your return.' (Not long back some clot jettisoned a canister of incendiaries in the first leg of the route out of the target and gave every night fighter within 50 miles a clear signal of the route being flown from the target.)

'Set target pressure (estimated atmospheric pressure) as you enter the aircraft and use the Broadcast Bombing Wind, multiplied by 1.1.' (These settings were for the bombsight, with the 'multiplied by 1.1' to prevent any German radio interception operator from making any sense of our broadcast, and so be unable to substitute a false message.)

'The Signals Officer will give the time of this broadcast. All aircraft are carrying flashes. Captains, keep your aircraft straight and level while the red light is on and let us have some really good photos tonight.'

That sounded easy in the Briefing Room, but with other aircraft, slipstream turbulence, not to mention searchlights and ack-ack, it was not quite as simple as that over the target, and our camera had fogged up with condensation on our last three trips.

'Bomb-aimers, obtain your pro-formas and bomb-stations for your aircraft from the Bombing Section after the briefing. Any questions?'

The CO then called the Gunnery Leader. 'Just a word to all gunners! Enemy night fighters are particularly active in this area, so keep an even sharper watch in your search pattern than usual.' (Comforting news, I don't think, but then he was not likely to tell them that there were no fighters about and that they could go to sleep, was he?)

'You all know your search plans. Cover all the sky, all the time. Load your guns while you are still in your dispersal area and do not unload or leave your turret until you are back in your dispersal area. Jerry may try an intruder raid with night fighters again, and it could be tonight, so stay alert even when approaching base.'

The CO now called the Signals Leader. 'R/T call signs of the Master Bomber, Deputy Master Bomber and R/T link are "Snodgrass 1, 2 and 3". The Main Force bomber stream is "Press On". Channel "C" on VHF and "1196". Wireless operators listen out on your Marconi set on the wavelength shown on your "flimsies", which are available at the back of the briefing room. Remember, skippers, if you cannot get the Master Bomber on VHF, tell your WOP to select "1196" and press button "C". Broadcast wind velocities will be broadcast at 0015, 15 minutes before "H" hour, and will be the usual five-figure group preceded by "X". Aircraft on "Darkie" watch on the return trip will be *"G-George"*, Flying Officer Dowling; *"T-Tommy"*, Flying Officer Harrison; and "K2", Flying Officer Creeper. Do these captains know what you have to do?'

'Yes sir,' we replied.

'On the return journey listen out on Channel D for any aircraft in trouble or lost. Very well, that's all. Any questions?'

Now it was the turn of the Intelligence Officer, Squadron Leader Leatherdale, a First World War pilot, who was always worth hearing. 'Your target tonight is the old world city of Dresden. The attack is divided into two parts. 5 Group are opening the attack at 2230, 2 hours before your "H" hour, with a slightly different aiming point. You should see their fires still burning when you get there. Jerry is shifting all his government offices with staffs and records for the Eastern Front to Leipzig – raided by 4 Group last night – Dresden and Chemnitz. These three cities are roughly in a triangle. Dresden has not been attacked before as there were no targets there, but now, with the "Big City" being evacuated partly to Dresden and with large concentrations of troops and equipment passing through to the Russian Front, the city is crammed full and needs disorganising. As you can see from the target map, the city is fairly easy to identify, and, on your bombing run from approximately north to south, you have several good pin-points to help you check your run.

'Now for the route. Base to Reading, to Beachy Head, to the Rhine, keeping clear of Mainz to starboard, then on until you pass just slightly starboard of Frankfurt. Frankfurt has a large searchlight area and some ack-ack guns, so keep clear and stay on track. Turn slightly north, then run up as though heading for Leipzig, or when you pass to port of that, as though the "Big City" is your target. Just north of Leipzig, you head east and across through this searchlight belt, and you may have quite a few lights put up there, but there should be little or no flak. North of Dresden you have a turn of nearly 90 degrees, so watch out for other aircraft and so avoid collisions. You have a reasonably long run-up, and, after bombing, you hold the same course until you have completed this short leg, then turn south-west towards Stuttgart and Nuremburg. Keep on track and pass south of these two places or you may have trouble. Then you head west, cross the Rhine on the south-east corner of France, and keep clear of this area, where they are still active and getting too many of our aircraft. Cross the coast at Orfordness at 6,000 feet at least, then lose height across The Wash to base.

'The defences of Dresden are not considerable but they may have brought back mobile flak guns from the Eastern Front, so the flak may be moderate, but I doubt if you will find it heavy. *Oboe* Mosquitoes are marking the target at "H-2" with a single red TI. Then the flares will go down and Pathfinders will drop their TIs. Red and green TIs cascading together will be used only if they can positively identify the Aiming Point. If there is cloud over the target, 'blind-marker' crews will use sky-markers, which will be green flares dripping red stars. Your order of preference for bombing will be: 1. Master Bomber's instructions. 2. Red and green TIs. 3. Sky-markers on the exact heading of 175 degrees True at 165mph indicated airspeed. 4. H_2S run. Any questions?'

The CO now walked out to the map, summarised the briefing and told us the heights at which to fly on each leg of the route.

'Phase times for return: First Phase, 10 minutes before ETA. Second Phase, on ETA. Third Phase, 10 minutes after ETA. Use Aldis lamps for taxiing out and taxi slowly, even on return, when you will have some daylight! Position yourselves on the circuit on your return and we will get you down much more quickly. Any questions? Have you anything to say, sir? (This was addressed to the Station CO.)

'Yes. I just want to impress on you chaps the necessity to be very careful to keep a very keen look-out at all turning points and so avoid any risk of collisions!' (Didn't he think we knew that? About 200 aircraft all heading for the same point within 6 minutes at the most, with no lights on, was enough to make anyone 'keep a very keen look-out'! We could not guess that within two weeks he would be the one who would have a mid-air collision over France when the 'Met blokes' 'boobed' and we would have to climb through 15,000 feet of cloud. After the other aircraft crossed on top of him, wiping out all four of his propellers and his canopy, he dropped back down into the cloud and was the only survivor, losing the crew he had 'borrowed' for the trip!)

'All right chaps, that is all. Have a good trip and hit it really hard.'

We all filed out to the locker room to change into our flying clothes. Jack and Maurie collected their pro-formas and flimsies on the way. Jock and Curly started their long job of getting dressed in electrically heated flying suits, socks and gloves, while Peter and I changed too. Max had gone back to the Navigation Section. It was a cold night on the ground and the 'Met bloke' said that the temperature at 20,000 feet would be –25 degrees, which would not be as bad as the –45 degrees we had had once or twice, but it would still be quite cool so I put on my long wool and rayon underpants and long-sleeved singlet. As 'T-Tommy' was not a cold kite, I did not put on my big hip-length socks, but put on my usual pair of woollen socks and a pair of woollen 'knee-warmers', before getting back into my trousers, then my flying boots. My shirt collar was left undone and tie loosened but left on, in case of diversion to another airfield on return. It would be awkward to go around without a collar and tie. I left the front collar stud in place, as there was a small compass built into the back of it, for use if I had to try to get back from Germany on the ground. I put on my 'once white' silk scarf to keep the wool of the rollneck pullover away from my neck, as it got very irritating after a few hours rubbing on the stubble of whiskers, then a sleeveless pullover, and the big rolled-neck one that came down over my hips, eliminating any draught between trouser top and battledress when seated.

Then, with my torch and small-scale map with the whole route on it stuck into the top of my right boot and my flying rations down the left one, I was ready. I put 'George', my fur dog mascot, into my battle-jacket, then went to see how the rest of the crew were getting on. I carried my three pairs of gloves (silk, chamois leather and outer leather-zippered gauntlets) and found Peter ready and waiting for me, similarly attired, except for all the gloves. John needed practically nothing extra as he sat on top of the heater unit, while Maurie had a few extras similar to Peter, and also a big scarf, as it got draughty with his head down in the open-ended perspex 'bubble' while he was keeping a look-out for night fighters homing on to us from below.

Curly and Jock were in their electrically heated suits and socks, and now Curly pulled on the waterproof outer flying suit I had loaned him, as his issue buoyancy suit was too bulky to let him and it into his turret together. (No doubt it was Curly who was too bulky, but this arrangement 'suited' him very well.)

Jock put on his big rollneck sweater, a sheepskin vest (by courtesy of the Australian Comforts Fund through the hands of his skipper in the cause of another warm and happy gunner), then his battledress jacket. Long knee-hip socks and heated flying boots completed their outfits, with their heated gloves.

Max had not come in yet, but would follow later so we went to get the crew bus out to the aircraft in the dispersal area. Many crews had the same idea, and after finding the right bus in the darkness and telling the WAAF driver our aircraft letter, we piled into the back and waited until the thing was full to overflowing with other crews. We visited several other 'B' Flight dispersals and wished the other skippers well.

'Have a good trip. Doug!'

'Same to you, Stan. I bet I beat you home tonight!'

'So you ought to. You have a start on me. I'm in the second phase!'

We arrived at our dispersal and again Peter and I went right around the aircraft, thoroughly checking for leaks, looking at the tyres for pressure, and seeing that the aileron and rudder chocks had been removed. After checking inside again, we were ready to run-up, and when everything was in order we switched off and climbed out for a final smoke, spit, swear, yarn and a 'leak' before take-off. We had about half an hour to go, and the boys on the ground crew took the wheel chocks away, as I would not be running up again, while I went over to the ground crew hut to sign the aircraft maintenance Form 700. I just took a quick look to see that it had been signed up by the various maintenance types, then signed it as taking the aircraft in satisfactory condition. The main thing was that the Flight Sergeant in charge of the aircraft said it was OK. If he said it was OK, then you could bet your boots or your life that it was!

Max arrived, got in and sorted all his gear out, with his charts, etc, in their right

Lancasters 'M' and 'Q' of 15 Squadron. (Theo Boiten via M.J. Peto)

places. The 'Doc' came round with his 'wakey-wakey' tablets, and Peter took charge of them, except for two each for Jock and Curly. We very rarely used them, but it was handy to have them in case anyone felt really tired! They had an effect for about 4 hours and I wanted to know who took them, and how often. Everyone now had their Mae Wests on, and the rest of the crew had on their parachute harnesses, as their parachutes were stored separately near where they were stationed, while I sat on mine and strapped the harness on when I got into my seat at the controls. It was about 10 minutes before we were due to take off, so we all climbed aboard, with a final 'See you in the morning about 6 o'clock' to the ground crew, and their reply, 'Right – have a good trip, Skip!'

We sorted ourselves out in our various positions and started up the engines. We confirmed with Max that the Distant Reading compass was correct, then tested and left the oxygen turned on. With a 'thumbs up' to the ground staff by torchlight, we were signalled out on to the perimeter track, having the radio on in case of a change of runway, etc. Maurie shone his Aldis signalling lamp on the edge of the asphalt about 50 yards ahead, and with engines just idling we taxied slowly along. Peter kept a look-out on his side (starboard) and called the distance between the starboard wheel and the edge of the track, and kept an eye on the brake pressure gauge. Jock kept the lookout behind to ensure that no one taxied into us from the rear. The Lanc was heavy to taxi with a full load, but answered to the brakes and motors, although you could feel the weight on the corners. At the controls you felt that the air was its natural element and it 'suffered' this crawling along the ground, only because it was necessary so that it could become airborne again.

This taxiing took so long that we seemed to be taking an age to get to the take-off point, but then everything took so long on these operations. We were about three-quarters of the way to the start of the runway and about half-way down a slight slope beside the bomb dump when I noticed a truck coming round on the track from the airfield controller's caravan, and its lights suddenly disappeared behind something in front of us. I had Maurie shine his lamp directly ahead and there seemed to be a dark shape out there, probably an aircraft, but no lights were visible. Then suddenly torches and lights shone from everywhere out in front, with frantic signals for me to stop. As if I needed to be signalled to stop! I had a fully loaded aircraft, some unidentified obstacle was blocking the perimeter track in front, there was grass, probably soft, to port, and a drop down to the entry to the bomb dump to starboard – where did they think I was counting on going?

I turned on the landing light (which we never used for taxiing in case it got into the eyes of a pilot taking off, and we did not use it for landing either) and it revealed two aircraft ahead in an unfriendly embrace! Just what we did not want at this stage, a taxiing accident! Peter was already worrying me about the engines overheating, as we had been taxiing downwind most of the time since leaving the dispersal. I warned the crew that there had been a taxiing accident and we might be late taking off. Max was not amused as he would have to watch all his timing calculations very carefully now to see that we set course on time or, at the worst, try to make time on the way, which was not easy with a fully loaded aircraft. Jock was now shining his torch out the back to warn any aircraft behind us not to taxi into us – I knew that there were three following us.

After a few minutes, which seemed a very long time, we were signalled to turn off the perimeter track on to the grass in order to pass the obstruction. How I would have liked to break radio silence to warn the others of the obstruction and to get confirmation that the grass was firm enough to take our weight without getting us bogged. But we really had no alternative. I could not go forward, I could not turn to starboard and the track behind was blocked by other aircraft waiting for me to show them that it was safe to turn to port, then swing wide to starboard round the trouble ahead.

I became reconciled to having to risk getting bogged, and I was convinced that the airfield control types out there signalling to me to move did not really know if I would get bogged or not, but they also had no alternative to offer. Peter reminded me again that the motors were getting 'bloody hot, Skip!' I 'bit his head off' by telling him didn't I already know that and what did he want me to do about it? I couldn't turn into wind here and we had other problems at the moment!

'Tell me when the gauges get well into the "red" just before they blow off!'

'They are into the "red", Skip, and I thought you should know that we haven't got very long before we have real trouble with them!'

I realised that I was getting 'edgy', and as I started to turn off the track I said, 'Sorry, Pete, but I don't like this going on to the grass caper after old Foggo's warning about the soft grass up at the corner of the runway.'

'I don't like it either,' he replied, 'but it seems all right so far, Stan.'

We made our way slowly around the two aircraft to a clear section of perimeter track, and I got an enthusiastic 'thumbs up' signal in the light of a torch from a very relieved airfield control chap, who had solved one of his problems and, in a few minutes, would have only the taxiing accident to sort out. We had a clear run to the ACP's caravan, and now the pre-take-off drill was done, with each item repeated aloud, so that Peter could check them all. Maurice came up out of his position in the nose for the take-off and sat beside Max. I flicked my lights to the ACP to indicate that I was ready, and immediately he gave me the 'green' from his signalling lamp, as all the aircraft from the other side of the perimeter track had taken off while we were sorting out our problem.

We taxied out slowly, keeping as near to the end of the runway as possible in order to use every yard of it that we could for take-off. We rolled forward a short distance to straighten the tail wheel, then stopped again. The friction nut on the throttles was tightened firmly so that they would not work shut if my hands came off them for any reason. Gyro was set on 'zero' and 'uncaged', ie it was free to spin and to indicate any change in direction in the darkness up beyond the end of the two rows of runway lights.

I opened the throttles to the 'gate' (normal maximum power position) for the two inboard engines as Peter reported, 'Fuel pumps on. All set for take-off!'

The motors were not the only thing revved up, as the adrenalin was flowing and I always got a feeling of 'goose pimples' with the sound of the Merlins at full throttle. The ACP flashed another 'green' indicating that the runway was clear. I told the crew, 'Righto, here we go!'

With the throttles for the outboard engines neatly half opened, and Peter holding the inboard throttles open, I released the brakes and pushed the control column as far forward as I could to get the tail up as quickly as possible. The aircraft had been vibrating with all this power on and the wheels locked with the brakes. Now it surged forward in spite of the full load. I corrected any tendency of the aircraft to swing with the thrust of the engines by using the starboard throttles, and, when we had the tail up and were heading straight along the runway, I took the outboard throttles to the 'gate' also and called to Peter, 'Full power through the gate!' He pushed all four throttles past the gate to the 'Emergency' position and locked the friction as tight as he could get it so that the throttles could not creep back when he took his hands off them.

'Full power locked on!' he reported.

I felt the extra power as a thrust in my back. A quick glance at the gauges for revs and boost confirmed that all the engines were OK and, with both hands now on the control column, I concentrated on those two rows of lights between which we now raced. I held the aircraft down so that we were not bumped prematurely into the air as we went over a slight rise about three-quarters of the way down the runway, as this would have us in the air in a poor flying attitude and one in which it took longer to build up speed. As we came to the end of the runway I eased back on the control column and we climbed away.

'Undercart up!'

Peter repeated the order and selected 'Up'. The red warning lights came on, then went out as the undercarriage became fully retracted. We had reached 135mph, which was the minimum flying speed at which you could stay in the air with three engines and a full load. I always relaxed a little and breathed more easily once we had 135 on the clock. (Fourteen trips later I was very busy for a while at this stage, as I had to shut down the port outer engine due to a coolant leak at a height of 400 feet!) Now I asked Peter for 2,850 revs and +9 boost, which brought the throttles back to the normal 'full power' position, at a height of 400 feet.

'Flaps up in easy stages.'

Peter repeated and complied, raising them 5 degrees at a time, while I retrimmed the aircraft to accommodate these changes. A mistake made with this operation, with the flaps raised too quickly, would cause the aircraft to lose lift, then a stall and a crash could occur! With training and growing confidence between the two of us, I did not hesitate to call on Peter to operate the flaps on both take-off and landing, and, although he had had no training as a pilot, he now had a good understanding of changes in conditions, which required slightly different operation of the flaps. A crew that understood what each had to do and co-operated so that it was done most efficiently was on its way to being a good crew, and good crews had the best chance of surviving!

With the flaps up and a climbing speed of 145–150mph, I asked for '2,650rpm and +7 boost'. Peter repeated the details and brought the throttles back to our 'climbing power' setting. We climbed on a heading of 270 degrees, and shortly Max told me to turn back to base, then, when back over base, we set course on our first leg to Reading and we were on our way at last! Large bombing raids certainly took a long time to get under way and were not a case of 'sit in the dispersal hut and scramble when the siren sounded' as in the Battle of Britain days for fighter boys. 'Otto' and 'Karl', our two legendary German night fighter boys, who patrolled the northern and southern sectors of Germany, were probably sitting around waiting to hear where we were heading tonight!

At 10,000 feet we lowered the engine revs to save both fuel and the engines, and completed a check of the oxygen flowing to all of the crew, also checking the emergency intercom. On this run to Reading we kept a very sharp look-out for other aircraft as they climbed from the various airfields to join the main bomber stream, all heading for this first turning-point. I tested the autopilot, and after an initial 'kick-up' 'George' engaged, which I anticipated, settled down and functioned quite well. I then disengaged it and we continued our climb. At Reading we had the benefit of all the other aircraft still having their navigation lights on, but I still had to dive a little to avoid one clot who turned without checking that we were there!

We set course for Beachy Head, and that bacon and eggs for tea seemed well down now and I nibbled some chocolate, interrupting Peter's log-keeping to give him some. He answered with a 'thumbs up' 'thank you' before going back to his log and 'gallons per hour used', etc. I called to each of the crew in turn to ask how things were in each position and to see if the gunners' heated gear was working OK. All replied 'OK, no problems', and Maurie merely rolled over and went back to snoozing. His time for looking for fighters and later guiding us to the target had not yet arrived.

After altering course slightly at Beachy Head we were out over the Channel. Here I got to thinking that the tension, although under control, was too high. I thought of offering a prayer for a safe return and wondered whether or not I might be a good leader and set an example to my crew. I was having trouble maintaining our required rate of climb, so I asked Peter for a slight increase of 50rpm, which meant that he had to re-synchronise the four engines. If this was not done correctly, the sound of the engines developed a 'beat', which seemed to go right through your head after a few minutes, and the best way of doing this was to look along the line of the two propellers on each side. The 'shadows' of the props appeared to move when they were out of 'sync' and remained practically still when the engines were synchronised to the same rpm. A small thing really, and I suppose I should not have let it get to me, but in my book it was just 'tidy' flying and one less thing to get on the nerves of skipper and crew.

I switched off the external lighting master switch and the boys checked that the lights were all out. (Some chaps went over Germany with their lights on, and a few of them even returned!) We were climbing again and Jock now had on his 'village inn', the automatic gun-laying turret. After he had adjusted the settings it worked well, giving warning 'beeps' on the intercom when another aircraft came within range of its radar scanning beam. The 'beeps' got louder and more frequent as the other aircraft came closer, building up the tension until Jock identified it through the small infra-red telescope mounted near his gunsight. All our aircraft were fitted with two infra-red flashing lights in the nose and these were visible in the rear gunner's telescope. The rate of exchange in the frequency of the 'beeps' is what I listened for, and when there was little or no change it usually meant that another Lanc had drifted across our track and Jock would come through with 'It's OK, Skip, it's one of ours'.

Maurie was now lying on his stomach with his head down in the perspex bubble, keeping a look-out down below. Max gave me an ETA for the next turning-point, then muttered some suitable comments about the Germans and the radar jamming in particular, as his *Gee* set had just become unusable because of the jamming signals obscuring everything else on the screen.

I asked him about the H$_2$S airborne radar. 'How is your "Y-set"?'

'OK so far,' he replied, and on we flew.

Five minutes later Max was back on the intercom and very annoyed! The 'Y-set' had packed up now, and this was serious. We were over cloud, unable to see anything on the ground, and had no means of establishing our exact position, with a long way to go to the target and back again, as well as keeping clear of those heavily defended areas mentioned at briefing.

Jack had just received the first Broadcast Wind which he gave to Max, who commented, 'I hope they're accurate tonight because we haven't got anything else.'

He was not the only one who had that hope. I quietly thought to myself what a big place Germany was to be flying over with no navigational gear, except a compass, a watch, and a Broadcast Wind! It would be bad enough after the target, as I always said that we could get home by flying 'west with a bit of north in it', but the route going in was going to be tricky, if those Broadcast Winds were not accurate or if we missed them when they were broadcast.

'Jack,' I said, 'you will be careful not to miss those Broadcast Winds won't you?'

'That's for sure, Skip, you can count on it!'

I quietly thought to myself, 'Yes, I knew I could', and it was that feeling of complete confidence in each other, which had grown up through our training together, that was so important now. As I thought about it I realised that I had the same confidence in the other crews in the Squadron and in the other squadrons, who would be sending back their calculated details of the wind, as we had done on other trips, so of course the Broadcast Winds would be accurate! That is what made Bomber Command the force that it was!

'How's the heat tonight, Stan?' Jack was doing his usual thorough check of all his responsibilities, as well as making sure of receiving the Broadcast Winds, and, I suspected at the time, was just making sure the Skipper was not brooding on the loss of the 'Y-set'.

'OK, thanks, Jack!'

'All right with you, Max?' he asked, but Max was not really paying attention to the heating or anything else, except his navigational problems after the failure of his equipment.

'It's fine, but if you have any spare heat you could try to unfreeze that scanner,' he replied.

'No hope of that, I'm afraid,' said Jack.

'Aye, what about the poor bloody frozen gunners?' Jock had joined in the talk. 'It's all right for you lot with all your mod cons. Curly and I have got minus 23 degrees back here!'

'Isn't your electrical heating working, Jock?'

'Aye, it is, Skipper, but it's still bloody cold!'

'Don't let your turret freeze up will you?' (I realised that it was quite a while since I had felt the slight swing of the nose of the aircraft, caused by the rear turret being turned from one side to the other and then back again to check free movement.) Curly joined in. 'No chance of that, Stan!'

'Good, Curly,' I replied, smiling to myself at the immediate 'banding together' of the two gunners against any implied criticism. A minute or two later I felt the nose swing slightly one way then the other as Jock checked his turret and I had another quiet smile to myself.

We were lucky as we approached ETA Frankfurt as there was a break in the cloud ahead to port, and we could see the searchlights. Max was pleased, as this put us bang on track, so we turned on ETA alongside Frankfurt. So far, so good, and all was well!

Maurie said, 'I think we're going into those lights!'

They always looked closer than they really were, particularly from his position out front. I did not know if he thought that I would fly straight into a group of searchlights, which were not defending our target, or if he was just getting a little 'on edge'. We were right on track with not too much further to go, and this was the turning-point that I was worried about when we lost the 'Y-set', as being only slightly off course would have put us right over the defences of Frankfurt.

'Nice work, Max! We hit that turning-point right on the nose!'

'Good, Stan. Those winds must be spot on, thank heavens!'

'Blast the idiot!' Some clot had jettisoned his load of incendiaries. They were strung out, burning on the ground, marking our new course for every night fighter this side of Stuttgart to see! Thank heavens the clouds were moving across again so that they were being screened. Occasionally, another aircraft was seen near us and identified as friendly, either visually or by Jock through his infra-red telescope.

Max now wanted a slight increase in our speed to make our next turning-point on time, so Peter had to re-synchronise the engines, while still keeping a look-out on the starboard side. Occasionally we 'hit' the slipstream of another aircraft, and this threw us around, but it was a good sign as it meant that someone else was flying our course, and we hoped that his navigation equipment was functioning correctly so he was right on track. It also meant that we were not the only aircraft on this area for the German radar-predicted flak guns to concentrate on, if there was a unit near here.

Even when experienced many times, the effect of 'hitting' the slipstream of a four-engined aircraft still caused the old heart to thump a bit, for it was as though some giant hand had taken hold of the aircraft and twisted it one way and up or down at the

Ju 88G-6B 4R+AR of 7./NJG2, equipped with SN-2, Naxos and Flensburg AI radar. (Collection Luis van Kampen via Theo Boiten)

Lancaster II DS771 in flight.

same time! There was nothing you could do about it, except to push the control column forward and apply full opposite 'bank' to avoid a possible stall and to level the wings. After a matter of a few seconds that felt like hours, the aircraft would dive through the area of affected air and return to normal 'feel' and control again.

As we sat there flying steadily on towards the target, I did not realise that the tension was gradually mounting until something very simple annoyed me, then I had a quiet talk to myself. 'Relax, you silly goat. Things are under control!' The clip for the oxygen tube to my face mask had slipped off the strap of my parachute harness, so that the whole length of the tube was dangling from the face mask and was dragging it whenever I turned my head, which was nearly constantly at this stage of the trip. I had got annoyed at the fool of a way of securing it, as it would not stay in place, but at the next try it remained fixed and all thoughts of animosity towards it and its inventor died without trace.

I checked through the crew again with some casual remark to each of them, and judged by their replies whether their oxygen supply was OK and for any signs that they were tensing up.

'Any icicles out the back, Jock?'

'No, not yet, Stan, but it's none too warm, ye know!'

He was all right and wide awake. 'How are things on top Curly? Can you see anything?'

'No. Everything is quiet up here, Stan. Where are we now?' (Evidently my turn for a test!)

'Just running north of Leipzig, Curl.'

'Leipzig. OK.'

'Anything down there, Maurie?'

'Yes. A heck of a lot of cloud, but nothing else!'

'What petrol are we using at this rate, Peter?'

'About 185 per hour, Stan. I'll check on my tables if you like.'

'No, that's OK, thanks. Is that a chink of light through the curtain there?'

'Whereabouts, Stan?'

Instantly, Peter was searching the blackout curtain between us and the navigator's area for any sign of light. 'It's all right, Pete, it's only a reflection from the perspex in your bubble.' (This 'bubble' in the side window on the starboard side allowed Peter to look down and it had caught some stray light from outside and reflected it into our area.)

'What is our ETA at this last turning-point, Max?'

After a while Max replied, 'Well, it's hard to say as I'm only running on DR (Dead Reckoning) based on Broadcast Winds. I hope they're somewhere near accurate!'

'How do you think they are?'

'Not too bad so far, I think, Stan. Our ETA is 2357.'

'How does that make us for time?'

'About a minute late, so step it up a little, if you can.'

'OK, Max, I'll try 170, but this kite is getting old now.'

'Righto, Stan, but we need a bit more speed.'

'2,350 revs, thanks, Peter.'

'2,350. Right, Stan.'

The revs were increased and I kept checking the airspeed to see if I could coax that extra 5mph. In a newer aircraft I would have just put the nose down for 200 to 300 feet, then level out when we had 170 and slowly pick up the height again. 'Tommy' was reluctant to go much over 17,000 feet, and it would be a hard job to pick up the height that we had lost. After a while, with no increase in speed visible, I asked Peter for 2,400 revs and eased the nose forward slightly to gain that extra speed. As the speed increased I carefully kept it and coaxed 'Tommy' back up again to approximately 17,500 feet. (The Lanc was very hard to accelerate by use of engines alone; anything up to 300 revs increase had to be used to get the extra speed, but then only 50 revs over the original was needed to hold it, so the easiest way to increase revs by the amount necessary to the hold speed, and actually gain that speed, was by losing height gently followed by slowly regaining the lost altitude.)

'You can put the bomb sight on now, Maurie!'

'OK, Stan. Is "George" right out?'

'Yes, and has been for over an hour!' (Bombsight gyros needed time to settle, and it was best to give them about half an hour.) Up ahead we could now see the bright patch on the clouds caused by a searchlight belt and we were thankful that the cloud was there shielding us. There was nothing to do but search the sky for fighters and fly on and continue to search.

'What's that over there on the port bow?'

'Yes, there was something black there!'

I searched for it by looking lightly away from where I thought it was, then I saw that it was another aircraft, which looked like a Lanc. 'Curly, can you see that aircraft on the port bow, slightly up?'

After a short wait, 'Yes, it's another Lanc I think, Stan.'

The aircraft did not close in or move away, and gradually I could make out the twin fins and rudders and the four Merlins. He was close enough, but he was above us and headed our way! On we flew and I started to look for the time to turn at the last turning-point before the target.

'There are some fighters about, Stan, I think,' said Jock. 'I've just seen two of their flares out here behind us (small flares were used by the night fighters to indicate our route). Try looking right back past the port rudder fin. I can just see the two tiny orbs of red light dropping slowly.'

'Yes, you're right, Jock. Keep your eyes open for them now, the pair of you.'

'Aye, I will! Jock replied in his broad Scots accent.

'Yes, right,' said Curly, and our nervous system got another notch tighter.

'How's our ETA, Max?'

'Two minutes to run, but we're still a bit late, so we have to turn early and "cut the corner", OK?'

'Yes, OK, Max. What is the next course?'

'179, Stan – I'll tell you when to turn.'

'179! Right, Max.' I resumed searching from side to side and back again, and repeated this again and again and again, as there were likely to be other aircraft 'making good' this turning-point after some slight variation from their proper track, while others might be going to 'cut the corner' earlier than we were, and could be coming across us.

'All right, start turning now, Stan.'

'Turning on to 179! Thanks!' Making sure it was clear, we came round to 179. 'Steering 179 now, Max.'

'OK, Stan. I think we should just about be right on time at this speed! Twenty-one minutes to run to the target.'

'Twenty-one! OK.'

As I looked ahead I saw a glow in the distance and realised that it was the glow of the fires started by the earlier attack by 5 Group! After all this flying we were at last getting near the target!

'OK Max, I can see it ahead and there is a break in the clouds so should get a good run.'

Rather agitated, Max asked, 'How far is it ahead?'

'Oh, quite some distance yet – about 15–20 minutes I would guess.'

'Oh, righto. I thought you meant we were nearly there and that I had boobed and got us here too early!'

'Not likely with you worrying over our times all the way, Max!

This course will put us bang on target too! Turn on the VHF will you, Jack?'

'She's on, Skipper.'

'OK, thanks.' I selected channel C and after a few seconds the background noise told us that the set had warmed up and I left it turned on waiting for the Master Bomber to start broadcasting. A few more fighter flares were seen, so they knew where we were and everyone was now very wide awake and searching the sky intently. Jack received the Bombing Wind and, after Max converted it, passed it to Maurie.

'3-1-5, 25. Right, thanks, Max.'

Maurie set it into his bombsight. We were tracking nicely towards the target and suddenly a voice came on the headphones. 'Snodgrass 1 to Snodgrass 2. Here is a time check. In 20 seconds it will be 0015. 10 . . . 5, 4, 3, 2, 1. Now! Over.'

'Snodgrass 2 to Snodgrass 1. Loud and clear. Out!'

It was all so very British! Here we were running into the target in the heart of Germany after 4½ hours flying with no navigational aids, and wondering how we were going to make it, and now, when we were at last in sight of the target, we were being greeted by a couple of typically English chaps with very English call signs, quietly checking that they had got the time right, down to the last second! Our reception was all right, so we did not have to worry about the other sets. The illuminating flares were going down now and they hung in the sky in rows like gigantic yellow lanterns. More and more of them dropped and the whole sky in that area was lit up.

'Just hold it steady about there, Skip, and we should be right on it.'

'OK, Maurie!'

'Curly and Jack, keep that search going. They're dropping more fighter flares. Are you in the astrodome Jack?'

'In the astrodome, Skipper!'

'Aye, I've got my eyes wide open, Skip'.

'She's right, mate,' replied Curly.

The TIs were being dropped now and Maurie was satisfied with our track towards the target. 'Yes, there go the TIs, Skipper. We're right on track!'

'How are we for time, Max?'

'Three and a half minutes to run.'

'Fair enough!'

The target was now obscured from my view, as it had passed under the line of the nose of the aircraft. Peter was busy pushing 'Window' down the 'chute to confuse the German radar operators.

Again a voice came loudly out of nowhere. 'Snodgrass 1 to Press On. Bomb on the red and green TIs. Bomb on the red and green TIs. Out.' This was repeated by the R/T link.

'The red and greens. OK, Skip,' said Maurie. 'Left! Left! Steady!' he chanted, and I repeated and executed these instructions as he alone now guided the aircraft to the bomb release point.

'Steady!'

I replied 'Steady' as I tried to keep the aircraft straight and level while still watching out for other aircraft near us on our level, directly above and slightly ahead. The greatest danger over the target was not from searchlights, flak or fighters (who usually stayed clear of the area immediately over the target to give the flak gunners an 'open go'), but collisions or being bombed by an aircraft above us. I was watching another Lanc on my side that was slowly crossing our course slightly above us, when Peter pointed out one on his side also. I watched these two as we continued our run-in.

'Left! Left! Steady!' These were repeated and executed, and Maurie's chant became, 'Steady! Steady! Steady!' The aircraft on the starboard side had crossed OK and was now just clear of us, but the one on the port side was going to be a nuisance! There were not many searchlights, and little flak, thank goodness! A very bright searchlight came very close, but at the last moment before catching us it swung away. There was no more noise than usual while the sounds of bombs exploding, as heard in Hollywood movies, proved that the producer had never been here! Exploding flak was usually seen, but was only heard when it was very close, and if you could smell the cordite as well it was time for a 'damage report'!

'Steady! Steady! Left! Left! Steady!' chanted Maurie, and I complied. 'That aircraft is getting closer!'

We might just make it as the release point must be close.

'Steady! Bomb bay doors open!' I repeated and executed.

'Snodgrass 1 to Press On! Bomb the centre of the red and green TIs. Bomb the centre of the red and green TIs. Out.'

'Did you get that, Maurie?' I switched off the VHF to cut out the R/T link's voice, which might have interfered with Maurie's instructions.

'Yes. Centre of red and greens,' Maurie replied quickly.

'Steady! Steady! *Steady!*'

I felt a slight bump, like someone kicking the wooden seat of a chair you are sitting in.

'Cookie gone! Incendiaries going,' reported Maurie.

The red camera light started to blink in front of me but I was more concerned with the aircraft that was coming from the port side and was now nearly above us. As his bomb bay doors were open, I turned away to starboard.

'Sorry Maurie!' I said. 'Another photo gone west, but he nearly bombed us!'

'OK, Skip, take it away.'

We had bombed at 18,000 feet, having lost our extra 500 feet running in from the last turning-point. As we straightened up again I brought the rev levers up until we had 2,500 and, with nose down, we headed out of the target with 220 on the clock.

'179 is the course, Skip', Max came through, as though we were just leaving a practice bombing range.

'OK, Max. Are things quiet up there with you, Curly?'

'Yes, OK, Skip, but I think there are fighters about as there's a lane in these searchlights.'

'OK. Keep that search going well.'

'*Corkscrew port, go!*'

I heard the turret machine-guns open up as Jock's call came through. With a warning of 'Down port!', I threw everything into the corner, full port bank, full port rudder, and control column forward. We heeled over and dived to port, and as the speed built up we came out of it as I dragged back on the control column, calling to the gunners 'Changing – up port!' With the build-up in speed we went up like a lift. Before we lost all this speed I called 'Changing – up starboard!' Then, as we lost speed, 'Changing – down starboard!' As we started to dive again, Jock called, 'Resume course, go! It's OK, Skip, he passed us by, but he's disappeared up in the starboard beam so keep your eyes open for him, Curly.'

A Lancaster explodes in mid-air after taking a direct hit in the bomb bay. (via Keith Percival-Barker)

'Starboard beam up. OK, Jock.'

We settled down again on our course, with everyone alert and searching intently.

'Next course is 2-1-5, Stan.'

'OK, turning on to 2-1-5.'

'All clear starboard, Stan,' reported Peter. Aircraft that were visible in the glare over the target could not be seen now, but we did see one or two that turned close to us. We settled on to the new course and, after a few minutes, I looked back to starboard and saw Dresden burning. While I watched, I saw a fire start in the air, and there, against the target, appeared the perfect miniature outline of a Lanc. The port wing burned furiously, and, after flying level for a few seconds, the aircraft heeled over and dived down as the wing fell off. We were too far away to see if any 'chutes came out. 'One of our aircraft is missing.' Max logged the time, height and position.

'Are you busy Max?'

'No, not for the moment.'

'Well, you wanted to see a target.'

'Righto, Stan.'

Max came out from behind his curtain and asked, 'Where?'

I pointed to the rear over my left shoulder where the yellow of the flares, the white of the incendiaries burning on the ground, the searchlights and the pin-point of light in the sky (from the flak at the stragglers from 'last phase') could clearly be seen. Clouds of smoke rose thousands of feet into the air. With the last of the red and green TIs, it completed a technicolour nightmare of Hell.

'Aagh! I never want to see that again,' said Max. 'I'll go back to my charts. You can keep that.'

But he stayed a bit longer to look hard at the scene, before disappearing back behind his curtain. I suppose it was an awful shock to suddenly be confronted with such a

A Lancaster over the burning pyre. (via Keith Percival-Barker)

sight, and I realised that the rest of us had become used to this type of scene, while Max had spent his time on each trip at his charts without knowing what was actually happening outside the aircraft and what it looked like. I never did find out what his thoughts about it really were, but I suspected that he actually was a very sensitive type, who disliked being suddenly confronted with such a scene of destruction. I never knew anyone who really liked the job, but I suppose there were some who did.

'It looks like we've done our job,' remarked Peter.

'Yes,' I replied. 'I don't think we'll have to come back again . . . All right, now, let's see that none of those fighters jump us on the way home. Are you going down in your bubble, Maurie?'

'Yes Stan. I'll give you a call when I want a rest from flying upside down.' (When he did I rolled the aircraft over until Curly could see down under us and called, 'All clear, starboard', then I rolled it over on to the other wing-tip and waited for his call, 'All clear, port'.)

'We're on the job too, Stan, you can count on it,' said Jock.

'That's right, Stan,' joined in Curly.

'Good, I'm glad to hear it. How long to our next turning-point, Max?'

'Not for quite a while yet, Stan. This is a long leg and I'll let you know in good time.'

'Right, Max.'

I noted that, as usually happened, the crew tended to be informal in speaking to me, except during take-off and landing, and when we were near the target area, when it became 'skipper' or 'Skip'. I assumed this was an unconscious recognition of their reliance on me, but that reliance was really on each other, so perhaps it was only a matter of naturally looking for a leader in times of stress and danger.

'Can I have the "1196" in for our "Darkie" watch please, Jack.'

'Yes. It's on now, Stan.'

'Thanks.'

I thought back on the attack and the roles of the various participants, from the Master Bomber who often marked the Aiming Point from only 3,000 feet, to the marker crews from the Pathfinder Force, to the Flare Force aircraft and to the Main Force, a very complex machine of destruction. The Marker crews and Flare Force aircraft dropped their TIs and flares over the target, then turned away, flying around and rejoining the stream of Main Force aircraft coming into the target, then dropping their bombs on their second run through the target. Once through the target was enough for me, but before not too many more trips we were selected as a Flare Force crew, finally joining the Pathfinders for the rest of the war.

We flew on and on, making the next turning-point and turning more westerly, now that we were past Nuremburg. Presently I saw a patch of light in the sky to port and wondered what searchlights they were, until it dawned on me that they were the lights on the shores of Lake Constance, Switzerland! I wondered what they thought of the war, apart from the money they were making. Being neutral certainly paid off, when you could be the world's clearing house! I told Max and he was quite satisfied. We were slightly off track to the south, but we were clear of Stuttgart so we waited until we were very close to the light before altering course to nearly due west, along the Swiss border towards France.

I was tired and hungry, which was no wonder, as we had now been in the air over 9 hours. My last piece of chocolate tasted very good, poor quality or not, and a cup of sergeants' mess tea from Peter's thermos tasted wonderful and helped get the eyes open again. I had 'George' doing the work now, but had my hand on the lever to disengage the autopilot the moment anything happened, so there was only a partial relaxation. Across the Rhine now, we altered course for England, losing height as we went so that our airspeed built up to 200 on the clock. If the Jerry fighters wanted us they would have to find us and catch us. My thoughts wandered. Dresden had certainly copped it, but hang this supporting 'Joe Stalin' and his boys – it was just too damn far. Helping Monty and his merry men was much more 'the shot' that appealed now. Peter broke into my wandering thoughts to ask if I had changed the supercharger control down to 'medium' as we had descended into that range. He was happy to know that I had and it was good to know that he was still right on the job, although like all of us he was now very tired.

Half-way across France Max told me that his *Gee* set was working again. 'We are only 15 miles off track, Stan, but you had better alter 30 degrees to starboard to avoid that possible trouble spot they mentioned at briefing.'

'Righto, Max. Altering 30 degrees to port. Now.' (Trouble spot? Briefing? That all seemed days ago. I seemed to have been sitting in this seat for a week.) Only 15 miles off, after more than 4 hours' navigating back from the target by dead reckoning and the Broadcast Winds, was a terrific effort and I congratulated Max, who merely uttered that 'George', our dog mascot, must have really been looking after us.

The French coast was crossed, then the Channel, through the fence of lights at Orfordness, navigation lights 'on' and nose down for base. As we approached I listened out and heard the various boys calling up as they reached home, and I checked out who had arrived back safely. Our beacon flashing 'BK' was a very welcome sight. There was no 'story book' or 'Yankee film' welcome, just '"Tommy", 1,500 feet' from the control tower. I knew that my call for permission to land had been heard in the debriefing room, where we would be posted up on the 'Returned' board.

It all happened very quickly now, and after more than 9^{1}/$_{2}$ hours in the air I shook myself wide awake to make sure that nothing could go wrong in the last few minutes. We had permission to join the circuit. Maurie was out of the nose. I called 'Downwind' and immediately Doug called me, 'Keep in close, Stan, I'm right behind you.'

'Right, Doug,' I replied in strictly non-RAF R/T procedure.

I flew a tight circuit on the ring of lights surrounding the circuit area, cut in close at the 'funnel' leading to the start of the runway, and wasted no time. Doug Creeper would have swung a little wider and turned into the funnel a little later than usual to give me time to get clear of the landing area so that he would not have to go around again. After nearly 10 hours in the air, having to waste time by flying round the circuit again was something no one wanted, particularly when we landed 23 aircraft in less than 33 minutes.

'"Tommy". Funnels!'

'"Tommy". Pancake!'

'"Tommy". Pancaking. Out. Full flaps. 2,850 revs.'

Peter complied. I managed to grease it on and Jock gave his greatest praise – complete silence! As soon as I touched down, Control called, 'Keep rolling, "Tommy".'

'"Tommy" rolling,' I replied, with a quiet smile to myself. I was not likely to stop in front of my mate and have him land on me, when we had just worked things so that we could both get down quickly. I suppose our talking between ourselves was not heard officially, but they 'officially' warned the aircraft that had just landed that another was landing immediately behind. At that time of the morning it was all a bit much for me.

We arrived back at our dispersal and were greeted by the ground crew who were pleased to hear that we had no trouble with the aircraft and that there was no damage to it that we knew of. In the crew bus going back to the crew room we greeted other crews, talking tiredly about the trip and any trouble they may have had. Jack dumped his gear quickly and hurried to the debriefing room to put our name on the board, and so reserve our place in the queue of crews waiting to be debriefed. The rest of us arrived shortly afterwards. By way of an informal report, the Squadron Commander asked me, 'How was it, Stan? Much flak, any damage, good run to the target?'

'A pretty quiet trip, thanks, sir,' I replied. 'Only light flak and a few fighters about, but I don't think we have any damage.'

'Good – it was a long one and you will be looking for bed. Tell your crew to turn in straight away too.'

'Right. Thanks, sir, I will.'

As I turned away I thought that there was something odd about that last remark, but then one of the other skippers spoke to me and the thought went out of my head. As I headed for a cup of tea, the Doc was there quietly running his eye over each of us without any fuss.

'How was it?' he asked.

'Not bad, Doc, but it was a long one. Nine hours 45 in the air.'

'Yes, a good night's sleep is what you need. Do you want anything?'

'No thanks, Doc. I have no trouble. I'm off to sleep as soon as my head hits the pillow. I just have to stay awake while "Bags of Flak" rambles on over there,' indicating a table at which one of the crews was being interrogated by the WAAF Intelligence Officer, known to all as 'Bags of Flak', due to her habit, during the interview with returning crews, of asking, 'How was the target area? Bags of flak?'

The Doc smiled, as he was in on all the jokes and sayings round the Squadron, and knew what ops were like, having closed the rear door of the Flight Commander's aircraft five times, from the *inside*. 'That's good. If there is anything when you wake up, just drop over and see me.'

The tea and biscuits tasted wonderful and Jock and Curly were arguing as usual over whose turn it was to have the tot of rum that I didn't drink, as well as the tot each had already had. Jock knew very well that it was Curly's turn, but this was a harmless way to 'unwind' a bit after the trip, and the rest of us joined in with suitable comments, while silently cursing 'Bags of Flak' for taking so long with each crew. At last it was our turn.

'What time did you bomb? What did you have in your bombsight?' she asked. (I would never forget her look of dismay and then disbelief when later, after a daylight raid on Cologne, with an Aiming Point near the cathedral, Maurie, who was bored stiff with this same question time after time, decided to liven things up by replying 'Two nuns and a priest!')

'Was there much flak?' (Someone must have told of her of her nickname') 'What did you think of the raid?'

'We had a quiet trip,' I replied. 'A very concentrated attack. One aircraft seen shot down shortly after we left the target.'

'Anything else?'

'No, I think that's the lot, thanks.' I signed the report and at last was on my way to breakfast. While eating my bacon and eggs I vaguely heard the CO say that he thought we might be on again that night, but I was too tired to care or connect. I was only interested in a good long sleep. I said 'Cheerio, see you later' to the others in the mess. No one was missing from the trip so we were all happy. I fell into bed at 7.45am but little did I know that I would be woken at 12.45 to be told that we were on the Battle Order for that night! After a late lunch, the whole routine, just complete, would be repeated and, after another trip, of 9 hours 20 minutes in the air to Chemnitz, I would fall into bed tomorrow morning, exhausted and with only one assurance that there was some limit to how often we were expected to be able to continue these operations. The Doc would tell me to get 'a good, long sleep', and when I replied, 'Just like yesterday Doc?', he would quietly say, 'No – if they try to put any of you who have flown these last two trips on a Battle Order for tonight, I will declare you "medically unfit".'

Thank God for the Doc!

22: Nearly a nasty accident (3)
Flight Sergeant Ken Westrope

I DIDN'T HEAR IT. I felt it, an almighty thump, and our Liberator just fell out of the sky. We were on the bombing run. We had just dropped our bombs and got the photo. The intercom and hydraulics had all gone. The only thing to do was to get out of the turret, unplug the intercom and oxygen, open the doors, get out, and put your parachute

1,000lb bombs from R-Roger, *a 70 Squadron Liberator, are just about to hit 'V-Victor' of 37 Squadron, 205 Group. (Ken Westrope via Steve Snelling)*

V-Victor heads for home with a smoking port inner on 16 March 1945 after being hit by a 1,000lb bomb over the target. (Ken Westrope via Steve Snelling)

on. It was 16 March 1945 and our target was the Monfalcone shipyards in northern Italy. Our bomb load was six 1,000lb and six 500lb, fairly general for all aircraft on these raids. I was 25 years old and the rear gunner on *V-Victor* in 37 Squadron, 205 Group, the only RAF heavy bomber group in the Middle East, based at Tortorella airfield near Foggia. This was my 20th or 21st operation. We flew 'Wells' up to Christmas 1944 in 37 Squadron and changed over to 'Libs' in January 1945.

Our Liberator had plunged 5–6,000 feet. It just dropped down, and I thought 'This is it'. I just didn't know what had happened. We had experienced nothing like this. We had had one or two things happen because of duff engines. During a training flight on Wellingtons we had been forced to land at Beirut airport on a single engine, but we didn't suffer any damage from enemy action. Flak had been the main threat, more than fighters. We had done all sorts of trips, including supply dropping to Tito's troops and dropping mines outside the northern Italian ports.

I hadn't given such dangers as bombs hitting us a thought. There had been the odd problem on supply drops when parachutes came down through when some aircraft were flying higher, but you were able to see and avoid them. It wasn't in our minds. We didn't realise or think it could have happened. As far as I could gather, I had been watching this aircraft, *R-Roger*, a 70 Squadron Liberator, flying more or less parallel and coming up on our port side. I got in touch with our mid-upper gunner and told him to watch it.

'OK', he said, then I lost sight of him.

Then he came alongside and suddenly must have turned left and come straight over the top of us. When bombs drop, they do not just drop straight down. They go forward.

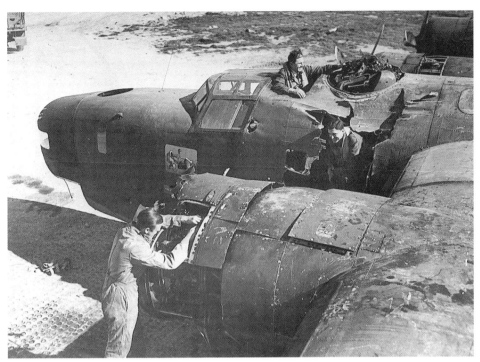

A shattered V-Victor *back safely at Tortorella shows what a miraculous escape Wally Lewis, the mid-upper gunner, had. Cliff Hurst, the wireless operator, got the worst of it.* (Ken Westrope via Steve Snelling)

By the time I could get out of the turret, unplug and open the doors, Squadron Leader Lionel Saxby, the skipper, had *V-Victor* under control. Then eventually we got on a level course again. I went forward and I saw this big hole in the aircraft. It was a bit shaky. The hole was about 6 foot by 4 foot. The bomb, or maybe there were two bombs, had fallen on the mid-upper turret. Wally Lewis was jammed in his seat. I don't know if he was unconscious; he was a bit bruised, but miraculously not badly hurt. Cliff Hurst, the wireless operator, got the worst of it. He was sitting on the starboard side with his back to the hole. Oil and steam were pouring out of the port inner but there was no fire in the engine. However, the prop was completely knocked off.

Pieces of the engine had entered the wireless operator's back. He was a tent-mate of mine. At first we laid him on the flight deck. He was unconscious for some time, then he came to. I suppose he must have felt the pain, but there was no question of being able to do anything about it. You could not give him morphia. That would have knocked him out, and he never asked for it. His set, everything, was out of order, and even though he was wounded, he managed to repair the wireless and get a message through to base to tell them what had happened. I held his parachute harness away from his back so it did not chafe on him.

It was a bit of a struggle on the flight back and obviously we slowed down. Lionel Saxby was a very experienced skipper. We just sat hunched up on the flight deck so that if anything happened we could all get out together, or attempt to get out, as there was no intercom to warn us when to go. You could not hear anything. It had to be by signs.

We all got into ditching positions for the landing. They cleared all the runway and were waiting for us. We did not know if the wheels were locked. We had to be prepared for anything. As it was we left bits and pieces of wreckage strewn on the runway. Cliff Hurst made a full recovery and was awarded the DFM. The pilot was not decorated. He got a green endorsement in his logbook, which represented a 'good show'. We did not think about decorations. We just did what had to be done.

23: Operation Plunder
Squadron Leader Malcolm Scott DFC

FOR MORE THAN A WEEK during March 1945 the Mitchells and Bostons of 2 Group had been pounding targets in the Rhineland in close support of the 21st Army Group fighting its way to the great river barrier; 22,000 British, Canadian and American casualties had been suffered in clearing the area between the Maas and the Rhine. Xanten, one of 2 Group's earlier targets and more recently the recipient of a devastating night raid by Bomber Command, was now occupied by British and Canadian troops. The last strong bastion of the German troops on the west side had fallen and within a few days the rest of the territory was cleared and the Allied armies stood on the west bank looking at the remains of the Wesel bridge blown up by the retreating Germans.

For the six squadrons of 137 and 139 Wings in 2 Group (I was a Mitchell navigator in 180 Squadron) the targets now shifted to the east side of the Rhine. At least two, occasionally three, raids were made each day on marshalling yards, communication centres and bridges, oil dumps, billeting areas and barracks, artillery emplacements and troop concentrations. Some penetrations were deeper to important rail centres, but

Mitchell IIs of 180 Squadron taxi out. (IWM)

mostly attacks were concentrated in the Weser–Emmerich–Munster area where 'Plunder', the code name for the overall operation covering the Rhine crossing, was to take place. Maximum effort had been ordered, and quite often up to 15 aircraft per squadron took part instead of the usual dozen aircraft in two boxes of six.

Montgomery's preparations for the Rhine crossing were, as always, massive and painstaking: troops being ferried to the rear echelons to practice 'boat drill' and the handling of small craft up and down the muddy banks of the River Maas at night in preparation for the real thing. There could be no misleading or attempted feints this time. Within a mile or two, the Germans could estimate where the Allied crossing would be made. As Kesselring wrote, 'The enemy's operations in a clearly limited area, bombing raids on headquarters and the smoke-screening and assembly of bridging materials, indicated their intention to attack between Emmerich and Dinslaken with the point of the main effort on either side of Rees.'

The only questions facing the enemy were when and how. Always before, the Allies had launched a parachute and glider attack as a prelude to the full force of the main assault. Kesselring could but wait to see where the paras dropped, or so he thought.

In the meantime, RAF medium bombers and Typhoons and the 9th USAAF Marauders and Thunderbolts carried on with their now familiar role of 'softening up' the area around the chosen points of the great river and the hinterland of the proposed bridgeheads on the east bank. One important road and rail junction town and troop-billeting area was Bocholt, which became the object of almost daily attacks and quickly gained a reputation for providing a very warm reception. On 18 March it was bombed and again two days later. We all got back but with our aircraft and a few aircrew heavily peppered by shrapnel.

The next morning, 21 March, Bocholt was again listed as the target. On the bombing run No 1 in the box was badly damaged and an air gunner's leg was almost shot away, but the pilot retained control and made an emergency landing at Eindhoven. No 2 in the box received a direct hit as the bombs fell away and virtually disintegrated, taking down No 3, an all-Australian crew, from which one parachute was seen to emerge.

Douglas Boston III L of 226 Squadron. (M. A. Collins Collection)

This belonged to an air gunner, who, although captured on landing, was freed eight days later by advancing British troops. The pilot of No 4 was severely injured, shrapnel smashing through his right thigh bone, but he managed to retain consciousness long enough to get his aircraft back over friendly territory after bombing, before passing out. The mid-upper gunner then took over the controls and managed, under the pilot's guidance, to crash-land at the first airfield en route without further casualties. The leading aircraft of the second box was seriously damaged by flak, wounding an air gunner, but the pilot pressed on, bombed and led his formation back over the Rhine before breaking away to force-land at Eindhoven. Bocholt deserved its thick red ring on the map as a place to be avoided if possible!

Of the 12 180 Squadron Mitchells that had left Melsbroek earlier, only seven returned to base, all with varying degrees of flak damage and some with wounded aboard. Only six aircraft took part in the afternoon show, but the other two squadrons operated 24. The next day they were joined by 11 aircraft from 180 Squadron, attacking an enemy strongpoint near Dingden in the morning and Isselburg in the afternoon. Notification was received of an immediate award of the DSO to the wounded pilot, Pilot Officer Perkins, a CGM to his air gunner, Flight Sergeant J. Hall, who carried out the emergency landing, and a DFC to the leading pilot of the second box, Flight Lieutenant G. Howard-Jones.

On 23 March the Mitchells and Bostons bombed strong-points near Wesel in the morning and, on return from a second visit to Isselburg in the late afternoon, we were told at debriefing that this was 'R-Day' and that British, Canadian and American troops would be crossing the Rhine that evening at various points on either side of Wesel and Rees. An early night was suggested, and while we slept Bomber Command put in a heavy attack on Wesel.

Long before dawn on the 24th, 'R-Day + 1', we were called to attend briefing at

Mitchells of 180 Squadron en route to their target. (John Smith-Carrington Collection via Theo Boiten)

A ground crew pause while bombing up a Mitchell of 226 Squadron. (137/139 Wing Association)

05.30. The target was set in the forest of Diersfordterwald, north-west of Hamminkein, where we would be making the final bombing raid before 'Operation Varsity', the airborne assault, came in. Our bomb load was six clusters of 20lb APs. The bombing height was to be between 11,000 and 12,000 feet and the approximate heading on the bombing run 075, turning right off target after bombing.

By 07.35 we were checking over our individual equipment in the aircraft, and half an hour later we took off leading 'Grey' Box, while 'Brown' Box tucked in behind as we set course. We picked up our Spitfire escort as we set course for Xanten, where we contacted 'Cosycoat', the MRCP controller. Within minutes we crossed the Rhine but the flak was minimal and not particularly accurate. Bomb doors were opened as the pilots followed the instructions given by 'Cosycoat' on the run-in to the target, and the six clusters dropped clumsily away from each bomber. Flak was now more accurate but, judged by earlier standards, only moderate. 'Cosycoat' signed us off and took control of another box running in. It all seemed very impersonal as the bombing details were entered in the log and the pilot was given the new course, and it was not until we'd made our right turn off the target that I became aware of all the activity taking place below. Even during the Ardennes breakthrough in the snow of the previous December and January I saw nothing to match the scene below us.

On either side of the river we could see the ripple of flashes from gun batteries and tanks and the occasional puff of dust and smoke as a flurry of shells landed. The little boats (from our height) handled by the Navy were ploughing back and forth across the river and we could see the spans of the demolished bridges lying in the water. Already pontoon bridges were being thrown across the great waterway looking like threads of cotton. We knew, although we couldn't see them, that the Army and Marine Commandos alongside various infantry units were fighting around Rees and Wesel and our tanks were already in action on the east bank, having 'swum' across during the night and early morning. Smoke was still drifting about and we could see Tempests, Typhoons, Mustangs and Thunderbolts diving in to attack enemy positions. We learned afterwards that Churchill was there on a high vantage point with Alanbrooke, Eisenhower and Tedder, but I don't think they got the marvellous view we did.

As we left the Rhine behind us we could see, coming in from the west, several thousand feet below, the vanguard of the Airborne Divisions. Dakotas, C-46 Commandos and C-47s loaded with paratroopers and their equipment occupied the first waves of the assault, heading three great columns stretching back as far as the eye could see. Following the paratroops came the gliders towed by Halifax, Stirling and Albermarle tugs, and, of course, the ubiquitous Dakotas. Our south-westerly course was gradually taking us away from this awe-inspiring sight. We hoped our bombing had been of support and had reduced in some measure the opposition that the Airborne were bound to encounter.

Our fighter escort left us over Goch and we were all back at base by 10.10. There was the inevitable 'turn round' call; the bomb trolleys were waiting to fill the empty bellies of our aircraft as we taxied in. Another briefing was on at 10.45 and the Squadron was airborne again by 12.50, attacking another strong-point near Brunen. The great colonnade had gone. All that remained of it were masses of 'broken' gliders and splashes of discarded parachutes. Smoke and gunfire were still in evidence, but it was not the same. The morning of 'R-Day + 1' was the only time that I really appreciated to the full our true role in tactical air support.

Appendix 1: Bomber Command Battle Order, 5 June 1944

Sqn	Station	Aircraft	Command
7	Oakington	Lancaster I/III	Bomber
9	Bardney	Lancaster I/III	Bomber
12	Wickenby	Lancaster I/III	Bomber
15	Mildenhall	Lancaster I/III	Bomber
21	Gravesend	Mosquito VI	2nd TAF
35	Graveley	Lancaster I/III	Bomber
44	Dunholme Lodge	Lancaster I/III	Bomber
49	Fiskerton	Lancaster I/III	Bomber
50	Skellingthorpe	Lancaster I/III	Bomber
51	Snaith	Halifax III	Bomber
57	East Kirkby	Lancaster I/III	Bomber
61	Skellingthorpe	Lancaster I/III	Bomber
69	Northolt	Wellington XIII	2nd TAF

Lancaster Mk 1 R5868 S-for-Sugar of 467 Squadron, RAAF, collecting PoWs at Brussels at the end of the war. (IWM)

Sqn	Station	Aircraft	Command
75	Mepal	Lancaster I/III	Bomber
76	Holme-on-Spalding Moor	Halifax III	Bomber
77	Full Sutton	Halifax III/IV	Bomber
83	Coningsby	Lancaster I/III	Bomber
88	Hartford Bridge	Boston III/IIIa	Bomber
90	Tuddenham	Stirling III/Lancaster I/III	Bomber
97	Coningsby	Lancaster I/III	Bomber
98	Dunsfold	Mitchell II	2nd TAF
100	Grimsby	Lancaster I/III	Bomber
101	Ludford Magna	Lancaster I/III	Bomber
102	Pocklington	Halifax III/IIIa	Bomber
103	Elsham Wolds	Lancaster I/III	Bomber
105	Bourn	Mosquito IX/XVI	Bomber
106	Metheringham	Lancaster I/III	Bomber
107	Lasham	Mosquito VI	Bomber
109	Little Staughton	Mosquito IV/IX/XVI	Bomber
115	Witchford	Lancaster I/III	Bomber
138	Tempsford	Halifax II	Special Duties
139	Upwood	Mosquito IV/IX/XVI/XX	Bomber
156	Upwood	Lancaster I/III	Bomber
158	Lissett	Halifax III	Bomber
166	Kirmington	Lancaster I/III	Bomber
161	Tempsford	Halifax V/Hudson III/V	Special Duties
171	North Creake	Stirling III	100 Group
180	Dunsfold	Mitchell II	2nd TAF
190	Fairford	Stirling IV	Bomber
192	Foulsham	Wellington X/Mosquito IV	ADGB
196	Keevil	Stirling IV	38 Group
199	North Creake	Stirling III	100 Group
207	Spilsby	Lancaster I/III	Bomber
214	Oulton	Fortress II	100 Group
218	Woolfox Lodge	Stirling III	Bomber
226	Hartford Bridge	Mitchell II	2nd TAF
300	Faldingworth	Lancaster I/III	Bomber
342	Hartford Bridge	Boston IIIa	2nd TAF
346	Elvington	Halifax V	Bomber
464	Thorney Island	Mosquito VI	2nd TAF
487	Thorney Island	Mosquito VI	2nd TAF
514	Waterbeach	Lancaster I/III	Bomber
550	North Killingholme	Lancaster I/III	Bomber
571	Oakington	Mosquito XVI	Bomber
576	Elsham Wolds	Lancaster I/III	Bomber
578	Burn	Halifax III	Bomber
582	Little Staughton	Lancaster I/III	Bomber
617	Woodhall Spa	Lancaster I/III	Bomber
618	Skitten	Mosquito IV	Bomber
619	Dunholme Lodge	Lancaster I/III	Bomber
620	Fairford	Stirling IV	38 Group
622	Mildenhall	Lancaster I/III	Bomber

Sqn	Station	Aircraft	Command
625	Kelstern	Lancaster I/III	Bomber
626	Wickenby	Lancaster I/III	Bomber
627	Woodhall Spa	Mosquito IV	Bomber
630	East Kirkby	Lancaster I/III	Bomber
635	Downham Market	Lancaster I/III	Bomber
640	Leconfield	Halifax III	Bomber
644	Tarrant Rushton	Halifax V	ADGB
692	Graveley	Mosquito IV/XVI	Bomber

S-for-Sugar. *This famous RAF Avro Lancaster Mk.I (R5868) flew 68 operations with 83 Squadron as* Q-for-Queenie *at Scampton, Lincolnshire, and 69 operations with 467 Squadron RAAF at Bottesford. The Goëring quotation was added in mid-March 1945 by LAC E. Willoughby.* S-for-Sugar *completed its 137th and final sortie on 23 April 1945, to Flensberg. She now takes pride of place in the RAF Bomber Command Museum at Hendon, London; a fitting testament to the men of Harris's Command.* (Author)

Appendix 2: Harris's letter to Bomber Command, 12 May 1945

'SPECIAL ORDER OF THE DAY'

FROM AIR CHIEF MARSHAL SIR A. T. HARRIS
KCB OBE AFC

Date: 12 May 1945

Men and women of Bomber Command.

More than five and a half years ago, within hours of the declaration of war, Bomber Command first assailed the German enemy.

You were then but a handful, inadequate in everything but the skill and determination of the crews for that sombre occasion and for the unknown years of unceasing battle which lay beyond horizons black indeed.

You, the aircrew of Bomber Command, sent your first ton of bombs away on the morrow of the outbreak of war. A million tons of bombs and mines have followed from Bomber Command alone; from Declaration of War to Cease Fire a continuity of battle without precedent and without relent.

In the battle of France your every endeavour bore down upon an overwhelming and triumphant enemy.

After Dunkirk your country stood alone – in arms but largely unarmed – between the Nazi tyranny and domination of the world.

The Battle of Britain, in which you took great part, raised the last barrier, strained but holding, in the path of the all-conquering Wehrmacht, and the bomb smoke of the Channel ports choked back down German throats the very word 'Invasion': not again to find expression within these narrow seas until the bomb-disrupted defences of the Normandy beach-heads fell to our combined assault.

In the long years between much was to pass.

Then it was that you, and you for long alone, carried the war ever deeper and even more furiously into the heart of the Third Reich. There the whole might of the German enemy in undivided strength and – scarcely less a foe – the very elements, arrayed against you. You overcome them both.

Through those desperate years, undismayed by any odds, undeterred by any casualties, night succeeding night, you fought: the Phalanx of the United Nations.

You fought alone, as the one force then assailing German soil; you fought alone as individuals – isolated in your crew stations by the darkness and the murk, and from all other aircraft in company.

*Air Chief Marshal Sir A. T. Harris KCB OBE
AFC.*

Not for you the hot emulation of high endeavour in the glare and panoply of martial array. Each crew, each one in each crew, fought alone through black nights rent only, mile after continuing mile, by the fiercest barrages ever raised and the instant sally of the searchlights. In each dark minute of those long miles lurked menace. Fog, ice, snow and tempest found you undeterred.

In that loneliness in action lay the final test, the ultimate stretch of human staunchness and determination.

Your losses mounted through those years, years in which your chance of survival through one spell of operational duty was negligible; through two periods, mathematically   nil.   Nevertheless survivors pressed forward as volunteers to pit their desperately acquired skill in even a third period of operations, on special tasks.

In those five years and eight months of continuous battle over enemy soil, your casualties   over   long   periods   were grievous. As the count is cleared, those of Bomber Command who gave their lives to bring near to impotence an enemy who had surged swift in triumph through a Continent, and to enable the United Nations to deploy in full array, will be found not less than the total dead of our National   Invasion   Armies   now   in Germany. In the whole history of our National Forces, never have so small a band of men been called upon to support so long such odds. You indeed bore the brunt.

To you who survive I would say this. Content yourselves, and take credit with those who perished, that now the 'Cease Fire' has sounded, countless homes within our Empire will welcome back a father, a husband, or a son, whose life, but for your endeavours and your sacrifices, would assuredly have been expended during long further years of agony, to achieve a victory already ours. No Allied Nation is clear of this debt to you.

I cannot here expound your full achievement.

Your attack in the industrial centres of Northern Italy did much toward the collapse of the Italian and German Armies in North Africa, and to further the invasion of the Italian mainland.

Of the German enemy, two to three million fit men, potentially vast armies, were continuously held throughout the War in direct and indirect defence against your assaults. A great part of her industrial war effort went towards fending your attacks.

You struck a critical proportion of the weapons of war from enemy hands, on every front. You immobilised armies, leaving them shorn of supplies, reinforcements, resources and reserves, the easier prey to our advancing forces.

You eased and abetted the passage of our troops over major obstacles. You blasted the enemy from long prepared defences where he essayed to hold: on the Normandy beaches, at the hinge of the battle for Caen, in the jaws of the Falaise Gap, to the strong-points of the enemy-held Channel ports, St Vith, Houffalize, and the passage of the Rhine. In battle after battle you sped our armies to success at minimum cost to our troops. The Commanders of our land forces, and indeed those of the enemy, have called your attacks decisive.

You enormously disrupted every means of communication, the very life-blood of his military and economic machines. Railways, canals, and every form of transport fell first to decay and then chaos under your assaults. You so shattered the enemy's oil plants as to deprive him of all but the final trickle of fuel. His aircraft became earthbound, his road transport ceased to roll. Armoured fighting vehicles lay helpless outside of battle, or fell immobilised into our hands. His strategic and tactical plans failed through inability to move.

From his war industries supplies of ore, coal, steel, fine metals, aircraft, guns, ammunition, tanks, vehicles and every ancillary equipment, dwindled under your attack.

At the very crisis of the invasion of Normandy, you virtually annihilated the German naval surface fleet then in the Channel; a hundred craft and more fell victim to those three attacks.

You sank or damaged a large but yet untotalled number of enemy submarines in his ports and by mine-laying in his waters. You interfered widely and repeatedly with his submarine training programmes.

With extraordinary accuracy, regardless of opposition, you hit and burst through every carapace which he could devise to protect his submarines in harbour. By your attacks on inland industries and coastal ship-yards you caused hundreds of his submarines to be stillborn.

Your mine-laying throughout the enemy's sea lanes, your bombing of his inland waters, and his ports, confounded his sea traffic and burst his canals. From Norway throughout the Baltic, from Jutland to the Gironde, on the coasts of Italy and North Africa, you laid and re-laid the minefields. The wreckage of the enemy's naval and merchant fleets litter and encumbers his sea-lanes and dockyards. A thousand known ships, and many more as yet unknown, fell casualty to your mines.

You hunted and harried his major warships from hide to hide. You put out of action, gutted or sank most of them.

By your attacks on Experimental Stations, factories, communications and firing sites, you long postponed and much reduced the V weapon attacks. You averted an enormous further toll of death and destruction from your Country.

With it all you never ceased to rot the very heart out of the enemy's war resources and resistance.

His Capital and near 100 of his cities and towns, including nearly all of leading war industrial importance, lie in utter ruin together with the greater part of the war industry which they supported.

Thus you brought to nought the enemy's original advantage of an industrial might intrinsically greater than ours and supported by the labour of captive millions, now set free.

For the first time in more than a century you have brought home to the habitual aggressor of Europe the full and acrid flavours of war, so long the prerequisite of his victims.

All this, and much more, have you achieved during these five and a half years of continuous battle, despite all opposition from an enemy disposing of many a geographical and strategical advantage with which to exploit an initial superiority in numbers.

Men from every part of the Empire and most of the Allied Nations fought in our ranks. Indeed a band of brothers.

In the third year of war, the Eighth Bomber Command, and the Fifteenth Bomber Command, USAAF, from the Mediterranean bases, ranged themselves at our side, zealous in extending every mutual aid, viewing in every assault upon our common foe. Especially they played the leading part in sweeping the enemy fighter defences from our path, and finally, out of the skies.

Nevertheless, nothing that the crews accomplished – and it was much, and decisive – could have been achieved without the devoted service of every man and woman in the Command.

Those who attended the aircraft, mostly in the open, through six bitter winters; endless intricacies in a prolonged misery of wet and cold. They rightly earned the implicit trust of the crews. They set extraordinary records of aircraft serviceability.

Those who manned the Stations, Operational Headquarters, Supply lines and Communications.

The pilots of the Photographic Reconnaissance Units, without whose lonely ventures far and wide over enemy territory we should have been largely powerless to plan or to strike.

The Operational Crew Training Organisation of the Command, which through those years of ceaseless work by day and night never failed, in the face of every difficulty and unpredicted call, to replace all casualties and to keep our constantly expanding first line strength in crews trained to the highest pitch of efficiency; simultaneously producing near 20,000 additional trained aircrew for the raising and reinforcement of some 50 extra squadrons, formed in the Command and despatched for service in other Commands at home and overseas.

The men and women of the Meteorological Branch who attained prodigious exactitudes in a fickle art and stood brave on assertion where science is inexact. Time and again they saved us from worse than the enemy could have achieved. Their record is outstanding.

The meteorological reconnaissance pilots, who flew through anything and everything in search of the feasible.

The operational Research Stations whose meticulous investigation of every detail of every attack provided data for the continuous confounding of the enemy and the consistent reduction of our own casualties.

The scientists, especially those of the Telecommunications Research Establishment, who placed in unending succession in our hands the technical means to resolve our problems and to confuse the every parry of the enemy. Without their skill and labours beyond doubt we could not have prevailed.

The Works Services who engineered, for Bomber Command alone, 2,000 miles of runway track and road, with all that goes with them.

The Works Staff, Designers, and Workers who equipped and re-equipped us for Battle. Their efforts, their honest workmanship, kept in our hand indeed a Shining Sword.

To all of you I would say how proud I am to have served in Bomber Command for four and a half years, and to have been your Commander-in-Chief through more than three years of your saga.

Your task in the German war is now completed. Famously you have fought. Well you have deserved of your country and her Allies.

(sgd) A. T. Harris
Air Chief Marshal
Commanding-in-Chief
Bomber Command'

Glossary

AA	Anti-Aircraft
AAA	Anti-Aircraft Artillery
ADLS	Air Delivery Letter Service
AF	Air Force
AFC	Air Force Cross
AI	Airborne Interception (radar)
AM	Air Marshal
Anvil	Use of aged PB4Y-1s as radio-controlled bombs
AOC	Air Officer Commanding
Aphrodite	Use of aged B-l7s as radio-controlled bombs
ASH	AI.XV narrow-beam radar used for low-level operations
ASR	Air-Sea Rescue
ATS	Air Training Squadron
AVM	Air Vice Marshal
BBC	British Broadcasting Corporation
BEA	British European Airways
BG	Bomb Group (USAAF)
Blip	Radar echo or response
Bogey	Unidentified aircraft
BS	Bomb Squadron (USAAF)
BSDU	Bomber Support Development Unit (RAF)
C-scope	CRT showing frontal elevation of target
Capt	Captain
CCU	Combat Crew Unit
CH	Chain Home (early warning radar station)
Chaff	American *Window*
CHEL	Chain Home Extra Low
CHL	Chain Home Low
CO	Commanding Officer
CoG	Centre of Gravity
Col	Colonel
CRT	Cathode Ray Tube
Day Ranger	Operation to engage air and ground targets within a wide but specified area, by day
DCM	Distinguished Conduct Medal
DFC	Distinguished Flying Cross
DFM	Distinguished Flying Medal
Diver	V1 flying bomb operation

Drem lighting	System of outer markers and runway approach lights
DSC	Distinguished Service Cross
DSO	Distinguished Service Order
Düppel	German code name for *Window*. Named after a town near the Danish border where RAF metal foil strips were first found.
e/a	Enemy Aircraft
ETA	Estimated Time of Arrival
F/L	Flight Lieutenant
F/O	Flight Officer
F/Sgt	Flight Sergeant
FIDO	Fog Investigation and Dispersal Operation
Firebash	100 Group Mosquito sorties using incendiaries/napalm against German airfields
Flensburg	German device to enable their night fighters to home in on *Monica* radar
Flg	Flieger: Airman (German)
FNSF	Fast Night Striking Force
Freelance	Patrol with the object of picking up a chance contact or visual of the enemy
Fw	Feldwebel: Sergeant (German)
G/C	Group Captain
GCI	Ground Control Interception (radar)
Gee	British medium-range navigational aid using ground transmitters and an airborne receiver
Gen	General
GP	General Purpose bomb
Gruppe	German equivalent of RAF Wing
Gruppenkommandeur	Officer commanding a Gruppe (German)
H_2S	British 10-cm experimental airborne radar navigational and target location aid
HE	High Explosive (bomb)
'Heavies'	RAF/USAAF four-engined bombers
HEI	High Explosive Incendiary
HMS	His Majesty's Ship
Hptm	Hauptmann: Flight Lieutenant (German)
HRH	His Royal Highness
IAS	Indicated Air Speed
IFF	Identification Friend or Foe
Intruder	Offensive night operation to fixed point or specified target
IO	Intelligence Officer
JG	Jagdgeschwader: Fighter Group (German)
KG	Kampfgeschwader: Bomber Group (German)
KüFlGr	Küstenfliegergruppe: Coastal Flying Wing (German)
LAC	Leading Aircraftsman
Lichtenstein	First form of German AI radar
LMF	Lack of Moral Fibre
LNSF	Light Night Striking Force
LORAN	Long-Range Navigation
Lt	Leutnant: Pilot Officer (German)
Lt	Lieutenant

Lt Cmdr	Lieutenant Commander
Lt Col	Lieutenant Colonel
Luftflotte	Air Fleet (German)
M/T	Motor Transport
Maj	Major
Maj	Major: Squadron Leader (German)
Maj Gen	Major General
Mandrel	100 Group airborne radar jamming device
MC	Medium Capacity bomb
MCU	Mosquito Conversion Unit
Met	Meteorological
MG	Maschinengewehr: Machine gun (German)
Monica	British tail warning radar device
MTU	Mosquito Training Unit
NCO	Non-Commissioned Officer
NFS	Night Fighter Squadron
Night Ranger	Operation to engage air and ground targets within a wide but specified area, by night
NJG	Nachtjagdgeschwader: Night Fighter Group (German)
Noball	Flying bomb (Vl) or rocket (V2) site
OBE	Order of the British Empire
Obgefr	Obergefreiter: Corporal (German)
Oblt	Oberleutnant: Flying Officer (German)
Oboe	Ground-controlled radar system of blind bombing in which one station indicated track to be followed and another the bomb release point
Obst	Oberst: Group Captain (German)
Ofw	Oberfeldwebel: Flight Sergeant (German)
op	Operation
OSS	Office of Strategic Services. The US intelligence service activated during the Second World War, and disbanded on 1 October 1945
OT	Operational Training
OTU	Operational Training Unit
P/O	Pilot Officer
PFF	Path Finder Force
PoW	Prisoner of War
PR	Photographic Reconnaissance
PRU	Photographic Reconnaissance Unit
R/T	Radio Telephony
RAAF	Royal Australian Air Force
RAE	Royal Aircraft Establishment
RAFVR	Royal Air Force Volunteer Reserve
RCAF	Royal Canadian Air Force
RCM	Radio Counter Measures
RNorAF	Royal Norwegian Air Force
RN	Royal Navy
RNVR	Royal Naval Volunteer Reserve
RP	Rocket Projectile
S/L	Squadron Leader

S/Sgt	Staff Sergeant
SASO	Senior Air Staff Officer
SD	Special Duties
SEAC	South-East Asia Command
Serrate	British equipment designed to home in on *Lichtenstein* AI radar
Sgt	Sergeant
SKG	Schnelles Kampfgeschwader: Fast Bomber Group (German)
SOE	Special Operations Executive
Staffel	German equivalent of RAF squadron
Staffelkapitan	Squadron Commander (German)
Sub/Lt	Sub-Lieutenant
TI	Target Indicator
TNT	TriNitroToluene
'Torbeau'	Torpedo-carrying Beaufighter
U/S	Unserviceable
Uffz	Unteroffizier: Sergeant (German)
UHF	Ultra-High Frequency
USAAF	United Sates Army Air Force
VC	Victoria Cross
VHF	Very High Frequency
WAAF	Women's Auxiliary Air Force
W/C	Wing Commander
Window	Metal foil strips dropped by bombers to confuse enemy radar systems
W/O	Warrant Officer
W/T	Wireless Telephony
Y-Service	British organisation monitoring German radio transmissions to and from aircraft
*	Bar to an award

Index